STA\

...I could say ...**ething brilliant**
at any moment

RAY CLARK

pop publishing

STAY TUNED
…I could say something brilliant at any moment!
Ray Clark
First published 2023 by Poppublishing (2nd printing)
Text © Ray Clark 2023
This work © Poppublishing
Published in paperback and ebook

**For further information about this book please contact
poppublishing@gmail.com**

Cover design: David Roberts
Front cover photo: Ray Clark in his home studio,
Burnham-on-Crouch, January 2023 © David Roberts

Visit Ray Clark's website: www.rayradio.co.uk

To my lovely wife Shelley
who has to put up with all
this nonsense every day x

To my Mum, Dad,
Trish & Jacky
Thank you for an idyllic
childhood – and for buying
me the tape recorder

Foreword by Emperor Rosko

Greetings good people.
There are a few guys that I keep in my little black book when
I have queries on UK radio. Ray always seems to know
the answers to my questions. So if you need info about
the "Pearl and Dean" in Radio, and the history and who's
playing what, where and when, the number one go-to-guy for
me is always Ray. You know the saying… "When the going
gets tough, Ray gets going."
I thought it was all over and now he has another must
read book.
More knowledge, more history.
More crazy things he got up to and a good plug for me!!
Raymondo, make sure you send my copy air mail.

I hope you enjoy reading it.

Emperor Rosko
LA. California

*P.S. Ray I told you "go get a manager,
you would have gone National" – but you
didn't listen to me did you?*

Chapter One

"Are You Sitting Comfortably?...
Then I'll Begin"

It might have been Dean Martin, or perhaps it was Domenico Modugno, singing in Italian, but it was certainly 'Volare' that was playing on the 'wireless' as I wandered happily along the passageway from our tiny mid terrace cottage, past Mrs Went's open back door. I can still hear that song, and picture in my mind, that little boy on that lovely late summer's day more than sixty years ago.

Volare, oh oh, cantare, oh oh oh oh,
Nel blu, dipinto di blu...

I was just four years and a few months old and enjoying life in my busy carefree way, during the early days of an idyllic, happy childhood. To be honest, I'm still living it, I really don't know what I'm going to do when I grow up! Anyway, the wireless was on, the sun was shining, I'm pretty sure it was Sunday and probably September 1958, as both versions of 'Volare' were in the hit parade, and Mrs Went was certainly listening to *Two-way Family Favourites* on the BBC Light programme, linking listeners with family members living abroad or serving in the armed forces. It was unlikely to have been anything else, there was no alternative, this programme was on everyone's wireless as Sunday dinner was prepared across the land.

I am so lucky to have a memory that recalls the strangest, most obscure, but usually the happiest of memories in detail. More than that I have an ability to 'feel' memories.

I can relive those special moments that have stayed with me through the years, just waiting to be recreated should they come to mind. Recalling the weather, the mood, the atmosphere ... the feeling of being there.

I am almost capable of transporting myself back into many situations – albeit very briefly.

That's my baby

Raymond Colin Clark, age 1 year 10 months, of 2. The Willows, Ostend, Burnham-on-Crouch.

My first public appearance - Essex Weekly News: 'Raymond Colin Clark, age 1 year 10 months, of 2 The Willows, Ostend, Burnham-on -Crouch'

Back to 'Volare', I've always liked it, even though for many years I had no idea what it was called, but whenever I hear it, I am taken back to what I am sure is my first memory of music on the radio, or wireless as it was called then. We had a wireless, a polished wooden cabinet about two feet long, twelve inches deep and eighteen inches high. There were four Bakelite knobs on the front – one for changing the wave band, one for adjusting the volume, one for tuning in … and one just for show. 'Gadgets' don't have 'knobs' nowadays, do they? Anyway, above the knobs was a raffia facia hiding the loud speaker – I took great interest in this dull looking front a few years later, when I found that if I turned the volume up to the limit, a cloud of dust would appear as the raffia front pulsated to the music, until I was yelled at to turn it down. Along the front was a glass panel that glowed in a dull shade of yellow, if you were to twiddle the tuning knob a red marker would travel past wonderful sounding places: Athlone, Hilversum, Andorra, and, as the marker hovered over these names, unrecognisable words in foreign languages could be heard amongst the whistles and crackles coming from this magical box. While Mrs Went's wireless played music, I only have memories of words coming from ours, at least in my preschool days.

At work with my Dad (Ray left)

My dad worked on the farm and would come home at what we called dinnertime. Nowadays it would be called lunchtime, but we would eat our main daily meal as soon as dad walked in around 1.15pm. Half an hour later, as he left the house and returned to work on his bike, the wireless went on. It would take a while to 'warm up' before we heard musical notes played on a xylophone, followed by a plummy voice asking, *"Are you sitting comfortably? ... then I'll begin."* Daphne Oxenford was the presenter with a story and a couple of nursery rhymes, and of course, a tune on her piano that she would sing along to. *Listen With Mother* was a daily 'must listen' in our house. I also have vague memories of occasionally listening to *Toytown* with Larry the Lamb on the Home Service, *Children's Hour*, which was broadcast later in the day, but poor old Larry soon lost out to *Torchy the Battery Boy* once we had a television.

We had another listening appointment in our house, a regular visit to Ambridge for *The Archers*. Back then it really did feature 'the everyday story of country folk', and with dad working on the farm, it rang true, so we tuned in daily. I'm not so sure what rural farming families think of *The Archers* as an essential listen nowadays, it seems the programme is probably more popular with those listening in Islington and Notting Hill today. But at an early age I knew of events at The Bull and Home Farm, and I could tell you what they looked like … in my mind - I would probably have recognised Walter Gabriel, one of the 'rustic' characters had I met him. The pictures on the radio have always been so clear to me and as a small child the sound of Sidney Torch and his Orchestra striking up 'Barwick Green', the iconic theme tune, ending each episode, signalled bedtime.

I was probably seven years old when my grandad gave me a wonderful find from his old shed – a pair of ex RAF headphones. Two Bakelite earpieces with a very uncomfortable metal expansion headband and a fraying brown coloured cable. Rushing home with my latest treasure, my dad, never very practical when it came to DIY, searched for a longer length of 'flex'. The 'stripped back' wires were then plugged into the extension speaker socket at the back of the wireless and held in place with two broken matchsticks. This elongated lead then went out of the kitchen window, up to my back bedroom window, and back into the house. The rubberised surround of the bare wires, which in turn was shrouded in a frayed mauve fabric, was then connected to the bare wires from the headphones.

Although bedtime was at seven o'clock, I could now listen to *The Archers* on my headphones while sitting up in bed and there was no fear of falling asleep while still wearing them – they squashed my ears and hurt my head, they were the most uncomfortable things imaginable.

Real excitement occurred at the start of the 1960s when a new record player was delivered to our house. There was no instant sale and collection from a modern warehouse stocked with every conceivable bit of kit, capable of playing whatever media you wanted - our record player had to be ordered from *Smarts* furniture shop in Southend and was almost certainly paid for on HP – Hire Purchase, with payments spread over a year or so. There was no choice of brand either – this was the only record player that the store sold – take it or leave it … 'Why', by Anthony Newley and 'Seven Little Girls Sitting In The Back Seat', by The Avons, were our first, and for some time, our only two records, I still have them, stored with several boxes of other long since played vinyl records.

I became fascinated by these small pieces of black plastic with their blue Decca, red Parlophone and green Columbia labels, together with the colourful paper sleeves. They cost 6/8d each (approx. 35p), but with dad's wage in the early 60s at less than £10 a week, it's easy to understand why our record collection took time to grow.

I was captivated by those 7-inch discs revolving at 45 RPM (revolutions per minute) on the turntable, the pick-up arm rising and falling almost indiscernibly as the stylus followed the groove set into the vinyl.

The valves of the inbuilt amplifier glowed brightly, protected by a piece of hardboard with hundreds of holes drilled into it. I loved the warm electrical smell from the simple electronics, but best of all was the sound – hearing those voices and musical instruments all contained on that small disc via the very basic mono loudspeaker – stereo would be something for the future. I would really have preferred our record player to have been one of those two tone grey machines made by Bush, they looked so stylish with the white sloping front panel and a friend of mine had one. This model was obviously more expensive than our basic 'no name' record player, but to its credit, the sounds that came from our machine were fine to my ears, and nowhere near as 'low-fi' as a Dansette.

As an aside, a couple of years ago we went to Felixstowe for a midweek, out-of-season drive and in the window of a

'collectors' shop' were three of those Bush record players –
unused, though more than fifty years old. I did ask the price -
£60 each. I really should have reached for my wallet; I'll never
have that chance to buy one again.

The only alternative to listening to the BBC was to tune
into Radio Luxembourg, broadcasting from the Duchy of
Luxembourg on the Belgian-German-French border on 208
metres Medium Wave. I must have heard the programmes
from the 'Station of the Stars' for the first time around 1961,
but the programmes were only audible in the UK at night, with
reception improving as the night went on. 'Luxy' played pop
music aimed at a British audience, but as commercial radio
was outlawed in the UK, the broadcasts came from mainland
Europe, financed by commercials such as Horace Bachelor's
'dead cert' method of winning thousands of pounds on the
football pools. Listeners were invited to send money to Horace,
via his office in K.E.Y.N.S.H.A.M. He always repeated the
spelling in a very precise manner, and in exchange for a Postal
Order he would send you details of his 'secret method' of
winning, that only he had mastered. Thousands responded, in
the hope of becoming rich, but obviously they hadn't worked
out that Mr. Bachelor's claims were dubious. If his system was
so good, why was he wasting time advertising it on the radio
and not benefitting from it himself?

While my teenage cousin Josephine was baby-sitting me,
mum was in hospital with my little baby sister. For the first
time I was introduced to commercials on the radio and short
excerpts from the pop songs of the day as Jo was a regular
listener to 208. However, apart from Horace and his Treble
Chance Football Pools, Radio Luxembourg seemed to be
playing Dorothy Provine's 'Don't Bring Lulu' and Sue
Thompson desperately calling for 'Norman' all the time. Oh
the frustration of the long, slow, fade as the signal drifted
away, usually, just as the hook of the song was approaching,
or worse, when the 'announcer' (disc jockeys hadn't yet been
invented in the UK) was about to tell you who it was by.

In later years whilst listening to 208 metres, I would find that the signal was far better in Cornwall or Scotland than in Essex – we just lived too close to continental Europe to benefit from a stronger signal. Although well-informed radio engineers could explain about the way that radio waves work – I just wanted to listen to the songs they were playing...and the 'announcers' playing them.

By 1962 I was really starting to get into the music - or at least the Top 10 - and making lists. Don't most kids go through this stage of making lists of some sort? Well, I was listing pop singers as there weren't too many pop groups around at this time. I think I had one copy of *New Musical Express* that I used as a guide and I would list every name within the paper, explaining why the likes of Bobby Rydell made the list – I'd be hard pushed to name one of his songs now. Strange to think that music papers and magazines were so difficult to come by in the early sixties, especially if you lived 'out in the sticks'. I can remember being very embarrassed as an eight year old going into the newsagents to ask for a copy of *Boyfriend,* a colour magazine with full page posters of the stars. I still squirm, as I remember saying it was for my sister ... She was just four years old!

Idyllic Childhood Christmas with sisters Ug and Itsy (Jaqueline and Patricia)

One show on the BBC Light Programme at the time left a particularly big mark on my memory. It was the only place to have any chance of hearing just a little 'popular' music during the daytime. I was off school, unwell, and the wireless was on and I'm guessing that the show came from the BBC's Paris studios in Regent Street. It involved yet another plummy-voiced announcer interviewing members of the public who appeared to be just passing by. They were first asked what song they'd like to hear, and immediately the record library staff were tasked with finding the record whilst the interviewer asked more questions of the 'guest': "Where are you from?", "Where are you going?", "What's your name?" Once the record had been located in what was seemingly a huge record library within another part of the BBC, a buzzer sounded, the interview came to a halt and the song was played. Well, having heard this, the afternoon was spent presenting my version of the programme with our very limited selection of records and one guest, my mother.

"And what record would you like to hear?"

"Would you play 'Little White Bull' by Tommy Steele... again?"

There was little opportunity to hear new records on the radio, the BBC seldom played pop music and although Radio Luxembourg offered a selection of chart hits, we were now watching television in the evening and at weekends, rather than listening to the radio.

The TV show that I looked forward to was *Jukebox Jury*, where excerpts of new records were played and judged to be 'a hit' or 'a miss' by 'stars' of the day. Often these stars had little or no connection to the pop music scene and, like most people on TV in those days, they were old. There was also *Thank Your Lucky Stars* on ITV. This became the place to hear, and see, the latest pop songs performed by the artists themselves and by now I'd also discovered the Top 10 charts, listed each week in the *Daily Mirror*.

My teenage cousin, Jo, was now regularly attending the

Odeon Cinema music tours when they visited Southend, and although I was much too young to go with her, she would buy me black and white photographs of the music stars that she'd seen, including Cliff Richard, Adam Faith and Frank Ifield.

'I Remember You', 'The Locomotion' and 'It Might As Well Rain Until September', were all in the charts during September 1962 and I still associate these songs with our first family holiday. They seemed to be playing everywhere we went. We stayed in a 'chalet', to be honest it was an extended shed, at Leysdown on the Isle of Sheppey – it was called *Perseverance*, named, I guess, after Percy and Vera who must have owned it. I think mum saw an advert in the newsagent's window and the place still exists to this day. I went to Leysdown a few years back to search it out, it's a bit poshed up now with double glazed windows,and probably electricity and hot water but sadly it's no longer named after Percy and Vera, bless 'em.

Anyway, not only do I remember that holiday as something special, I also remember seeing a group of strange looking structures off the coast, a first view that is still very clear in my mind. They were the Red Sands and Shivering Sands wartime defence forts, positioned out at sea in the Thames estuary, just a few miles off the coast of the Isle of Sheppey. I would later develop a fascination with these Jurassic giants and the part they were yet to play in British pop music culture. But for then, late summer 1962, they were just twenty-year-old abandoned relics from the war.

By Christmas 1962, the family record collection had grown considerably. 'Bobby's Girl' for my sister, 'She Taught Me How To Yodel', for dad … and for me, and it still sounds so exciting, the fabulous 'Telstar' by the Tornados, it was so ahead of its time, and almost as good, on the flip side, 'Jungle Fever'.Try listening to it with headphones turned loud, it's brilliant to hum along to and I can picture that dark blue Decca record label spinning around on the record player turntable at 45 rpm with the anticipation added to by the crackles at the start of the vinyl record. I still have that original copy and really ought to retrieve it from my collection, clean it, buy a new Decca records paper sleeve from ebay, and make sure that it survives into the future.

We were lucky to have a small independent cinema in the town where I grew up…it still exists, amazingly, and I still live in the same town. 'Jungle Fever' was one of the tunes played while the cinema was filling for the Saturday afternoon matinee. I loved the Princes cinema, it's now called The Rio … it still smells the same, wonderfully musty, but we do have the latest films, really cheap seats and sweets that the owner buys from a supermarket and re-sells at low prices. Everyone, by law, should be made to go to the Burnham-on-Crouch Rio at least once in their life. I've seen all the 'must see' films from the last 60 years in this amazing place, including every one of those pop music movies from the 60s and 70s: *Ferry Cross the Mersey, Catch Us If You Can, A Hard Day's Night, Help! Grease*, they all came to the Princes cinema in Burnham … eventually.

But it was to the Embassy cinema in Maldon, a grand Odeon-styled building with a balcony, that my cousin Jo took me to see *Summer Holiday*.

What a film – well that's what I thought at the time, it certainly captured my imagination. I don't know if it was the double decker bus, the idea of driving to the sun, or being in a pop group, but for the next few weeks it was all I could talk about. Even acting out the part of Cliff Richard in front of Mrs Harris's class at Burnham County Primary School – I'm still embarrassed to think of it, and worryingly, I know people who STILL remember my performance! Later I would drive a double decker bus for a living. I suspect Cliff was responsible in some small way for this, and for my present-day addiction to eating Paynes Poppets. March 5th 1963 is written in history as the first time I'd tasted these wonderful little chocolate covered toffees. Sadly, they're not readily available nowadays, and certainly not from the foyer of the beautiful art-deco Embassy cinema, which was bull-dozed to the ground in an act of wicked vandalism in the 1980s, replaced by a modern, ugly 'Granny Home' building. However, Poppets, although no longer made by Paynes, are still available in bulk online - I have a supply. The former art-deco Paynes Poppets sweet factory in Mitcham, South London is now a BMW dealership.

I amaze myself at some of the things I know – if only I could make a living by reciting these odd facts!

And then the Beatles arrived: 'Love Me Do', 'Please Please Me', 'She Loves You', suddenly music changed, seemingly overnight, becoming just so much more exciting than it had ever been, and although I was only nine years old I was so aware of these fab new songs and changes in style of pop music. When Mr. Sandford, our headmaster, played 'I Wanna Hold Your Hand' on the school record player at the Christmas party I realised that this 'new' music was here to stay. My Christmas present from Cousin Jo this year was 'I Like It', by Gerry and the Pacemakers. Like it?, … I absolutely loved it.

As the Fab Four and all the other great 'Merseybeat' acts and their songs swept across the land throughout 1963 I was just at the right age to become music aware. These days I have copies of the songs that the Beatles wrote or performed on vinyl, CD and as downloads, but the first Beatles' song in our collection back then was 'She Loves You', although not by the Fab Four. This was a cover version, together with covers of five other hits on the Rocket record label. Available only by mail order and advertised in *Reveille*, a newspaper style magazine of the day, these records were a forerunner to the *Top of the Pops* LPs, which became hugely popular in the late 60s and 70s. Entire albums featuring cover versions of current hits, costing much less than the original recordings, with LP sleeves picturing very attractive girls in hot pants, tight tops and short skirts which made them even more appealing to teenage lads. These records regularly featured in the album charts and in a very strange and tenuous way that Rocket record would link to my future interests and career, which will become obvious later in the book.

It was around this time that we got a tape recorder, bought by mail order from a company called Headquarters and General Supplies. They were always advertising in the Saturday newspapers – radios, bicycles, telescopes, typewriters and tape recorders, all described in a way that made them sound better than anything else on the market, and all of them made in Russia or Japan. Now, in 1963 the legend 'Made in Japan' suggested a product might be at the pinnacle of new technology but unfortunately this masterpiece of Far Eastern engineering was yet to be perfected, but then it only cost £4-19-6d - expensive at the time, but a bargain when compared to 21 guineas for a more up-market model that had been made in England.

That cheap Japanese tape recorder has a lot to answer for
(Photo: radiolondon.co.uk)

I loved this small, portable machine and spent hours recording silly stories and general nonsense on it. One masterpiece was set at a race course with commentary and sound effects of horses going over the jumps, made with a plastic beaker and 'clicking' the teeth of a comb. Oh, how I wish I had those recordings now. The tape reels, just three inches in diameter on this *'superb hi-fi, solid state tape recorder'* started to speed up once the tape had transferred more than halfway from one reel to the other, the faster reel speed resulting in the recorded voice playing slower and slower – it was great for adding unusual effects to my quirky recordings… and it made my voice sound much deeper. The clues regarding my future career were already starting to show.

There was an explosion of interest in the new wave of pop music everywhere it seemed. Local pop groups of spotty-faced teenagers would play in church halls, television shows would feature the new musical stars and pop music was suddenly becoming far more accessible, though still seldom played on the radio. In October 1963 even our local carnival, a huge event in the town's social calendar, was reflecting the new, exciting music scene.

My home town, Burnham-on-Crouch, holds an annual Carnival. It is still a very popular event, but back then it was a massive attraction for the thousands who flocked to our small riverside town from all over the Southeast on the last Saturday of October.

As the evening procession wound its way through the narrow streets, it produced a blaze of colour and sound, with many of the tableau playing music, including the *Queen of Toyland* where, on this occasion, I was standing to attention as a nine year-old toy soldier. As the procession lined up a couple of hours before the official 'move off', we were queuing outside a house with the curtains and the front door wide open, even on a chilly October evening. Inside the TV must have been on full volume and from our position on our float we were entertained by Brian Poole and The Tremeloes belting out 'Do

You Love Me?', giving it their all, on the television, another of those songs that will take me back to that very moment in time, forever etched in my memory. But the deluge of pop music became increasingly evident as the parade slowly moved into the small town centre where *Stevens Carnival Funfair* filled every part of our broad High Street. I've always been in love with the excitement, colour and sound of a travelling fair, but to a young lad smitten by pop music, this fair, in our town at this time, was just so amazing. The roar of the generators and the distorted loud speakers screaming out the most amazing sounds played on a record player suspended by 'bungees' in the paybox to prevent the pick-up arm skidding across the vinyl record. The music slowed down or sped up depending on the 'load' placed on the generators, as the rides - The Twist, The Swoosh, The Sputnik Chaser and the De-Luxe Dodgems - started and stopped. It's difficult to imagine just how exciting this explosion of sound and colour was in a normally quiet sleepy town, tame perhaps by today's standards, but more than half a century ago it was about as exciting as life got. It was just magical!

And then, the next day it was all over and we were back to craving the pop music that was clearly available but somehow overlooked by the broadcasters. Sunday lunchtime's *Two Way Family Favourites,* played very few of the current pop songs, but at least it featured music, unlike the radio shows that followed, *The Navy Lark* or the *Clitheroe Kid,* both comedy shows, but both very much in the 'middle class, white collar' style of BBC humour. *The Billy Cotton Band show* was another Sunday broadcast. It had a huge audience, but there was nothing else to tune into. As the father of the future head of BBC Television, Bill Cotton, welcomed his listeners with a cheery 'Wakie Wakie' and his band struck up music hall hits. Radio was just so unbelievably DULL! Television was slightly better, *Thank Your Lucky Stars, Juke Box Jury* and *Ready Steady Go!* were all 'pop music' shows and there was always one chart song on children's TV shows such as *Crackerjack.*

I remember the show featuring the hit tune 'Nutrocker' and, although it was by B Bumble and The Stingers, I only remember seeing one man on a piano. A great name, but the Stingers had buzzed off it seemed. ITV's *Five O'Clock Club* also featured a chart hit performance and was hosted by Wally Whyton and Muriel Young, together with Pussycat Willum, Ollie Beak and Fred Barker (all puppets). Peppa Pig is nothing new!

But it wasn't just the music that I was aware of, although I knew little of the importance at the time; I became aware of big news stories. I know exactly where I was when the announcement was made that President Kennedy had been assassinated - Mr Rand's coal yard in Southminster. It was Dad's payday and we were there to pay the coal bill. I wasn't sure who President Kennedy was, but I knew his death was an important story, especially if my dad and the coalman were discussing it. Other than that, I seldom remember any references in our house to anything remotely connected to politics. It was the same when Marilyn Monroe died. Again, I didn't know who she was, but I could paint a picture of where I was, how I heard about it and even what the weather was like: Wrekin Farm in Althorne, my dad's boss's wife at about 4.15pm … beautiful blue skies and a warm August day. "Marilyn Monroe is dead," she called out. I figured she must have been very important.

Fortunately, one story that I was protected from at this time was the seemingly imminent end of the world during the Cuban missile crisis. I don't think young children nowadays are as protected as we were from daily reports of horror and death as they have access to all forms of media now.

I was only nine years old when I was offered my first job. We lived in a cottage in a tiny hamlet called Ostend, not the town in Belgium, that was where our mail would often go before postcodes were invented – more than once my birthday cards, or worse, birthday presents arrived some months later after taking a European tour.

Our Ostend was a mile from Burnham-on-Crouch, and our cottage was just as far as the paperboy would deliver. However, Mr Pye was a farmer living another half mile further on and he wanted his *Daily Telegraph* delivered every day. So as 1964 started I was earning the princely sum of 6d a week, 1d a day (one old penny) for walking to and from Elm Farm in all weathers, rain and shine, just to ensure the occupant could sit and read his daily newspaper, although I was given Sunday off.

Now, all these years later I've been doing a little research on my paymaster, Mr Pye, and the interesting thing is, he was the son of the founder of W G Pye Ltd – the famous Cambridge based radio company. Harold, my Mr.Pye, was a bit of a wizard at design and had been responsible for the famous art deco Pye wireless, hugely popular in the 1920s and 30s. By the early 1960s he was worth heaps of money and he retired after the Pye company merged with the huge EKCO radio company, based in nearby Southend and Mr Pye became a farmer, hence his connection to Elm Farm, just up the road from my home.

Considering that at the age of nine I trudged back and forth to his house every day in all weathers my labour was grossly undervalued – a trait that was to haunt me throughout my working life, but I can claim to be one of the last living survivors who worked for just one penny a day. Strange to think that I worked for the guy who designed and built some of the most iconic of 'wireless' sets, without realising the significance at the time.

Then suddenly it was Easter 1964, and the world was about to become a far more exciting place for me and millions of radio listeners in the UK.

Chapter Two

"We Love the Pirate Stations"

Just how millions of us got to hear about this new radio station broadcasting from a ship just a few days after its first transmission of pop music was a mystery. There was no official announcement – it just appeared on the radio, but in our house, we were certainly aware of it. I can picture it now, the Easter Monday edition of the *Daily Mirror*, it had news of the radio station on the back page: '*Pop pirate ship ... non stop music ... outrageous... BBC challenged... shouldn't be allowed ... bla bla bla*'. I can vividly remember saying to my mum, "that's the radio station that we've been listening to."

Having been involved with Radio Caroline in more recent years, you'd be amazed at how many people claim to have tuned in over that first weekend in 1964: "I've been listening since day one", they say, and perhaps they have.

Radio Caroline was on the air, and listening to the music and announcements from a ship anchored not far from where we lived on the east coast, it had me hooked from the start. Although I didn't know it at the time, it would have a huge influence on my life.

Talk at school was of this new radio station. Our wonderful teacher, Mr. Hosegood, as always, was on the ball and mentioned it when we returned to class after the Easter holidays. The songs they were playing in those first few days are still so familiar: 'You're My World' by Cilla, 'I Believe' by The Bachelors, 'Juliet' by The Four Pennies, 'Can't Buy Me Love' by The Beatles and so many more.

The BBC had lost the chance to shine, it was always going to be Caroline from now on in our house. A few weeks later and the second shipborne radio station, *Radio Atlanta* appeared, "I don't like that as much as Caroline", I remember my mum saying to a friend of hers, "It sounds far too American for me."

It wasn't long before Atlanta and Caroline merged to become Caroline North and South. Interestingly, the man behind Radio Atlanta, Allan Crawford, was the guy who operated Rocket Records, the company producing those cover versions of the hits of the day, including the first Beatles song in our record collection.

The pirate stations certainly attracted my interest, broadcasting from ships with huge aerial masts, the music, certainly in the very early days, slowing down as the generators struggled with their job of keeping a shipborne radio station on air, just like the generators at the fair. The disc jockeys gave us listeners a 'behind the scenes' insight into what was going on. To me, it was like another world coming at me from our radio, even though, as I would find out many years later, it was quite a mundane existence for much of the time, with very little glamour for those onboard. But if brave souls were prepared to go through hell in rough seas on small ships, as they battled against seasickness, just to play me the latest Beatles record then me, and millions of other listeners, were prepared to give them our support. Wherever you went you would hear the Caroline bell '*ding ding*'.

"This is Radio Caroline on 199, your all-day music station".

As is the way with nine year-olds, I was inclined to get a bit carried away with the truth, or perhaps it was just exaggeration, but I remember telling one of my school chums that Simon Dee, the first Caroline DJ, was my uncle – this is the same uncle who'd also been Freddie Garrity from Freddie and The Dreamers a few months earlier. I soon dropped those stories and changed my ways when the mother of a school chum challenged me about it, but, at least, Freddie Garrity had the same hairstyle as my uncle Don.

In June 1964 my 10th birthday present was a brand-new turquoise and orange Raleigh bike (those colours were all the rage) with the latest 'twist grip 3 speed gears' and it was by far the best bike in the school bike shed. But that wasn't all.

Thanks to my mum saving five wrappers from Armour baked bean cans and a ten shilling postal order, I received a state-of-the-art transistor radio.

It was tiny, Japanese, about 8 inches by 4 inches and 2 inches deep, made of newly available moulded plastic and wrapped in a faux leather case, with strap. The recent invention of transistors, replacing those huge glowing electric valves found in the older wireless, allowed the Japanese to flood the market with these little radios.

The sound quality was awful when compared to today's standards, but the pirate stations were broadcasting on AM and we'd never been able to have portable music before. Tuning was difficult too. Move the dial a fraction to the left or right and you'd lose the station, but with the 'quality earpiece included' - the newspaper ads always listed that - and the leather case and strap, you were made aware that you were listening 'off-channel' instantly, by the static screeching in your ear.

What a wonderful 10th birthday I had, and it just got even better. The small amount of cash I received enabled me to join the Caroline Club. For 5 shillings (25p) sent as a postal order to 6, Chesterfield Gardens, London W1, listeners were promised a booklet giving full details of the radio station, the ships and the disc jockeys, plus a personalised club card and a car sticker. Even the application was a major operation and involved a trip to the Post Office to buy a postal order, but with my envelope neatly written and posted, I waited eagerly for my package to arrive… it took ages, so much so, that I had to write and ask if my application to join had been lost, which resulted in me eventually getting two packages, with two personalised cards and, until the club fizzled out when they realised it was costing too much, two separate packages of photographs and updates every time they were issued.

During that summer's school holidays my new bike and new radio were in regular use. With the strap to tie my radio onto the handlebars, I had music on the move – I thought I was so cool!

Caroline's output was so exciting that summer: 'House Of The Rising Sun' by The Animals,'Have I the Right' by The Honeycombs,'When You Walk In The Room' by The Searchers, 'Shout' by Lulu and Manfred Mann's 'Do Wah Diddy Diddy'. Every song coming from that tiny radio speaker was special.

By now, Radio Caroline had been joined by two more 'pirate' stations, Radio Sutch and Radio Invicta, broadcasting, not from ships, but from the old war time forts in the Thames Estuary, the same structures that I'd seen off the coast of Kent a few years earlier. These more recent radio stations were far less professional than Radio Caroline, but I was fascinated by them. The broadcasts seemed very basic, it was as if the disc jockey was playing his own personal record collection with just the occasional hit added and it was obvious that their record library contained very few records. The broadcasts were erratic and low powered, the announcements sounded as if they were being made from a big metal box which in effect, coming from the steel towers positioned atop concrete legs, they were. Although the broadcasts relied on adapted domestic and army surplus equipment, I could receive them loud and clear as I cycled down to the River Crouch at Creeksea.

These days, as a grown-up desperately trying to stay fit, I regularly return to Creeksea, still on my bike and now I realise why those low powered radio broadcasts boomed into my little transistor. On a clear day you can see those towers on the horizon, the wonderfully named Shivering Sands and Red Sands Forts. If they'd turned the volume up, I could almost have heard the songs playing without a radio.

Those Thames forts fascinate me. I have been on several boat trips out to see them up close. They are amazing relics, built in Gravesend and floated into position during the war and still standing, but in desperate need of renovation. I fear they will ultimately rust away and fall into the sea, although with their military and social history they deserve at least some form of preservation for the future.

The great record releases back in that summer of '64 kept on coming. Sitting by the river in the sunshine I'd listen to The Rolling Stones 'It's All Over Now', Dusty Springfield 'I Just Don't Know What To Do With Myself' and then The Beatles with their latest album, *A Hard Day's Night*. Caroline played every track and I was able to listen to all of this on my very own, tiny, and tinny sounding, transistor radio.

This was the Swinging Sixties, and, just by tuning in I was a part of it, though obviously not able to enjoy the full benefits as those a few years older could.

Eventually the seemingly endless summer came to an end, and with it a return to school. The weather soon turned colder and wetter and with less time to spend outdoors I returned to our trusty record player. Now it was more than just a means to play our few, ageing pop records - it became my very own radio station at weekends.

"That was the Avons singing 'Seven Little Girls Sitting In The Back Seat', and coming up next, 'Telstar' from the Tornados". It was just like my interpretation of the BBC request programme that I'd re-enacted a few years earlier, but this time it included the top news stories and the weather forecast, copied from *The People* or *The Daily Mirror* newspapers and interspersed with comments about the supposed rough seas and problems with the generators that I was experiencing. All spoken in my version of a mid-Atlantic accent, with a particular East Anglian twang, and coming 'live' from my bedroom, as I attempted to fill the gap with meaningful speech while changing the records over on my one turntable.

I soon learned that talking, reading scripts and operating a record player at the same time was more difficult than it seemed, and transcribing weather forecasts and news stories from the newspaper took far longer than you'd imagine. I also became aware of the difference between sentences to be read aloud to an audience, albeit, an imaginary one, and sentences to be read to yourself. I still hear news reports from journalists today that are written to be read, but not to be said.

I also learned that while facing a microphone you couldn't see who was behind you. I remember turning around and catching my dad grinning as he entered the bedroom diligently 'tuned in' to my 'broadcasts.'

Those carefree childhood days just raced by, but with the end of summer there was always October half term to look forward to, heralding the return of the distinctive yellow and orange trucks of Joe Stevens' Travelling Funfair. The weekend's carnival events got underway at dusk on the Friday, when the Carnival queen was to be crowned on the dodgem track. The prospect of the first ride on the fair being free had us kids clamouring to take advantage, but the 1964 event promised to be even more exciting. The official guest for the whole weekend was to be a Radio Caroline disc jockey.

The personality was Carl Conway, one of the first voices to be heard on Caroline, who had quickly realised that being tossed around on a ship in rough seas wasn't for him. He elected to work on-shore, carrying out publicity events such as our carnival. The event had always attracted many thousands to our town, but in 1964 attendance was boosted noticeably, with the event promoted on the radio.

As a ten-year-old, I was keen to win one of the cash prizes in the children's fancy dress competition. My mum was very creative and had designed an intricate and colourful costume for me to wear.

I paraded with my fellow schoolmates in fancy dress, waiting to be judged, hoping for first place with a prize of 'half a crown'. Assisting the judges was the Carnival guest, Carl Conway, "and what are you?", he asked as the judging took place, "I'm a firework", I replied. I still have the photographs to prove it.

It couldn't get much better, I had a conversation with a real radio disc jockey, and I won first prize in my age group.

Many years later I would interview Carl at his home in Margate. By this time he had long since retired, but he did remember crowning the carnival queen in Burnham. Sadly,

I think he'd forgotten his conversation with a firework, but he was thrilled when I gave him photocopies of the local newspaper articles featuring his visit many years earlier when both he and I were much younger.

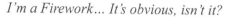

I'm a Firework... It's obvious, isn't it?

Just days before Christmas another offshore radio station arrived off our coast, quickly establishing itself as the most professional of the 'pirates', with disc jockeys like Dave Cash and Kenny Everett. "Biggest Sound Around, Big L' and 'This is Wonderful Radio London" they proclaimed. It was quirky and unpredictable and would cause Caroline (which I still preferred) to up its game, eventually changing its format and broadcasting style.

I always looked forward to our school holidays, weekends were fun, but spending days on end with your mates couldn't be beaten and pop music was becoming more important in my life.

I have vivid memories of a wet afternoon during the Easter holiday, playing Monopoly with school friends. My chum Peter's older brother had a weekend job which meant he had money to buy records, and his collection was large and it was Peter's family that owned the stylish two-tone grey Bush record player that I'd looked at with envy.

High in the pop charts that Easter was The Rolling Stones hit, 'The Last Time' - a wonderfully exciting record. As I sat there hoping that someone would land on my expensive property and pay rent for a hotel on Mayfair, we'd placed the record on the turntable and, leaving the auto-changer arm pushed to one side, the same record would play over and over again. We must have heard 'The Last Time' at least thirty times, until Peter's mother came into the room and told us that this really would be the last time we heard that record if we wanted to stay indoors.

As the school holidays continued I was able to tune into the radio throughout the day, the excitement of non-stop pop music was still something new to us children of the sixties. We also had our favourite DJ's playing the hits. Tony 'Tea Cosy' Blackburn was one, so named because of his hairstyle and another who stood out at the time was Keith Skues. All these years later Skues, a friend still, would be the first to admit that his style of presentation might be considered a little dated now. However, back in 1965 he was just so innovative, with his catch phrases and on-air puns: "I have a card here from a Mrs. Woman from ...", "On the news Cardboard Shoes" and other quirky phrases.

I distinctly remember July 1965, my last few days at primary school and, after walking home for lunch, hearing Skues getting very excited about one particular new record, "Here's a fabulous new record by a group called The Byrds and the song is 'Hey, Mr Tambourine Man." I shared his enthusiasm for the song.

Despite being obsessed with pop music and listening to the radio, I had somehow passed my 11+ exam and as the new school year started I was off to Maldon Grammar School, twelve miles from home and a fifty-minute bus ride.

Whilst I had thoroughly enjoyed my days at primary school, I was never really happy at my new school. I just didn't fit in academically. At primary school I suppose I was reasonably clever, coming fourth or fifth in the class, but now I was in a class made up of many children who had been first, second and third in their primary school classes. I wasn't at the bottom of the class, but I was never far from it.

I didn't particularly like too many of the teachers either and most of them certainly weren't impressed, or even aware of me. I didn't like the Grammar school ethos, it wasn't for me. I hated the way we were called by our surnames, how rude I thought. I still get angry when I think about that ridiculous idea, but here I was, signing up for at least five years at what my friends who hadn't passed their 11+ called 'the posh school.'

Oh, and another stupid idea, we were forced to wear a cap with our uniform for the first two years. Can I sue for losing much of my hair by the age of 21 to that stupid bloody cap? - I'm convinced that's what caused it.

I do remember our first English lesson vividly, despite it being so long ago, with Mr Harrison, who was one of the friendlier teachers. To his credit, he took time during that first lesson to ask our names, so at least we wouldn't be known by him as 'you boy'. As he went around the class I knew my turn was coming soon and one of my first public speaking roles was about to be played out in Room 13.

"So, what's your name?" he asked.

Now remember, I had grown up in a small rural town with ancestors living there for several hundred years and I had a very broad rural Essex accent, nothing like Estuary English which later became the norm in our county, and I certainly didn't speak 'posh' like many at the Grammar school.

"Thaat's Raaymund Claaark" I replied, as he and the entire class erupted into laughter, not out of unkindness, just in surprise that anyone of our age could have such an old-fashioned sounding accent. Within seconds I realised that if I wanted to be on the radio then the accent had to go.

Ironically, more than fifty years later and regional accents are most certainly all the rage. Just listen to the continuity announcements on TV – all of them with a noticeable accent – though I'm yet to hear an example of a really broad East Anglian accent.

I really didn't enjoy the 'big' school. I guess, to most of my fellow pupils the lessons were Important, perhaps that's where I went wrong, because all I wanted to do was listen to pop music on the radio and certainly not spend all day in a classroom.

Shockingly, some of my new classmates had never tuned into the pirate stations, their parents only allowing them to listen to the BBC. Those of us that were fans of pop radio would have heated discussions as to which was the best of the offshore radio stations. One school friend went sailing with his family and he told tales of sailing past the Caroline and London ships. I was so envious of my chum John who'd seen them for real.

Years later, I would experience the joy of sailing out to the Radio Caroline ships. John certainly got a better deal as he only had to contend with potentially rough seas three miles off the coast, by the time I got to go out there the ships were anchored more than twelve miles off the coast

In 1965 I joined a local entertainment group called 'The Higher Lights', a singing troupe, run by a local lady, Annie Brasted. Every year she'd put on a variety show featuring the youngsters from the town, aged 9 to15. Supporting local charities, these performances invariably played to packed houses.

Childhood school friends – The Higher Lights

We'd spend three months rehearsing, meeting every Tuesday evening in the hall at the back of The New Welcome Sailor pub, practising our songs and stage moves, ready for the show in the autumn. It wasn't the singing that appealed to me, but I did like the whole idea of entertaining and, I'd have loved the job of the compere. Sadly. that was left to a grown-up, though I do remember supplying him with a joke about the Isle of Wight ferry, which he used. Okay, seeing as you asked: 'What's brown, steams and comes out of Cowes?'

The best bit about my new school was the daily bus journey, I especially enjoyed the journey home. There was always music from at least one radio onboard playing those fab songs:'I Got You Babe' by Sonny and Cher. 'Hang On Sloopy' by The McCoys and the latest hits from the Kinks, The Who, The Stones and The Beatles.

Sometimes we enjoyed live music. Two of the older guys on the school bus, Colin and Tim, were in a band and would bring their guitars, entertaining us with their renditions of the Top 10, and they weren't bad at all. I remember their performance of one song in particular, and whenever I hear it, my mind goes back to that school bus journey.

A guy with the unlikely sounding name of Crispian St Peters had a hit song called 'You Were On My Mind.' Colin was the singer, breaking into song … "Well I woke up this morning …." he sang, "Pity" called out one of the older boys. We all laughed out loud and it still makes me smile thinking of it now.

In our chemistry and physics lessons we were taught various scientific charts, but the only chart that I was interested in was the pop music chart. I knew all the chart positions and I was aware of all the new bands and their songs - even the songs that the offshore stations featured that never became national hits.

It wasn't just the pop tunes that would permanently be playing in my mind, I was also captivated by the commercials. In those days television commercials often featured catchy jingles and as the pirates became more established and popular many nationally known companies appeared on air with great sounding ads:

"Square meal nourishment, that's what you get with Weetabix," "Four kinds of Sunsilk shampoo, one is for you?," "Shimmer into summer with eyes bright and beautiful, eye colour from Evette, exclusive from Woolworths beauty counters.."

But not only did these radio ads feature catchy jingles, the pirates, and Radio London in particular, played the most amazing station jingles.

It took a few years to discover the story behind the wonders of jingles and their production. I had no idea that in America every radio station played these amazing little songs all the time and that in most cases, as with those we heard on Radio London, they were made by a company called PAMS, Production and Marketing from Dallas. "You're hearing things …on … Wonderful Radio London."

Caroline had much to learn, their jingles were homemade, and it showed, although even their 'imaging' as it's called nowadays was better than the BBC. The closest they came to having a jingle was the Greenwich Time Signal.

One bitterly cold morning in January 1966 I woke up to dramatic news. It was the start of a really unpleasant winter's day that you remember from your school days. Bleak and dark, just a few days after returning to school after the Christmas holidays. Nothing to look forward to in the foreseeable future and those bright, hopeful spring days were a long, long, way off. My Dad called upstairs, "Radio Caroline has sunk." Well, it wasn't quite that bad, but the radio ship had been blown ashore after losing her anchor. The winter winds had been blowing for days from the North East, and living on the Essex marshes,it was noticeable that this was the coldest and strongest direction for them to blow in from.

Just up the coast, across a few miles of fields and three miles of sea from where we lived was the Radio Caroline anchorage, or, more to the point, where the Caroline ship should have been anchored before she lost her anchor and drifted, going aground near Frinton. The situation around the small ship became headline news, whilst the DJ's were rescued and safe, the ship was in great peril.

The next day there were amazing photographs across the national newspapers of the stranded ship high and dry on the beach. There were real fears that she would break up if she spent much longer being pounded by huge waves and stranded on the beach,

Us Caroline fans really suffered. Not only were we without our favourite radio station, but we were also forced to listen to Radio London for our fix of pop music and worse still, our friends who were staunch Big L fans ridiculed us for supporting a radio station with a wreck of a ship. These things mattered when you were twelve years old. It wasn't until years later that I learnt that the Radio London ship was just as much an old wreck and had itself gone adrift two nights before Caroline, though fortunately for them, they'd taken control of the drift preventing them from running aground.

There was a plus side to Caroline's misfortune, being fascinated by the ships themselves and with photographs hard to come by, the *Mi Amigo*, Caroline's southern ship was all over the newspapers and television news.

Eventually, some two days later the ship was freed from the beach and, although Caroline was publicly saying that all was fine, in truth the ship was holed and in danger of sinking. In later years I met and interviewed most of those who were on the ship at the time and heard the full story of events.

The newspapers said Caroline would be back in a couple of weeks but this period turned out to be the longest two weeks ever. The ship was towed to Holland for repairs, but then came news of a replacement ship, belonging to a Swedish offshore radio station. The Cheetah was to become the temporary home to Radio Caroline. Years later I would learn that the replacement ship was totally inadequate for live broadcasts, the transmitters and aerial were unsuitable, and much work had to be done behind the scenes, including removing parts from the Caroline ship in Holland and shipping them back to the coast and refitting them onboard the Cheetah. But I was impatient to hear the music. I would frequently tune around on our old wireless, straining my ears to hear my favourite radio station, but to no avail.

Occasionally I would pick up a loud hum. Could this be Caroline's transmitter ready to burst into action I wondered? But invariably it was a 'spurious emission' (what a wonderful phrase that is), caused by the signal from our own television. We also now had a modern portable radio, in cream and red, with a spinning tuning dial, all made of strong moulded plastic, but it used up battery power in huge amounts. Two huge square Ever Ready batteries made it work brilliantly, but within hours they needed replacing.

The days turned to weeks before I was to hear Radio Caroline again, but then, while tuning around on a Saturday evening in late February, I heard Nancy Sinatra's number one song, 'These Boots Are Made For Walking,' playing faintly in the background, almost swamped out by static, whistles and interference from other stations. More chart songs followed, until I was certain that Radio Caroline was about to return to my radio after such a long period of silence.

Those initial broadcasts were very erratic, another song of the time was '19th Nervous Breakdown' by The Rolling Stones, and whenever I hear this I always hear it as I did back on that dark February night in 1966. Not only was the broadcast quality very poor, but problems with the ship's generators caused the Stones' record to slow down and speed up as it played: I thought it improved it!

It took several days before a regular, reliable service started again on199 metres, albeit on low power, but at least us Caroline fans at school had some ammunition to return to the Big L fans who were bad mouthing our station.

As Easter approached there was still no sign of Caroline's Mi Amigo returning. I remember listening one evening after school and DJ Dave Lee Travis, obviously fed up with the situation, reported that now the replacement ship was being towed away for repairs as she'd sprung a leak, "...and now we're sinking", he said. Fortunately, repairs were soon sorted, and the station returned to the air, just as the original Caroline South ship arrived back in her position off the Essex coast. Disc Jockey Graham Webb announced "what a good Good Friday this is,"as the Mi Amigo came sailing over the horizon.

Within days the repaired ship, now with a more powerful transmitter, was on the air and on a new frequency. After almost three months of sporadic broadcasting Caroline showed that they meant business and were out to regain their missing audience.

For a few days during April 1966 and fortunately coinciding with the school holiday, there were two Radio Caroline South services, with broadcasts on two frequencies from the two ships, playing different songs and the DJ's on one ship telling us to re-tune to the other ship. It was fun, and a great time to listen to the radio and, in my opinion, we were about to enjoy the most exciting summer of radio listening ever, thanks to some incredible record releases.

I still think 1966 was one of the best ever years, not just for pop music and radio. So much was new and exciting, especially for kids of my age: Batman & Robin on TV, World Cup Willie Bubble Gum - I guess England winning the World Cup could also be included, oh, and Zoom ice lollies.

I just loved listening to all those fantastic, exciting new songs being played nonstop on the radio, and I paid attention to all the disc jockeys, some better than others, what they were saying, and took note of their individual styles. At last, here in the UK, we were able to enjoy the sort of Top 40 radio that American audiences had been listening to for years.

I can remember the point in the song where Caroline's copy of 'Substitute' by The Who would stick and I can tell you where and when I first heard 'Bus Stop' by The Hollies - it was one Sunday morning, just before eight o'clock, played by Tony Blackburn.

Writing these words years later, it's obvious I was smitten with listening to the radio and even at the age of eleven I knew what I wanted to do in the future. It's hardly surprising that I have spent much of my adult life living my childhood dream.

Just days after Caroline had, effectively, relaunched, there was yet another exciting radio occurrence off the Essex coast. A new pirate radio ship and this time it was home to two new radio stations; Britain Radio, a middle of the road station playing Sinatra and light melodies and Swinging Radio England - way ahead of its time in the UK, but presented in all American style - well almost all American, apart from two of the new 'Boss jocks'. Both were Brits: Johnnie Walker with the broadest 'Brummie' accent and Roger Day. Neither had ever worked on the radio before, and at the time, it showed.

Swinging Radio England, (SRE) was full on radio, slick presentation, all at breakneck speed, with echo on the disc jockey's voices, more songs per hour than any other station and huge production for the introduction to the news, '*This is Radio England Bannerline News – This news is BIG news in the world today*' and every song was followed or introduced by the latest American jingles '*you get a positive 'charge', here on Swinging Radio England*'. It was just so very exciting.

Many years later it would be one of those 'Boss jocks', Roger Day, who would offer me my first full-time job on the radio, so events around Swinging Radio England, all those years earlier were to have a huge effect on me. Strangely, even more years later, Ron O'Quinn, the guy who gave Walker and Dayo a job, was very complimentary about my style of presentation after tuning in whilst he was in the UK. 'I'd have given Ray a job", he said to a friend who was driving him to the airport.

The tests for Radio England and Britain Radio went on for some time, with the two radio stations alternating their frequencies. The difficulties in operating radio stations from ships at sea were enormous, although as listeners we were oblivious to the major feat of engineering taking place in rough seas off our coast.

I found it fascinating, turning the dial on our portable radio between the two separate broadcasts, coming from the same ship. The music was the very best of the charts. It was a copy of the American Top 40 stations that kids in the States were growing up with, like New York's *WABC* or *WMCA,* but this was all new to us here in the land where, until a couple of years earlier the BBC had ruled the radio waves.

My daily journey to school was enjoyable now as we had at least four radios on the top deck of our bus. Depending on where you were sitting, and that depended on which school year you were in, you could hear Radio Caroline, Radio London, Radio City and Radio England. It was possible to hear the number one song four times during the fifty-minute journey and most of the Top 10 hits as well.

I remember so very well one gloriously sunny, warm spring morning, I can picture it vividly, and my guess is that it was the last week of May 1966. We were travelling to school and the fast-talking American DJ on SRE went from 'Monday Monday' by The Mamas & Papas to 'Paint it Black' by The Rolling Stones. *"In swinging England this song is 'boss song' number one one one one one one..."*

How exciting, and even now, whenever I hear the first few notes of either of those songs, I am taken back to that beautiful morning, travelling on our double decker bus on the way to school.

Could it get any better? Oh yes! On weekends Radio England was playing oldies, flashbacks and golden greats they called them.

Nothing new nowadays, but back in 1966 the rock and roll back catalogue was still relatively new, so even the oldest oldie was no more than twelve years old. Prior to the arrival of the radio ships the BBC had played just a few new pop songs that it decided we should hear, and once they were out of the charts they were never played again, unless they were novelty songs that were featured regularly on *Children's Favourites* on the BBC Light Programme. I'd already outgrown 'The Runaway Train' and 'The Teddy Bears Picnic.'

I was learning, without realising it, about the mechanics of radio, just by listening to this new style of exciting radio. I became aware of differing formats and styles of presentation, promotions, and advertising, obviously intended to attract different audiences. The advertising campaigns would change throughout the year, depending on the season, and there were great competitions, such as Radio Caroline's 'Cash Casino' which gave the chance to win huge amounts of money (for the time, £2,000+), just by solving daily clues. I encouraged my mum to enter. Each entry had to be accompanied by a 'product proof of purchase' connected to the various advertisers involved, such as Weetabix, Libby's Canned Fruit and Findus Frozen Foods.

The crews on the ships changed every two weeks and that meant new voices, some never to return and occasionally, as with Tony Blackburn and Norman St. John, moving from Caroline to be rediscovered on Big L, Radio London, days later.

At the age of 12, I would compare the playlists of each radio station. Their individual pop charts were all different, Radio London's was well ahead of the others and often included songs that no other station was playing. It was obvious that some financial deal was behind many of the hits.

I was aware of The Kinks hit song, 'Dedicated Follower Of Fashion' being absent from Caroline's programmes, but played hourly on Radio London. I thought it was because of the lyrics. Years later I would realise that I'd misheard them, but at the time I was convinced that Ray Davies was singing something like, "Big L hugs and digs" in fact it was the line "… as fickle as can be". Go on, play it. You'll see what I mean. Although not always correct in my interpretations, I was pretty clued up as to how pop music radio worked.

Caroline was the first of the pirates, but there were many listeners who thought the output had been unadventurous when compared to Big L and Radio England. Now it upped its game. 'The Sound Of The Nation', on 259 metres, suddenly came alive with Emperor Rosko, Mike Ahern, Robbie Dale and Tom Lodge. Just great charismatic 'friends on the radio' playing the hits. Many of them still are played to this day and still sound great: 'Pretty Flamingo,' 'Summer In The City,' 'Wild Thing,' 'Good Vibrations,' 'Friday On My Mind.' And let's not forget The Beatles. The album *Revolver*, with fabulous, futuristic tracks like 'Tomorrow Never Knows,' and, in my opinion, the best Beatles single that never was - the B side of 'Paperback Writer.' 'Rain', complete with the fascinating effect of John Lennon's voice, reversed by a backwards running tape, and Ringo's fabulous drumming. It was as if every song released was trying to better the one before. Combine all that with the classic hits coming from the American charts - take time to listen to Billy Stewart's incredible version of 'Summertime,' and Lorraine Ellison oozing passion whilst singing 'Stay With

Me Baby' and you'll see why 1966 was such an amazing year for music.

I would daydream, in a way that schoolboys do, of having my own radio station in a shed in the back garden and playing all these great songs. I'd even draw plans for where the record decks and tape recorders would go.

Another of my favourite listens was Radio City, broadcasting from the former wartime defence forts in the Thames estuary. Whenever the disc jockey opened the microphone to speak, the constant ringing of the warning bell on the navigational buoy, marking the wonderfully-named Shivering Sands close by, could be heard. Events around this station would ultimately lead to the government crackdown on the offshore stations after the Radio City boss was shot dead.

Shivering Sands Forts – So much history...

There were also shipborne radio stations further north, a long way from Essex and I would try to receive their broadcasts by taking the aerial wire from the back of our wireless and holding the bare metal onto the chrome strip around the top of the fridge. I don't know if I was risking electrocution just to listen to the radio – I have had several close encounters with electricity over the years, but the signal of whatever I was listening to certainly increased. Sadly, it didn't allow me to listen to Radio 270, off Scarborough or Radio Scotland – but I did hear Caroline North, from the Isle of Man early one morning.

Waking early, around 5.30am on an already sunny morning I remember turning my faithful, tiny transistor radio on to hear a selection of Caroline news jingles followed by the introduction jingle that Caroline North always started with – it was different to Caroline South's start-up. The two stations were run as completely different outfits and I suppose I heard someone in the on-air studio playing the jingles, but they hadn't realised that the studio was 'live'. Another fascinating insight into what happened behind the scenes.

On this same morning, any chance of hearing anything other than the powerful Caroline South signal was then lost as the southern ship came on the air, now with a huge 50-kilowatt transmitter, always starting with the same, iconic song, 'Caroline' by The Fortunes. That drum roll smashing over the static. It sounded so good then and still does whenever I play it on the radio now, nearly 60 years after hearing it every morning at 6am.

You always knew when Radio Caroline was about to burst back into life after any closedown period. As the ship was anchored just a few miles away, the carrier, in effect the sound of the transmitter without music, was very distinctive. With a warm, but very slight hum - it was unmistakably Caroline.

*****

There were now thousands attending our town carnival by 1966, so a loudspeaker system, stretching almost a mile, was installed throughout Burnham's long main street to help with crowd control and to make announcements in between playing records.

Although I was too young to become involved, I listened intently to the announcements coming from the 'studio' based in the town's Clock Tower overlooking our broad High Street, which was filled with a large funfair and huge crowds. The style of presentation was obviously based on the output of the pirates everyone was listening to and the songs played were the same as the ships were playing. Broadcasting throughout our town from those cylindrical cone shaped Tannoy speakers came the hits of the day, The Four Tops with 'Reach Out I'll Be There',' The Sandpipers' 'Guantanamera' and 'Still I'm Sad' by The Yardbirds. It all sounded so exciting to me and by now I had decided that this was the sort of thing I wanted to become involved with when I left school.

It was Christmas Eve 1966, and the family went shopping to Southend on Sea. Christmas was always a special time in our house, Mum and Dad would go a bit bonkers with presents for us kids. Money was extremely tight throughout the year, but at Christmas we had everything we could possibly want, and certainly more than we needed. But on this occasion we made a stop at Curry's, the High Street electrical chain. These were the days before shopping malls and out of town retail parks; we were in the town's Southchurch Road, then part of a thriving town centre. My sisters and I were left outside speculating about what our parents were buying. We decided it was a portable typewriter for my eldest sister and when they came out of the shop their purchase certainly looked like a typewriter case. But on Christmas morning - Wow! Fidelity said the name on the two-tone grey moulded plastic case. It was a reel to reel tape recorder and, unlike the previous machine a few years earlier, this one recorded and played back at a consistent speed. There was also a reel of tape with a demonstration recording that is still very special to me. I only have a short segment of it now, but it was a Happy Christmas message from my mum, followed by a recording from a Christmas Eve television show, made long after I'd gone to bed, of Tom Jones singing 'Green Green Grass of Home'. It had been recorded from the television using the microphone, which, according to the instruction book, was to be placed about twelve inches from the TV speaker. Halfway through this recording the rustling sound of the microphone being dragged closer to the TV can be heard, followed by my dad justifying his reason for moving it: "Well that's a foot", says Dad, sadly the only recording I have of him.

Now 'Radio Ray' was really in business. Besides a record player in my bedroom studio, I had the means to play the hits of the day and jingles and commercials, all recorded from our big old wireless. Even better, unlike our first tape recorder, this one could be connected directly to the speaker output on the wireless, so I could make recordings of songs without the budgie chirping all over them.

I would sit at the kitchen table listening to the radio with the two mechanical 'record' levers poised, waiting for a particular song that I wanted to record. The art was to judge when the DJ had finished talking, giving me a clean recording of as much of the song as was possible. I had to be very selective as to what songs I recorded as the running time of my tape was just 30 minutes each side and I had just one reel of tape. I had no idea where you would buy extra reels of tape and I was pretty sure the cost would far exceed my pocket money.

I became a teenager in June 1967 and had enough money to buy my first LP record. It had to be *Sergeant Pepper's Lonely Hearts Club Band*. The Beatles fabulous new album had been released just a few days before my 13th birthday. A note from school was duly obtained to allow me to go into town at lunchtime and I eagerly awaited the 12.30 school bell. I practically ran to Miss Cater's record shop in the High Street, her window displaying coloured light bulbs that alternated between red, green and yellow. If you stood close enough you could hear the regular 'click' from the automated light switch. There was a selection of faded LP sleeves placed behind the 'light display' and in the corner a sign that read 'Honey For Sale.'

The princely sum of 32/6d, (£1.62p) - a lot of money for a 13-year-old to spend - was handed over for my first LP. Miss Cater took the beautifully laminated double-gated cardboard sleeve, complete with its wonderful images, from the pigeon hole behind the counter and placed it into a shiny, brown paper bag.

Walking back to school I peeked into the bag, hardly able to contain my excitement. There really had never been anything like it before, and one quick glimpse captured what looked like the lyrics to all the songs on the back of the sleeve. How wonderful was that? As I walked proudly into school clutching the album, my fellow classmates crowded around, just as eager as me to see, feel, smell, and read the album cover. It was already in danger of being handled too much. Fortunately, the crowd that had built up around me and my treasure faded away as the bell went for a return to lessons, and on this Wednesday afternoon, it was Music, in Room 13. We entered the recently built room where we were taught to translate classical pieces into a series of dots and quavers as we sat listening to, what were, as far as I was concerned, completely unfamiliar tunes, not even any hint of 'classical music's greatest hits. But I did take the opportunity to place my new album on the desk, so I could continue to stare at it with pride. As our music teacher, Miss Williams, walked by, she glanced at the sleeve, and even she realised what it was and, for probably the first time in my years at the school, acknowledged something that was of interest to me.

I was amazed that she knew who The Beatles were. "I could play this as part of the lesson," she said. Great, I thought: I wouldn't have to wait until the following lessons were over and the bus had taken me home before I could hear the Beatles. "But", she continued, "it's open day for the new parents and I don't think they'd get the right idea about the school if they heard The Beatles." And so I had to wait.

Home at last, I carefully removed the gleaming disc of black vinyl from its sleeve and placed it proudly on the record player.

The volume turned loud to enjoy the first track as the orchestra tuned up in the crowded auditorium. The album painted such beautiful pictures in my mind from the start, and then the wonderful introduction led to Paul McCartney singing "It was twenty years ago today..." Well, even after more than fifty years it is still a very special thing to listen to.

The tracks that followed were already familiar, having been played on the radio, and I loved them all, although George Harrison's Indian influenced 'Within You Without You' sounded decidedly strange to my ears, I felt a bit embarrassed by it at the time.

How times and attitudes have changed. Try listening to it again now, years later and it's as 'groovy' as the rest of the album, and like several of George Harrison's tracks, ahead of its time. 'Lucy In The Sky With Diamonds', 'She's Leaving Home', 'A Day In The Life'... it was some time before I stopped playing this record on a daily basis. My excitement was tempered by some worrying information as the school holidays got underway. It was the news that many radio listeners had been dreading. Since Radio Caroline had first appeared on air, more than three years earlier, the government had been threatening legislation that would outlaw the offshore radio stations and bring to an end our supply of non-stop pop music. The radio stations that millions listened to would become illegal overnight, forcing them to close down. Sadly, one by one the radio stations announced their imminent closure - all of them, except for Caroline, which remained defiant and announced it would stay on air.

I was so angry. I don't think I've ever forgiven those politicians for taking away my music. It was obvious that the radio stations needed to be regulated, but there really was no excuse for such draconian measures. I sat with my tape recorder listening to Radio London at 3pm on that Monday afternoon, August 14th, 1967. The last song played? It had to be, The Beatles classic, 'A Day In The Life.'

"Big L time is three o'clock, and Radio London is now

closing down"... and it did...*"crackle, hum, click..."* and then silence.

I spun the radio dial from 266 metres across to 259 metres, the home of Radio Caroline. "Welcome to the continuing voice of free radio ...", disc jockey Robbie Dale announced, then he explained that Caroline would still continue after the new act of parliament became law at the end of that day.

I tried to stay awake on the evening of August 14th as Johnnie Walker - I remember the jingle: *'He's in, Johnnie Walker, He's on,'* - announced that Caroline would continue and defy the new government ban. Although I was asleep long before midnight, I was up early the next morning, eager to see if Caroline was still on the radio, and fearing that the ship had been blown out of the water by the Navy. The programmes continued, but now with just three disc jockeys to broadcast 24 hours a day. Ah: if only I'd been a bit older...

Radio Caroline did honour their commitment to continue. At first nothing appeared to change, but after a while the lack of new records was noticeable and the few DJ's that the station had, were on the ship for weeks at a time, rather than changing over every two weeks. There were now more commercials on air than there had ever been, but there was a fascinating reason for this.

The new law had made it illegal for UK firms to advertise on the radio station, but, although there were a few obvious plugs for records and small businesses, Caroline attempted to hoodwink the authorities by playing numerous ads dating from the days when they were legitimately booked to be heard on Caroline. American commercials for International products could be heard and they even resorted to recording commercials from the television and playing them on air. The clever idea was to confuse the authorities as to which advertisements were real and paid for, and which were decoys. Caroline might have tried to cover up the paid plugs, but as an avid listener I could certainly tell the difference.

For six weeks Radio Caroline was the only place to go to for pop music, but the BBC had been given the task of replacing the pirates, something us listeners thought would never be possible.

Chapter Three

'Wonderful Radio 1'? - I Wasn't a Fan

I remember well the day that BBC Radio 1 started. It was Saturday September 30th, 1967, at 7am. Once again I was in position to record the opening on my faithful tape recorder. Just ahead of the first show from Tony Blackburn we listeners were asked by an old man in a suit to make the switch to Radio 1 or Radio 2, from the old BBC Light programme.

I got the shock of my life that morning, but not from the exciting new sound of 'Wonderful Radio 1'. The top of the mains plug on my well used tape recorder had worked loose and as I attempted to unplug the machine the top of the plug came off in my hand and as my fingers touched the inside workings of the mains plug I received one almighty electric shock. Attempting to remove an open-topped electrical plug from the mains is not something I'd recommend.

I was prepared to give the new station a chance. I'd even bought a copy of *Radio Times* that listed the new programmes and dipped in and out of most of the shows throughout the day. A quiz presented by former Radio London DJ, Duncan Johnson, followed by Keith Skues and Saturday Club. At mid-day, former Caroline presenter Emperor Rosko exploded onto the BBC. The British Broadcasting Corporation had never heard anything quite like this. Rosko's crazy, wild man style of presentation seemingly shocked the news reader, "And now the BBC News, read for you in English." he said. I gave it a fair chance and although this new radio station was doing all the things that the pirates had done - playing the hits with the new soundalike pirate radio jingles made by the same company - it just wasn't wonderful radio to my ears. It wasn't the same as the pirates and it certainly didn't excite me.

Radio 1 soon became the number one radio station in the UK.

Caroline continued throughout the hard winter of 1967, but by now supply deliveries to the ship became very erratic. New records were noticeable by their absence, with the American Hot 100 being featured rather than the UK chart, as these records were easier for them to get, sent out to the ship via Holland. The Marine etc.Broadcasting (Offences) Act 1967 had forced both Caroline ships to be tendered from abroad. By now there were no 'paid for' commercials, other than constant 'plugs' for songs on the Major Minor record label, which was owned by the man financing Caroline, record promoter Phil Solomon. It all came to an end as both ships were towed into port after the money had run out. Sunday March 3rd 1968 was a dull, damp day, made even worse by the vacant frequency on the medium wave band. I, like millions of others, spent all day tuning around, trying to find Caroline's signal. Maybe they'd changed their position on the dial, or perhaps just gone off the air for maintenance. Sadly though, after almost four years of fabulous radio this was the end, no more Radio Caroline, seemingly forever. Radio 1 was there, but I still wasn't a fan. It seemed like the BBC was 'the enemy' and to tune in would have been disloyal to the memory of the offshore stations. I even avoided watching too much BBC TV, preferring the Independent Commercial Channels, Anglia from Norwich, and Southern from Southampton. Many programmes on BBC television seemed far too stuffy, pompous and 'posh' for my taste.

Whilst Britain had outlawed the pirates, the Netherlands, just seventy sea miles away had failed to introduce a similar act to that of the UK, giving the exiled Caroline DJ's a home. I developed an interest in Holland and the Dutch. Although I didn't know any Dutch people at the time, they seemed okay to me.

The Dutch also had their own pirate radio station, Radio Veronica, which pre-dated Caroline, having started in 1960, it was hugely popular in the low countries. I tuned in and enjoyed the 'pirate sound' but unlike the UK stations, Veronica's shows were recorded on land and sent out to the ship on tape. Many of the records were familiar, with much of the Veronica pop chart, *The Tip Parade*, made up of UK recordings plus a few records from Dutch bands that performed in English. And, importantly. they had jingles.

I was soon listening after school to a guy called Lex Harding, who had a show aimed at teenagers with great songs, jingles, and commercials, in Dutch. I began to understand much of what was being said. I got the gist of the chat, fathomed out the commercials, most of which were for cigarettes, Pall Mall Export and Caballero, two stroke petrol for mopeds by Shellina, and Berdie, which I think was a dry cleaners specialising in suede and leather. There was also an ad, played frequently for a product called Clearasil which helped to clear acne from Dutch teenagers' faces, something that I had more than a passing interest in at the age of 13. I even managed to follow the stories on the hourly news bulletins from Veronica… and I can still count to 100 and recite a couple of Dutch tongue twisters too, it's still one of my party pieces.

I wasn't the only British listener. Before long Robbie Dale, one of the Caroline stalwarts, was given a regular show on the station to increase the British audience. Sadly, his show was broadcast in the evening and reception was difficult for me after dark, despite the ship being just 70 miles across the North Sea. I did write to the station though, and after a long wait received a package of photographs of the ship and DJs, a Veronica car sticker, and a copy of the Radio Veronica Top 40 chart. Medium wave reception was poor, we were yet to experience the clarity of FM listening and were quite happy to put up with the most difficult listening conditions to hear a foreign station that faded and often lost the battle against static with its relatively low powered signal. Mind you, the BBC's Radio 1 was only available on medium wave at this time, apart from when it joined up with Radio 2, which was also available on VHF(FM). Radio 1 was practically impossible to listen to because of interference, certainly after dark on the

Essex coast. It was made more difficult as Radio Tirana from the Albanian capital started its broadcasts at 4pm with their haunting, slightly frightening call sign of nine eerie trumpet notes. If you ever tried to listen to Radio 1 after 4pm on a winter evening in the UK then I'll guarantee you're humming that eerie tune as you read these words.

I was starting to come to terms with listening to Radio 1, at least for some of the time, and although Radio Veronica continued off the Dutch coast, it seemed certain that the magic of British pirates would be denied us for evermore, until... Easter Saturday, 1968, a few weeks after Caroline had closed down, and my slightly older school friends, Ian and Tony knocked on the door. "Quick, can we tune your radio into a new pirate radio station, it's on short wave". To be honest I'd not had many dealings with the short wave band, and the idea of looking there for pirate stations had never occurred to me.

With great haste I turned on the mains wireless and the three of us stood around in our kitchen, waiting for the valves to warm up, I turned the Bakelite knob and selected short wave. Taking control of the tuning knob we heard all the strange static, bleeps and whistles that were associated with short wave, until out of thin air came an announcement: *"You're listening to a broadcast test from Radio Victorious, please stay tuned"*. It's strange to think that an announcement such as this could hold so much hope of a return to exciting pirate radio once again. We waited and the message was repeated, "Obviously on a tape loop" I said, sounding knowledgeable about such things. By the third playing of the message the penny had dropped, "Ian, that voice sounds a lot like you."

Radio Victorious was coming from a transmitter operating, not from a ship out at sea, but from my mate's back bedroom just across the road! "Ha ha" they giggled.

I wanted to own a transmitter. I had no idea what they looked like and although the press had published the occasional photograph of the pirate radio ships and the bigger name disc jockeys, we'd never got to see what the technical stuff looked like, although I was pretty sure that a professional transmitter looked nothing like the one that my friends had built. The Radio Victorious transmitter was built into an Old Holborn tobacco tin and consisted of a nine-volt transistor radio battery and a few wires and electrical bits and pieces. By the next day all three of us had our own transmitters and used them to communicate with each other, being very careful not to mention our names, though the range was probably little more than the distance between our three houses.

The novelty soon wore off for Tony and Ian, but I connected the bare wires from this little gadget to a loud speaker that I'd been given and was able to play recordings of my favourite current songs that I had recorded from the Radio 1 chart show, *Pick of the Pops*, and listen to them on the huge old wireless that I'd recently acquired from a rummage sale, positioned on my workshop bench in my bedroom.

Like most teenage lads, I would spend more time in my room than out of it and I'd managed to take the family record player and our small collection of records with me. So, now I had a record player, my beloved Fidelity tape recorder, and a potential death trap of a wireless, which frequently produced sparks whenever I tried to connect it to the other equipment as the audio leads came into contact with the live metal chassis of this monster. It was housed in a heavy wooden casing with the tuner, volume and waveband changer all operated by a pair of pliers, as the Bakelite knobs had been missing when I bought it for five shillings. I knew a bargain when I saw one.

With time on my hands during the school holiday I was making plans for my very own radio station to go on air. Radio Viking would broadcast not only to my mum in the kitchen downstairs, but also via three long pieces of two core electrical flex connected together (taking a route out of my bedroom window and in through the kitchen window) to our next door neighbour. Mrs Amos was well into her 70s and assured me that she was going to be tuned to the non-stop groovy sounds of my bedroom radio station, Radio Viking.

The studio was now made up of two record players, the family auto-changer and a borrowed Dansette and my tape recorder. All of this was precariously balanced on the lid of our twin-tub washing machine supported between a bedside cabinet and a chest of drawers. Because of the difference in height of the two pieces of furniture, the whole set-up sloped towards the end of the room. Speaking, with any chance of my listeners hearing anything, required a very close microphone. technique, almost to the point of swallowing the small plastic microphone that was provided with my tape recorder. I'd found a way of using the tape recorder as an amplifier, but it meant that I could only play a recording or speak, but doing both at the same time just wasn't possible.

Radio Viking continued to appear at various times during my school holidays, but although it went on air at 8am it usually went off air 'for essential engineering' after about an hour. The frustrations of using equipment that really wasn't up to the job were too much to overcome and besides, my audience figures slumped catastrophically when mum left for work, even though Mrs Amos persevered, although her hearing wasn't too good.

*****

If I was going to become a proper disc jockey, what I really needed were professional double decks. Perhaps I could be a disco DJ if I couldn't get a job on the radio when I left school? My Radio Viking bedroom studio was about to undergo a serious upgrade.

My position in the seating hierarchy on the school bus had moved on considerably. I was now allowed to sit on the front seat although my seniority wasn't yet such that I could sit on the back seat, that was for the really cool guys. My new seating position enabled me to catch up with the lads from the band that had serenaded us with their songs and guitars a year earlier, when we were all still sitting downstairs. Now one of them, Tim, became more interesting to me. Not only did he have a selection of musical instruments, but he also had a couple of matching record decks at home that might be for sale. Those disc jockey double decks that I longed for were close to becoming a reality.

I'd seen copies of *Practical Wireless* magazine, and although the articles talking about diodes, watts and ohms were far too boring and complex for me to want to understand, there were advertisements for public address audio equipment, including the relatively new idea of disco kits.

I soon learned that the Garrard SP25 record deck was the one to get, but at something like £25 with the pick-up cartridge extra, they were far too expensive, made even more unattainable as I needed two of them. There were adverts for 50-watt power amplifiers as well and tall speaker columns. I could only gaze at these black and white adverts with their illustrations, dreaming of what I'd like to have. I knew what I wanted and what all budding disc jockeys needed, but there was no-way I could afford to have them. I was still at school and earning just 17/6d (75 pence) a week from my paper round. So, when Tim on the school bus told me he had some double decks for sale and that they were even fitted into a plinth, another DJ term (I was learning fast), and he was looking at £10 for them I was certainly interested. "Come round at the weekend and take a look at them", he said, "I'll pop in sometime", I replied in a laid-back sort of way. My mind was already made up, those double decks were going to be mine, although I hadn't got £10 of my own at the time, but in that innocent way that children have of knowing that mum and dad will always bail you out, I'd all but agreed to buy them long before seeing what was on offer.

It was another of those days that I can clearly remember, probably because I was so eager to get my hands on the double decks. I knew a little about Tim's family. What I did know was his father ran a band, playing at local events that finished late at night, so when I knocked on his front door, promptly at 10am, I got the feeling that I'd woken the whole family up. I'd also heard that Tim's father worked for a record company, and as the front door opened, I could see piles of brand new LP records stacked against the wall in the hallway.

"Wow, can I look at these?" I asked, as I dived towards them. Brand new, glossy LP covers of the latest albums including The Moody Blues, *In Search Of A Lost Chord*, *Their Satanic Majesties Request* by the Stones and so many more. Then piles of brand new singles, many on the brown and white Deram label, which was one of the new successful labels with exciting new songs, 'A Whiter Shade Of Pale' had been one of their first successes, and all of these records had a huge letter A on their label and the legend, *Demonstration copy only, not for sale…* I'd just walked into vinyl heaven.

"The record decks are in here," said my new best friend. I walked into a room off the hallway and there, next to a selection of guitars, drums and amplifiers were two of the oldest looking record decks I had ever seen. My heart sank.

Made in black Bakelite, they looked little changed from the old wind-up gramophones of years earlier. The turntables were certainly of that design, and they were sitting in a tatty chipboard stand – 'plinth' would be too grand a word. They were Garrard decks and obviously made very well, but whereas I was expecting something resembling the latest SP25's, these dated from the 1950's. But they were,sort of, what I wanted.

"Yes please, but I'll have to get the money sorted first", I said, "I'll be back."

I made my way home, knowing that they weren't what I really wanted. They didn't look anywhere near as modern and groovy as I'd hoped. I needed to get the pick-up cartridges for them, as they weren't included… and I'd have to have a proper plinth made for them, but, in a 'make-do' sort of way, they were the best I was going to get. Now to negotiate a loan, of the sort you never have to pay back, from the bank of mum and dad.

I got the money; I bought the decks and eagerly took them home to see how they looked in my studio/workshop/bedroom. Not too bad really, I thought, as I plugged them

Ray Clark

into the mains and watched the decks spin around, although I couldn't play anything on them as I had no audio cartridges, or stylus. I can't remember how I overcame that obstacle, I think it was a case of buying them over a period of weeks, but I do remember the first time I had two records lined up to play. My disco decks were connected into the back of my big old, near lethal, wireless which I used as an amplifier and I was now able to segue (it's called a mix nowadays) from one record, seamlessly, to the next. I was on the way to becoming a proper disc jockey.

My next project was to get a professional looking plinth made. Roger, our next-door neighbour, was a few years older than me and worked as a boat builder, so he knew all about woodwork and stuff, and he owed me a favour. When I got my copy of the Beatles *Sergeant Pepper* album a couple of years earlier, he'd asked to borrow it to impress his girlfriend, so now it was payback time.

"Rog, I don't suppose you've got some off cuts of marine plywood, have you?" I asked, and the plinth was built, the decks fitted. Then another favour: my chum Tony loved any challenge involving switches, solder and wiring. I now had a control panel. My twin disco decks were complete, but built in a very large, rigid box that, to be honest, looked a bit like a coffin covered in brown wood effect sticky-backed plastic – I was so pleased with it.

The first public appearance of the double disco decks was to be at school. I struggled half a mile to the bus stop carrying this huge plywood box with two prehistoric record decks built into it, but I was so proud, especially when the bus conductor looked quizzically at my music machine while I attempted to place it under the stairs of our double decker. For once I was looking forward to a day at school.

We'd got permission to use the school hall for a charity disco, although I don't think any money changed hands. A small group of us congregated in the school hall for 40 minutes after rushing our school dinner. We had a motley selection of records, there were a couple of recent chart hits, but most were an aged assortment of records from various collections belonging to parents, and I was about to use them to entertain an audience of some twenty schoolmates. I had the means to play them, all we had to do was connect my disco to the school hall public address system, which was surprisingly easy, and away we went.

Problem one soon became evident. Because of the construction of my plywood disco unit, the records skipped whenever anyone walked past, let alone attempted to dance, but that was soon solved by placing cushions underneath – sorted. Then I realised that without headphones and a built-in amplifier I had no way of cueing the next record. This problem was a bit harder to crack. Answer, bend down and place my ear as close to the pick-up as possible and listen for the stylus 'scratching' at the start of the record. Children of the sixties were so ingenious, if only kids of today could solve problems like we could.

Problem number three was the most difficult to overcome, there were very few dancers taking to the floor at this, the first of potentially many, Maldon Grammar School lunchtime charity discos. In fact, on thinking about it, nobody danced! Fortunately, one of the few teachers who appeared to be interested in the education of young people, came up with a piece of advice that would be far more useful to me in years to come than he, or I, ever thought likely at the time: "If you want people to dance you must play music that people can dance to", he said as he turned to stride briskly across the stage, not realising that the records were jumping with every one of his heavy-footed steps. OK, so maybe 'The Ballad of Bonnie and Clyde', by Georgie Fame and 'Thank You Very Much,' by Scaffold weren't the easiest songs to dance to, but my choice was very limited, and for good reason, they were the only current songs that I had. After a while the novelty of taking this huge box of aged gramophones to school started to wear thin, the lunchtime discos continued, not as frequently, but I continued to practise my newly found skill of mixing records at home. With my paper round money I was occasionally able to buy a new record but building up my collection was frustratingly slow.

Today it's possible to hear a song for the first time, identify it online and download a copy within seconds. In 1968 the logistics of buying a new record were very time consuming. I'd hear a new song that caught my attention, then, once the song had been identified and having found the money to pay for it, I then had to make a lunchtime visit to the record shop. This usually meant a visit to Mid-Essex Television in the town. This involved having a note from home requesting permission to go and invariably, the shop had to order the record. As deliveries of new records normally arrived on Tuesday lunchtime, I had to get another note for a return visit the following week and pay the money in exchange for my coveted piece of vinyl. No wonder I can still remember in detail most of my record purchases from those days. There followed an afternoon of at least three interminable hours in anticipation of playing the new record, then the bus trip home and eventually, around 5pm, I was able to play my new purchase. Far more complicated than logging on and downloading today.

My first visit to what could loosely be called an organised disco, was to the Tuesday Club, run by the Congregational church and held in the Marsh Mission. This was an old wooden hut that had spent many years on the farmland that surrounded Burnham and had been a place of worship for countless farm workers and their families in the past. Now, with its usefulness as a place of worship over, it had been brought into town to serve as a hall for meetings, such as WI and The Tuesday club – a youth club for teenagers. The club was run by a church minister who was quite a progressive guy in his time, he'd made the national newspapers for playing pop songs during his sermons. Bob Bailey, known as Beatle Bailey, because of his modern attitude and hairstyle, booked bands and a mobile disco once a week for the local youngsters. What we called dancing was actually mostly 'jigging along' to 'Baby Come Back,' by The Equals and 'Mony Mony,' by Tommy James and the Shondells. I looked forward to Tuesday evenings. Besides the opportunity to hear the latest hit songs played at a loud volume, it was also a chance to meet girls.

Me and my Mum – Are all teenagers that moody?

We usually took the long drive down to Cornwall for our family summer holidays, staying with my grandparents. It was always a week that I looked forward to, and now, many years later, I still try to spend a few days in Devon and Cornwall every year. One of the highlights of the week was a visit to Plymouth. This city has a large undercover market, and in the late sixties it had one stall that sold second hand records and a second-hand shop just around the corner from the market. "I'm off for an hour, I'll meet you here", I'd tell my parents. The experience of flicking through their collections of old single records was surprisingly exciting. Nowadays, just about every song and version of it is easily accessible, but imagine the sheer joy of finding a record that you'd only ever heard on the radio. And there it would be, in one of those wooden Britvic orange juice boxes – just the right size for holding 7 inch records – and better still, the price of these singles was usually no more than 2/6d (12p). I would always come away with a handful of collectable records, all of them bargains, and now my record collection was starting to grow. Not only did I pick up three gems from the second hand selection in Plymouth - 'I Spy For The FBI' by Jamo Thomas, 'Callow La Vita' by Raymond Froggett and 'The Walls Fell Down' by The Marbles - I also made the day for the record store owner in Newquay by spending nearly all of my remaining holiday money two days later. These purchases included the latest Beatles song on the brand-new Beatles label, Apple, 'Hey Jude', but with a Parlophone label number. 'Those Were The Days,' by Mary Hopkin was Apple 2. Oddly, there was never an Apple 1.

All this happened on a wet Wednesday and the whole family, all five of us, had a mixed grill in an upstairs restaurant, which seemed very extravagant. My dad joked that we'd be on egg and chips for dinner next week… Another illustration of my extraordinary capacity to remember events so vividly. If only I could use my memory to make money!

The holiday was soon over and the journey home in those pre-motorway days took ages. We made a break in Sunningdale before driving around London and with a little of my holiday money remaining, I searched out a small record shop. Children of our generation could track them down intuitively. I bought a copy of the new Bee Gees hit, 'I've Got To Get A Message To You'. I eventually arrived home with a very satisfying haul of vinyl.

Back home, the Southminster Flower Show was one of two great events locally, the other being the Carnival held later in the year. It wasn't the flowers or the garden produce or even the cookery displays that my chums and I wanted to experience - even though it was at this very event that I discovered the proper name for a jam sponge was Victoria Sandwich, until then I'd thought that was the name of the lady who'd made them. We were attending because of the visit by Nichol's Funfair, a mecca for the local teenagers, drawn towards the colourful fairground rides. Among those were The Big Wheel, The Hurricane jets, The Dodgems and, best of all, Nichol's 20th Century Speedway, known by some as The Noah's Ark. Us Lads stationed ourselves around the wooden platform surrounding the fast moving centre as it rose and fell, while travelling over the hills and dips of the ride. We appeared to be waiting for the next ride, but we didn't always rush forward to take up a position on the wooden motorbikes or the chariots. The bravest of us preferred, standing with our back to the outside of the ride, hanging on with all our might to the chrome safety bar, whilst secretly praying that the ride would slow down before you lost your grip and got flung onto the grass field below. Apart from using this as a ploy to make our money last longer whilst soaking up the atmosphere, it gave us an opportunity to listen to the music, and how exciting that music sounded. As the guy in charge of the ride moved the electrical 'knife' style lever to start the ride, a cascade of sparks signalled the slow start, draining the electrical power generated by the engine on the aged Foden fairground truck. This would cause the record playing in the pay box to slow down in sympathy. The heavy ride took the bulk of the power produced, just to get going, but, as the momentum increased the platform was soon hurtling around at an incredible speed, almost certainly faster than was really safe for anyone to deal with. The whole temporary wooden assembly shook and vibrated from top to bottom, packed with teenagers being spun around and throbbing to the distorted sound of the latest, scratched records being played at full volume through the torn loudspeakers housed in huge wooden boxes tied by thick ropes to the wooden roof supports. The record player was suspended on bungee ropes within the operating centre, with the operator flicking the light switches on and off to add to the excitement.

As the ride slowed and came to an end, the speed of the music increased as the need for power was reduced, adding to this amazing atmospheric experience that I still remember so well.

Many of the songs playing I'd never heard before. Reggae was becoming popular in the clubs, but few people outside the big cities had the chance to hear these raw, rough recordings coming out of Jamaica. So many were heard for the first time at the travelling fair, and several are now favourites in my collection today: The Cats and 'Swan Lake' - the classical tune, but put to a reggae backbeat and scratched dreadfully because of being played so often - wonderful! Another tune that took me more than forty years to eventually track down and get a copy of was 'Cat Nip' by the Hippy Boys. Oh, the delight of eventually finding it via Youtube, which must be the modern day equivalent of searching through the boxes of second hand singles on the market stall.

*****

Our school geography group went on a field trip to North Norfolk in July 1969. We stayed at the youth hostel in Sheringham and were there when man landed on the moon. This was the first time I'd been to the north coast of Norfolk and it was very special, I liked it a lot. But again, music accompanied me, supplied this time by the family's portable radio.

Travelling north on our coach, I tuned in to Radio Veronica and even Radio 1. I have a vivid picture in my mind of Norwich as we passed the old cattle market site near the castle and by the headquarters of Anglia Television, passing the window as Emperor Rosko on Radio 1 introduced the latest record from the Rolling Stones, 'Honky Tonk Woman.' I can honestly say I remember the first time I heard that song, around 12.30pm, travelling through Norwich city centre, on Saturday 20th July 1969. Even on a school visit my radio was still a very close ally, 'Living In The Past,' by Jethro Tull, seemed very appropriate as this was played during a long walk through the grounds of Holkham Hall. Now, you're wondering what was the link?

OK, here's the history lesson, which also goes to prove that I was listening to my teachers some of the time, as well as enjoying the radio. See, even then, I could do two things at once. Thomas Coke, 1st Earl of Leicester built Holkham Hall. He was a real go-ahead guy when it came to farming back in the 1700's. He practised strip farming, which helped the land to recover by rotating different crops over the years, and he encouraged new inventions and developments, and one of those new innovations was the seed drill, invented by Jethro Tull. He and Lord Coke became chums – not the guy who could stand on one leg, play the flute and sing, all at the same time – his name was Ian Anderson and he was the front man to a new pop group called, Jethro Tull. See, I was listening.

My trusty radio also earned me major Brownie points on that trip as Mr Matthews, one of the teachers accompanying us, asked if he could borrow it to listen to the first moon landing during the early hours of the next day. I slept through "one giant leap for mankind" – it was one long sleep for a 15-year-old, but my radio was there!

Because of the establishment taking away my favoured source of pop music, I was still very bitter towards the government and the BBC, even though the BBC had little to do with the actual closure of the pirates and had been forced to provide an alternative, Radio 1. But, I had decided that as I wanted commercial radio and there was none to be had, I would favour watching commercial television, rather than the BBC.

I enjoyed the less matronly attitude of *Magpie*, the ITV alternative to *Blue Peter* and, in general, the programmes seemed to me to be more appealing. In short, ITV was less pompous, more down to earth, and this was certainly the case with local news programmes.

Strangely, where we lived our small district was outside all of the ITV regions. The Anglia region finished to the north of us, the Thames TV (London) region stopped short to the west and the Southern region was, well, south of us. Consequently, we received various 'local' programmes which were dependent on the weather conditions. Usually it was Southern TV.

Despite living almost 200 miles away from the place, we knew everything that was happening in Southampton courtesy of Fred Dineage on *Coast to Coast*. I'm still a fan of Fred, who recently retired after 60 years on the telly. Occasionally we could watch *About Anglia*, which was certainly more geographically relevant, and if the weather was affected by settled high pressure we could watch the pictures from Dutch television, though we couldn't hear it, as they used a different broadcast system to the UK.

Time for another advance in my journey through life, experiencing a 'disco dance' in the most exciting of venues, the canteen at Bradwell Nuclear Power Station. The guy at this event was far cooler than the Tuesday club DJ at our youth club. Not only did he have two huge speaker cabinets, but he also had an ultraviolet strip light, and gave away prizes, one of which had my name on it. As he played 'Bad Moon Rising,' by Creedence Clearwater Revival, he asked, "what was their first UK hit?" It was, of course, 'Proud Mar*y,*' and knowing that vital piece of information won me a copy of 'Lay Lady Lay,' by Bob Dylan. What a smart arse I was. Most of those attending that evening had thoughts on dancing, I just wanted to check out the disco equipment. The 1969 family holiday took us to Great Yarmouth, back to Norfolk again and then on to Hastings. At the time I was trying to find a particular reggae record by Max Romeo. It was decidedly risque - just the thing to appeal to a teenage lad. I eventually found a copy in the Norwich branch of Boots The Chemist of all places. Understandably, Radio 1 didn't play it, even when it got into the Top 20, although you could hear it played regularly on Radio Veronica - but they were Dutch and very little shocked them. Legendary DJ Alan Freeman wouldn't announce the title on the BBC Top 20 show, he just said, "at number 15 a song by Max Romeo, not arf." I'll challenge you to find the title - it did have a great reggae beat though. The other record that I set out to buy at the time is still a favourite, a fabulous instrumental with Billy Preston almost making his Hammond electric organ speak, 'Billy's Bag' is a classic which I found in a tiny record store in Hastings. The shop was called 'The Disc Jockey' and I have a very poor quality black and white photograph of me, a moody looking teenager, posing with one of their plastic bags and trying to look cool.

With summer over I was back at school for my final year and having scored a moderate success with the school lunchtime discos, my thoughts turned to finding another excuse to play records in the school hall. This time a few friends, persuaded by me, hit on the idea of a lunchtime version of *Juke Box Jury*.

The format would copy the television show where a selection of new single releases were played to a panel - in our case four teachers who formed the jury, and were expected to vote the songs a potential 'hit' or 'miss'. Surprisingly we had no shortage of volunteer teachers wanting to take part, which was a very brave thing for them to do when dealing with a group of fifteen-year-old schoolboys, especially as the records of the day seemed to have found an 'x certificate' niche in order to sell copies.

The number one song of the day was a recording in French that included lots of gasping and breathlessness. 'Je T'aime, Moi Non Plus,' had been banned by the BBC. They even went as far as to replace the original hit recording with an instrumental copy for the TV show *Top of the Pops*, but we just happened to have a copy of the original version, which as you'd expect, we played, accompanied by giggles from the audience, most of whom were girls.

To be honest, my command of the French language certainly didn't enable me to translate the words from that song, but I got the gist of it …. and so did the R.E teacher, Mrs Jeffs, and she most certainly could translate it. She made it very clear that she wasn't impressed with our choice of records – she voted it a '*miss*'.

However, the rest of the jury voted it a hit. "It's very tuneful," said Mr. Ford, the PE teacher, with a chuckle; I think he was well aware of the song before we played it. It was at this time that I hit on a wonderful idea that might increase the size of my record collection, with no cost.

Reggae music was in its infancy in the UK, Desmond Dekker's hit 'The Israelites' had recently become the first reggae number one in the charts and I was aware, from reading *Disc & Music Echo* magazine, that there were many similar recordings being imported from the Caribbean, mainly catering for West Indians who had recently migrated to the UK. These records were also being played in the clubs in London, a world away from where I lived and the chances of me hearing most of them was limited.

I was already aware of the minor ska hits from a few years earlier: Prince Buster's 'Al Capone,' and the Skatalites, 'Guns of Navarone,' but now new releases were appearing every week on a selection of exotically named labels: Pama, Coxone, Unity, Crab and Trojan. So, my brilliant idea was to write a letter to Trojan Records, based in Neasden, North London:

Dear Sir,
At school I run a regular event where we play records.
Can you send me some copies of your fab records please?

I was very polite, and to the point and sometime later a package arrived at home containing a short note, also very much to the point, saying something like:

We can't afford to give you free records, you cheeky little so and so, but if you want to sell them to your school mates we can offer you a discount.

The tone of the reply frightened me off, and I think had a lasting effect that made me shy away from asking for anything in the future, but the package did contain three records: 'Mini Skirt Vision' by Max Romeo, 'Do the Moon Hop' by Derrick

Morgan and 'Wonderful World, Beautiful People' by Jimmy Cliff. I must have been one of the first people in the country to have a copy of the Jimmy Cliff single, which became a huge hit about six months later.

Maybe I should have taken up their suggestion and started selling records to my schoolmates. I might have become a hugely rich entrepreneur. Richard Branson was unknown and was yet to start buying and selling records cheaper than the record stores, and look where that got him.

Anyway, the next school *Juke Box Jury* had a distinct reggae feel, not least because of this supply of new material, but also because reggae was the next 'big thing'. We included two of the recently acquired records but replaced the newer Max Romeo song with his hit from a few months earlier, complete with the dodgy lyrics that left nothing to the imagination. We loved it, but Mrs Jeffs detested it. "Stop this right now" she stormed, and that was the last ever lunchtime session of *Juke Box Jury.*

I had been fascinated by the amazing jingles that the pirate stations had played through their brief spell on air, and it wasn't difficult to realise that many of them were edited copies of originals. I spotted an ad in the music press for original radio jingles for sale. Sending off my Postal Order, I received a small 3-inch spool of jingles from the biggest American top 40 radio station, WABC in New York City. I loved these great catchy jingles and played the tape repeatedly. The production on those jingles had a full, big sound with echo and effects that I tried to recreate on my basic Fidelity tape recorder.

I had discovered how to produce the fascinating phasing effect used by The Small Faces on 'Itchycoo Park'. By lining up a record and playing a tape recording of the same song alongside it, any song would produce this amazing sound once you managed to 'hit the phase.'

The art was to create a split second difference between the two recordings, but then you'd have to delicately slow one machine or the other, as the pair slipped further out of alignment. You can get the same effect instantly nowadays with the right computer programme.

Making my own jingles was fun and I think I still have examples hidden away on old reels of tape that nowadays are shedding oxide. The audio quality, poor at the time, makes these ancient recordings almost inaudible now. I practised what would more recently have been called, sampling, mixing tiny excerpts from records to make tunes and jingles, one in particular I used was 'Telstar'. You see, ahead of my time again!

I'd seen the advertisement for the WABC jingle tape in a copy of *Disc & Music Echo* and regularly checked out their small ads page: 'Recordings of the pirates', read another ad. I paid nearly one week's paper round earnings for those. Thankfully, I was the best paid paperboy in Burnham as I had the longest round: 17/6 (75p) a week for my three-mile route. But 12 shillings (60p) got me a recording of DLT, Johnnie Walker, and my favourite Caroline disc jockey Mike Ahern from a few years earlier. They were all in fine form, and even today, despite a change in presentation styles and the music played not to mention long since banned commercials for cigarettes, those recordings from nearly 60 years ago sound so exciting.

Chapter Four

"Radio? Have You Considered Working in a Bank?"

The arrival of the seventies saw the return of offshore radio. I was a bit bored and tuning the radio around on one of those cold, damp unpleasant January Sundays, desperate for something different to listen to, I found Radio North Sea International. A familiar voice returned to my radio: Roger Day, a former Caroline DJ. "We're on the air with a test broadcast, so if you're hearing me … and you must be hearing me say this, write to …" with an address in Switzerland. This message was played repeatedly, together with an instrumental: 'Man of Action' by The Les Reed Orchestra which became a sort of anthem of the first part of the seventies.

Now this was the real thing, a proper radio station, and the broadcasts were coming from a ship, and certainly not the house across the road. As the tests continued 'Oh Well,' by Fleetwood Mac and 'Instant Karma' by John Lennon were regularly played.

Record Mirror had an article about this new radio station and also a photograph of the ship that it broadcast from and despite the photo being in black and white, the varying shades matched the description of a multi coloured, psychedelically painted hull with a huge aerial mast towering above it. Once again, I was excited by what I could hear on my radio. Within a few weeks the tests came to an end and Radio North Sea International officially opened and disc jockeys Andy Archer and Roger Day, who I remembered from the Caroline days, were amongst the voices returning to my radio.

As with all teenagers my bedroom was my sanctuary and over the Easter school holiday, I redecorated it. I wanted to paint it black, it was the 'must have' colour for all teenagers. However, I had to settle for orange wallpaper, but with the go ahead to build a wooden desk and wardrobe. Well, that was how I described my design to my mum and dad, but in reality it became a work bench for my record decks, tape recorder and general stuff.

Additionally, as I thought, very tastefully, I displayed a large psychedelic poster bought at the Boys and Girls Exhibition, held annually in London. The event was a bit like the Ideal Home Show, but with acne. The highly-coloured poster depicted swirling shapes and clouds. I recently saw a copy online, the bidding was more than £100 - if only I still had it.

I also had a white painted road lamp hanging from the ceiling. They were everywhere back in the day, usually painted pillar box red but occasionally yellow. Mine had been partly squashed and dumped at the side of the road, but with the paraffin lamp taken out and a lightbulb and holder replacing it, the red lens looked groovy when the bedroom light was turned off.

The other major contraption hanging from my ceiling, and one that I was very proud of, was my self-built strobe light. This had to be seen to be believed. Now, should you want to buy a strobe nowadays they're easily obtainable and completely electronically operated. Mine involved building a box out of plywood, approximately 18 inches tall, 9 inches wide and 6 inches deep. Into this was placed an electric motor that I'd taken from a derelict tape recorder that I'd acquired, and a 40-watt light bulb and socket. Writing this makes me aware of just how potentially lethal this thing was. I'd cut a two-inch square hole for the light to shine out of and covered this with a piece of coloured, see-through plastic gel. Then I'd taped the power supply, basically bare wires, to both the light and the motor and then plugged it into the mains. That was stage one. I really should have registered this with the Patents Office!

Stage two was to construct a near circle of hardboard that I'd shaped with a blunt saw using my limited woodworking skills. This was attached to the spindle from the electric motor, and this had a chunk taken out for the light to shine through as it spun over the hole in the box. The whole piece of kit was covered in silver baking foil. It looked like a spacecraft and smelt very hot as the heat from the motor and the light bulb within the box increased.

Once plugged in, the wheel started slowly, usually needing a gentle nudge to get it going. Then, as the speed increased, it would begin to jump up and down alarmingly, to the point that, had it not been anchored to the ceiling, it would have walked out of the room. What a marvellous machine it was. I never got to own an ultraviolet strip-light that high-lighted anything white - something I always wanted - having seen one at the Tuesday club, but at least I had a strobe.

As 1970 continued, I tuned into RNI, Radio North Sea International, at every opportunity, listening throughout the spring and early summer as they played fabulous songs: 'Spirit In The Sky,' by Norman Greenbaum, 'Question' by The Moody Blues and 'In The Summertime,' by Mungo Jerry. But controversy surrounded the station as the 1970 General election approached.

Originally RNI had broadcast from off the Dutch coast, but in March 1970 Britain once again had a radio ship off our coast, this time anchored off Clacton. The government started to jam the output in an attempt to silence the broadcasts, something that had never been done before in the U.K. and, in response, RNI changed its name to Radio Caroline and fought back. Caroline had returned and encouraged its young listeners not to vote for Harold Wilson and the Labour party who had been responsible for closing the pirates back in 1967, but to vote Conservative as they had pledged to introduce commercial radio to Britain if they were elected.

The jamming signal, initially from Kent, was an annoyance but the station was still listenable by moving your radio around until the interference was minimal. But in the days leading up to the election, the power of the jamming signal increased from a new site, Canewdon, directly across the river from my hometown, Burnham. In fact I could walk to the quay and see the towering aerial mast they were using to transmit from The huge signal swamped everything and for a while we were unable to listen to practically anything on the radio, including Radio 1 - even the fridge and telephones were picking up the incessant beeping noise from the jamming transmitter. However, in between the noise I could still hear 'Everything is Beautiful' by Ray Stevens, 'Love Of The Common People' by Nicky Thomas and 'Never Marry A Railroad Man' by Dutch band Shocking Blue. Even now when I think of these songs, they still have a regular *beep beep beep* as part of the backing track in my mind.

Revising for my 'O levels' was done to an accompaniment of the hit songs from RNI and the repetitive jamming signal and perhaps that was the reason that I failed seven of the eight exams that I took. I would be leaving school soon afterwards, so it was time to think about my future employment. Further education certainly wasn't an option. I'd already decided that I would try for some sort of media job, although it wasn't called media in those days. I really wanted to be a disc jockey on the radio, but the school careers department knew nothing about working on the radio, in fact, such jobs were nonexistent in their world. Our careers department was one dear old man, Mr Anderson, who knew how to get jobs for school leavers in banks, but little else. It was a changing world but Maldon Grammar school wasn't about to be a part of it. I soon realised that any job I got would be off my own back and without assistance from the school.

Television sounded exciting, or at least the ads did. They were always better than the programmes and I loved the different ITV regional idents between every show and the stirring music that each station started their mid-afternoon programmes with. Listening to those customised classical pieces from Rediffusion, Southern, Westward and Anglia now, via youtube, still gives me goosebumps. Go and search them out, you'll instantly be taken back to more innocent times..

My memories went back to my journey through Norwich a year earlier, so I wrote to both Anglia TV and Southern TV in Southampton. I asked if there were any jobs for school leavers. Perhaps I could be a cameraman, or maybe even a continuity announcer - *"From Norwich this is Anglia Television", "And now on Southern, 'How' with Fred Dineage and Jack Hargreaves"*. I practised all the possible links, but, in the unlikely event of a job offer, I realised I would be a 16-year-old working away from home.

I'd not thought of the practicalities like, where would I sleep, or who would iron my shirts – I still haven't mastered that skill - so I asked if they had hostels for employees. Both companies replied encouragingly that there might be jobs for a school leaver, but they also pointed out that they could not offer accommodation. I also wrote to ITN, Independent Television News in London: "Sorry, we have no vacancies" was their reply. I think that was probably, 'we have no vacancies for a would-be disc jockey with one O level', even though my one exam success was a top grade in Economic and Public Affairs.

Having been a huge fan of the offshore radio stations I was still inclined to think of the BBC as 'the enemy', but I needed a job, so my next letter was addressed to the Careers Department, The British Broadcasting Corporation, Portland Place, London W1. *'Dear Sir or Madam (all letters started that way in 1970) I would like to work in radio, do you have any jobs please?'*

I was thrilled to receive their reply. *"Come and have a chat,"* they said. My interview took place in an office opposite Broadcasting House. The interview was very friendly, but my first obstacle was the distance as I'd need to travel from home to London's West End. It took a bit of fast talking to persuade my interviewer that it was possible to endure a daily journey to and from London, but it would mean a 12-hour day, with 4 hours of travelling each day. *'You'll be working in Programme Accounts'* they said. I was thrilled. Sadly, I wouldn't be reading the news, or presenting the breakfast show, but it was a job, and it was at the BBC. *'Enjoy your summer holiday and we'll see you in September… off you go, you'll hear more from us before then'* said the very nice, if rather posh-sounding lady.

As my last few days at school loomed, the leavers were summoned into the headmaster's office to be given words of advice for their future - a sort of half-hearted attempt to suggest we might be capable of doing a job, but certainly not encouraging us enough to believe in ourselves.

"And what do you see yourself doing for a living, Clark?" said this elderly man who had given his working life to education but was so completely out of touch with the youngsters in his charge.

'I'd like to be on the radio,' I replied, with my broad rural Essex accent. It was still there but after the embarrassment five years earlier when the whole class laughed at the way I spoke, I was still trying to perfect a sort of Mid-Atlantic twang.

I don't think I was expecting the response that I got from this learned man. He laughed out loud, "Oh, I really don't think that's likely, I suggest you think of something else, have you considered working in a bank?"

So, with those kind words of encouragement ringing in my ears, I went out into the big wide world armed with my one 'O' level. I'd been studying eight different subjects for the previous three years with a view to taking 'O' levels in each of them, it was obvious that my results would be poor, but I was particularly bad at French Grammar, so it was decided that I take an alternative course for one year in a subject that usually took two years to get to examination standard. And so it was that I got my grade one pass in Economic and Public Affairs, despite failing the other seven examinations that I took. Not only did I enjoy the subject, it included visits to Parliament, the Stock Exchange, and the Ford Motor plant, but I was good at it, although never thinking that years later it would be extremely useful in my daytime job, as an unqualified journalist. I suppose the moral of the story is, enjoy what you're good at because you never know when it'll be of use.

Cool Dude Teenage Ray

June, July, then early August came and went, and I'd still not heard from the BBC. With little more than a fortnight to go before the start of my working career I was getting concerned. I wrote and asked for details of where and when I should report to start working for The British Broadcasting Corporation. I received a letter, almost by return saying, in effect, *'Who are you? We have no record of ever having contact with you, but If you say we've promised you a job then you'd better come for another interview to prove it'*. So I did, and I secured the job all over again. So, I got my first BBC job twice, which set a trend, as I've now lost count of the number of jobs and contracts I've been offered by the BBC over the years.

*****

'It was the 1st of September, a date I'll always remember' as I stood squashed against the railway carriage door, dressed in my best blazer style jacket, shirt and tie, looking like the new boy, which I was. I was already thinking,'I wonder if I'll be standing up all the way to London for the rest of my working life?'

That September Tuesday, in 1970, was the first day of my first job, working at the BBC. My morning journey had started aboard the 7.23am train from Burnham-on-Crouch to Wickford, a comfortable ride along the Crouch valley, with plenty of room on the small three-carriage, branch line, diesel train. But, it was all change at Wickford and suddenly I had stepped into the overcrowded world of the commuter, squeezed into a packed carriage, with no seat all the way to London Liverpool Street.

Being nearest the door, I was almost pushed out on arrival at Platform 14. In those days military marching music was played during the morning rush to encourage this army of commuters to move swiftly on their way. My journey to work continued with a walk/march through the winding, dimly lit tunnel that led to the westbound platform of the Central Line and a further crush into the elderly, rattling tube train for an uncomfortably hot 20-minute journey to Oxford Street. This was followed by a climb up the steep escalator - I was in too much of a rush to just stand there - and a five-minute walk to my workplace, 33 Cavendish Square, a giant 1960s concrete and glass, 25-storey office block on top of Oxford Street's huge BHS store. As I walked into the building through the revolving glass doors, the elderly, smartly dressed commissionaire, complete with peaked cap, gave me a welcoming 'Good morning' nod, and directed me towards the lift - there were no passes or security checks in those innocent times. Up I went to the seventh floor and found my way to Room 734 and it was here that I entered the exciting world of life as an office clerk in the programme accounts department of the BBC.

The Programme Accounts department was the office that paid and kept records of all the fees due to anyone who appeared on any BBC radio or television show. Whether it was a one-off fee for a Radio 4 interview or the payment for a star performance on a top television variety show, all financial rewards came through our office. I'm sorry, I can't divulge any details as I had to sign the Official Secrets Act, so I guess I'm still subject to its restrictions, assuming it still exists. (I've just checked: The original 1935 act was replaced by a new one in

1989 – so I guess I still can't give you any further information, even if I could remember any of it).

Basically, my original job entailed putting numbers on pieces of paper. The contracts came into our office where we had a large card index held in files around the office. There were about ten of us in the office and we had to match the name on the contract with a number on our card index and write it onto the contract. At the end of the day all this paperwork, complete with numbers, was sent to a much larger office next door where the 'punch card girls' spent all day typing holes into index cards which were then sent to the cheque printing section. The cheques were then sent out at the end of each day and eventually payment was made.

Our office also kept records of the payments made by the BBC and then we informed the taxman. These details were contained within reams of paper piled high and squeezed into storage cupboards, and that's how I came to help a number of well-known actors and broadcasters and meet a Radio 1 disc jockey. But before that happened the job changed, or at least mine did and, as with many things in life, it was a case of being in the right place at the right time.

The BBC in 1970 was still a very 'establishment heavy' place to be, run as if it was part of the Civil Service and those in charge were, in many cases, former military types. The boss of my department was a former Wren called Miss Webb. "Would you like to come and see the new BBC accounts computer?" she asked, just a few days after I'd started work. So off I went to the floor below to discover a huge machine that looked just like a current day security scanner for luggage that you find at airports, but much, much bigger. This was the new computer, complete with whirling wheels and flashing lights. It looked very futuristic and took up the whole room. In the next room was a large dot matrix printer spewing out piles of paper and making an awful din. So big was its task, this printer needed a guy to constantly attend to it and feed it with paper. The person given this task had recently been moved from our office. I suspect this was because, as I soon grasped, he didn't seem to be that popular with any of the others.

Although the BBC now had its state of the art computer in the finance division, the payment system still relied on people writing numbers onto pieces of paper that matched numbers on the card index. If for any reason these didn't match up then the contract in question was rejected and no payment was made, or, sometimes, cheques would be returned if the incorrect information was stored in our records. Occasionally contracts were just kicked out because the computer didn't like the look of them, or so it seemed. These loose ends had to be tidied up, problems solved and payments made, to avoid irate calls from those wanting to know where their payments were.

So, within a couple of weeks of starting my new job, and the new BBC computer coming on stream, I was given the job of investigating and solving errors. Each morning I picked up a file of contracts which, for one reason or another had failed to produce payment on their journey through the system, and it became my job to find out why this had or hadn't happened. In many cases it was easy to see why; a figure 5 wrongly typed as a figure 3, that sort of thing - but occasionally, a complicated chain of events would lead to a huge cock-up with someone's payments. That's where it became my job to sort it all out.

By being in the right place at the right time, and at the age of 16 and a half, I had become the only person within the BBC who could solve these issues and ensure the big names got paid.

"Can I come in and check my payments?" asked Radio 1 disc jockey Dave Lee Travis in a phone call one morning. Days later he and his wife entered the office, and we helped them go through his BBC earnings. He wasn't the only 'celeb' to visit, but DLT was certainly of interest to me, 'cos I wanted his job. At this time, he was presenting the Sunday morning show on the 'nation's favourite', Radio 1, with one of the biggest audiences of the week. It was from this show that he would later move to the daily breakfast show, becoming known as

'The Hairy Cornflake'. Anyway, we were chatting away about records and radio, and I happened to mention that I'd listened to him on Caroline and still had a 'Travistacratic Declaration of Heritage' - a daily feature on his hugely popular show a few years earlier. He was very impressed, so I decided to chance my luck. "Would it be possible to sit in on your Sunday show and watch what goes on?" I asked. "I don't think that would be a problem" he replied, "just turn up at reception and you'll be fine".

It was as easy as that. I'd got myself an invitation to a Radio 1 studio while one of the country's top disc jockeys was on-air.

I never did take up the offer to visit DLT and sit in on his programme. Well, I had to travel to London every weekday and to miss a Sunday lie-in to be at Broadcasting House by 10am was more than any self-respecting 16-year-old should have to endure. What a mistake!: More than fifty years on, I still regret not following up on that offer.

Throughout the summer of 1970, Radio North Sea continued, despite various battles, to survive. One Saturday in early September I'd been listening to Rosko on Radio 1 and he'd been featuring clips from a recently released collection of American albums, the *Cruisin* series. These LPs featured recreated radio shows from America's iconic disc jockeys and radio stations, playing a selection of greatest hits from the past

As Rosko finished his show, I retuned my radio to RNI just in time to hear an S.O.S call as an attempted raid on their radio ship was underway. This was certainly the time to get my tape recorder going. It all ended safely after listeners were urged to call various telephone numbers to inform those on land of the dangers that the crew of the radio ship were facing. As a result, various rescue boats rushed to the aid of those onboard. It was all very exciting, and certainly not the sort of thing you would hear on Radio 1.

I recently included part of this recording in a montage of unusual and dramatic events that had occurred over the years and had been broadcast by the radio ships, whilst giving a talk in the original Marconi radio factory in Chelmsford, pointing out just how exciting listening to the radio could be.

My lunchtimes at the BBC were usually spent in the company of my work colleague Janet. We'd both started working there at around the same time and got on well. As a result, I remember visiting department stores in Oxford Street to buy pairs of tights. Not for me you understand! But it seemed that almost every day she was in need of tights. When not on tights buying duty the two of us would often make our way to the BBC canteen in Broadcasting House. The food there was inexpensive, and you could always be sure of spotting a well known face: a public figure, an actor or maybe even a disc jockey.

Janet and I would explore Broadcasting House every time we entered the building, always taking a different route. We'd enter through the huge brass doors at the front of this grand ship-shaped building into the reception, strolling in, unhindered, past the smart commissionaires, towards the ornate lifts. Then we'd select a floor number at random and just wander through the long corridors in the iconic home of British broadcasting while making our way to the canteen on the sixth floor of what was then, the new extension.to the original building.

Walking past offices and production studios, we'd glance in to see what was going on inside - perhaps, in my case, just hoping that a shout of, *"Find me someone who can present a radio show this minute?"* might be forthcoming. Surely there must be a producer missing a presenter with seconds to go before their show started, I would hope. I'd have been there ready, certainly willing and quite probably able to burst into action at a moment's notice.

On one adventure Janet and I found the BBC book library, hidden deep inside Broadcasting House. I don't know if it still exists, but I do remember borrowing a book about the Swedish pirate radio station, Radio Nord, a predecessor to Radio Caroline. I felt a real rebel and perhaps just a little disloyal to the BBC.

There was very little security in public buildings, such as Broadcasting House, at this time as there was little need for it. If you knew where you were going, or just gave the impression of knowing your way around, then nobody would challenge you. That said, attitudes did begin to change about security matters during my time in London.

I clearly remember the day after a huge IRA bomb blasted the prestigious revolving restaurant on the upper levels of The Post Office Tower, now the BT Tower. I would often gaze through our panoramic office windows, idling a few moments away, while watching the restaurant slowly rotating as diners enjoyed their meals. But on this Monday morning a huge chunk had been 'bitten' out of the structure and being on the seventh floor of our West End building we had an uninterrupted view of the damage. Everyone became a good deal more security aware after that.

Sadly, I was never asked to present that pop programme for Radio 1, but I now realise, many years later, that I might have missed yet another chance to 'infiltrate' the nation's favourite radio station.

Much as I enjoyed the challenge of my job, by mid-afternoon I was desperate to leave the confines of our modern office block and escape into the outside world. Taking the opportunity to wander around in the fresh air and enjoy the exciting hubbub of the West End of London, I volunteered for a task that nobody else was interested in taking on - the afternoon post run.

I had to visit a number of BBC offices to collect the new contracts that had been agreed and typed up. These were issued by different BBC departments for performers and contributors to forthcoming radio and television programmes, and needed to be ready to be processed the next day. My route took me across Cavendish Square, alongside The Langham (then a BBC building and now a luxurious hotel), and on into the lobby of Number 9 Chandos Street, yet another building where the BBC rented more office space. Then it was up into the rickety lift – I hope that's long since been replaced - and along a gloomy corridor with grubby skylights leading to the rooms containing the Drama section, the Music section, and the Light Entertainment section.

All three offices were staffed by females of varying ages, some just a little older than me, others appeared to be quite elderly. Mature ladies did in those days. As they paused in front of their typewriters to chat they were all very friendly and kind and, depending on their age, were either protective of this young innocent 16-year-old up from the country, or enjoyed teasing and embarrassing me just a little. Following our brief daily chat, I would collect the pile of buff-coloured A4 reusable BBC envelopes bursting with new contracts and sealed with string, before moving onto the next section.

The Light Entertainment office was slightly different. Most of the girls were younger than those in the other offices, though still a little bit older than me, and they were certainly more flirty. I enjoyed my daily visits, because of their attention but also because they were always listening to recordings of disc jockeys introducing pop records playing from a big old tape recorder.

It was at this point that I missed possibly my biggest opportunity ever. I didn't realise until it was much too late, and I'd long since left the BBC (for the first time), that these tapes were from prospective disc jockeys all clamouring for Tony Blackburn's job, for it was the Light Entertainment office that looked after 'the talent' employed by Radio 1.

This was where 'demo' tapes were either rejected or judged as 'possibles' before being passed onto the next stage along the 'hit and miss route' to becoming a star on the radio. To think, I could just have used a little bit of my innocent charm and cheek and asked for my demo tape to be played to the ears of those who had influence, by those girls that fondly teased me.

My job also involved calling colleagues in a department based in The Langham called Central Registry. If we had issues with contacting a particular artist in order to pay them, we would request files associated with the person and look for clues to eventually unite them with their overdue fee. The files were fascinating and contained all communication between well-known names and the BBC, including letters asking for auditions or work, together with reviews of their performances. They made for a captivating read, and if published would have made an instant bestseller… but no, I'm sorry, I honestly can't tell you more.

Still buying records, and now with a monthly wage of almost £60, I was able to add to my collection considerably. *Time And A Word,* an early album by Yes, was one of my first purchases. It included a track based on the 'Theme from the Big Country'. I'd heard *'*No Opportunity Necessary, No Experience Needed,*'* played on Radio North Sea, *'*Paranoid,*'* by Black Sabbath and 'The Witch', by The Rattles: all were 'Prog Rock' recordings that were popular at the time and all were bought with my first pay packet. I soon noticed that there wasn't much cash left after paying £20 for my monthly train season ticket and paying 'for my keep.'

Between lunch break visits to the BBC canteen and hosiery departments in nearby stores, my colleague Janet and I would search for record shops. Many of them in the early seventies were in boutiques with music blasting out. So, as I browsed the record department, Janet searched for yet more pairs of tights.

Cassette tapes, (now long out of fashion), were the next big thing, but they were very difficult to find. They would eventually be sold everywhere, but at this time you could only buy them from specialist shops, and one of the few shops stocking them was close to Tottenham Court Road station. I recall travelling from Oxford Circus one lunchtime just to buy one lone cassette tape for 50p. How the world has changed. Lasky's Radio was like an Aladdin's cave of electronics, stocked high with cassette tapes, jack plugs, flashing disco lights, amplifiers, and record decks. I would wander around looking at these fabulous gadgets, searching for the plugs, sockets and cables that would connect my hotchpotch of tape recorders and record decks that I had at home.

Practical Wireless was a magazine that my clever chum, Tony, read every week. Tony understood electronics and was very good at soldering and wiring audio plugs. He was a good guy to know. I'd look at the magazines that he would lend to me, not really understanding the articles but drooling over the adverts for shops selling disco equipment, amplifiers and even 'separates' stereo systems, again something that were yet to become available in mainstream stores.

A stereo unit then was still a piece of furniture with a record player inside, rather than a system made up of separate components. The fact that it was in a varnished wooden cabinet, often with turned legs, was more important than the practicalities of it being capable of playing stereo records. These items were just as likely to be available in furniture shops as in Currys electrical stores. But in Edgware Road, if you walked far enough north beyond Marble Arch, you would find several small shops manned by elderly men wearing brown dust jackets, selling electrical spares, such as cooker parts, electric fire elements, light bulbs and stereo system components, probably made in their own workshops and without the well-known brand names of Bush, Fidelity or Phillips.

There was one brand name that I was particularly interested in, Garrard. To own a Garrard SP25 record deck was the Holy Grail for would be disc jockeys. So, one cold Saturday in December 1970, I set off for Edgware Road, returning home later that day after struggling with boxes containing a Garrard SP25, a stereo audio cartridge and stylus, two small wooden loudspeakers and a 'no-name' solid state amplifier. The whole lot must have cost all of £25 and after walking two miles to Marble Arch station, travelling on the Tube to Liverpool Street, a further 45 minutes to Wickford and then waiting for the branch line train for the final part of my journey, I arrived home, exhausted, with my treasure.

I remember the sheer joy of listening to my new stereo, but preparation took some time before the big switch on. After carefully placing the speakers in two opposite corners of my room and running the thick, red coloured audio cable around the floor, my next task was to connect the record deck and amplifier to the mains. To do this I needed a new mains plug, and you just didn't have spares like that in those days and they certainly weren't supplied ready fitted. So it was a case of wiring the record deck and the amplifier into the same plug, borrowed from a table lamp, and with no wire strippers available, the procedure was to bare the red, black and green wires with my teeth. I'd become very good at that.

And then came that big switch on. There was a gentle hum from the speakers as I placed my newly-bought copy of the Beach Boys *Sunflower* LP onto the turntable, slowly lifting the pick-up arm onto the vinyl. There was a quiet rumble as the stylus found the groove of this pristine disc and then … the Beach Boys … in stereo.

To be honest, it was a basic stereo unit, but it was the best that I could afford, and I was so excited. Taking off the Beach Boys I increased the speed to 45 rpm and placed my other newly bought record onto the turntable, 'Ride A White Swan,' by T Rex, and it sounded wonderful.

As 1971 got under way the pirate station, RNI, was still my choice for radio listening. Despite working for the BBC, I was still very much a fan of the pirates, with their more exciting, less formal style of broadcasting. The ship, now anchored off the Dutch coast, was regularly playing records that would never get played on Radio 1, so I was hearing new releases from the USA and Europe.

One song that was played regularly at this time was called 'Underdog,' featuring the latest invention, a Moog Synthesiser. The record was by Giorgio, (Moroder) who, six years later, would become world famous as the guy who revolutionised disco music with Donna Summer's 'I Feel Love'. If you knew where to look, many of these records were available in the small Oxford Street record stores, and of course, the giant HMV store near Bond Street. I was eager to buy a copy of 'Resurrection Shuffle,' by Ashton, Gardner and Dyke, as soon as I heard it on the radio. I was the first person I knew to have a copy. I also bought several other records that seemed destined to become the next big thing, or perhaps not. Somewhere in my vinyl collection I have a copy of Ray Stevens' 'Bridget the Midget,' and the even stranger, 'Yamasuki,' by the Yamasukis, a Japanese rock song championed by John Peel's record label, Dandelion.

A huge new record store had recently opened at the end of Oxford Street, close to Tottenham Court Road, and everyone was talking about it. I had to check it out and bought the new John Lennon album *Imagine* there on the day it was released. As I passed over the money it was given to me in a plastic bag, overprinted with a huge logo, for Virgin, but I discarded the bag before taking it home as I thought the name was rude and I was too embarrassed to walk down the road with the bag emblazoned with Richard Branson's company name.

It was time to meet another Radio 1 DJ, who would become a friend in the future. Back then he was enjoying superstar status.

Working at the BBC gave me access to the ticket unit where, every Tuesday, the single telephone line opened at 9am and instantly became engaged. It seemed every member of staff of a certain age within the BBC was dialling 2122, trying to get tickets for *Top of The Pops*, the legendary pop music show, then in its heyday. I'd spend ages trying to get through, until about 10.30, by which time all the tickets had gone. While patiently dialling 2…1…2…2… on the old 'round dial' telephones, with no push buttons, it was always good practice to have a second choice of show to request tickets for once you eventually got through. I got to see many radio or television shows being recorded, but one I distinctly remember was a *Radio 1 Club* show from the BBC's Paris studio in Regent Street. It seemed to involve either dancing in front of the DJ podium or sitting in the auditorium of this former theatre listening to the music. The show was broadcast live and the disc jockey on this occasion was Michael Pasternak, better known as Emperor Rosko.

Rosko was doing his stuff as only Rosko could do in those days; I was fascinated by his performance, and the bank of equipment he had in front of him and decided that I should try to get a dedication played. After all, I worked for the BBC, so my friends listening at home would expect to hear their names on the radio, especially as I might have had them believe that I had special connections.

I wrote the message on a paper plate, "Hi Rosko, can you play a song for...", but then I needed to pass this important message on. In a split second I stood up, caught his eye, and spun the paper plate through the air. With an impressive lurch he captured it, grinned to acknowledge a couple of smart moves from both of us and the dedication was played. Twenty years later I would be offering Rosko a job on my radio station. Callers and visitors continually contacted our BBC office, some in person, most by telephone and they were usually perfectly reasonable people. But occasionally we would be subjected to obnoxious calls from pompous old farts who were too wrapped up in their own self-importance and were very, very rude.

Sir Robin Day had been one of the first newscasters (as they called them at ITN) and had later moved to the BBC to front *Question Time* and important political debates. He was certainly a BBC big gun in 1971, in fact he was probably the biggest political big gun on the books, but in my book his standing gave him no reason to display such rude and ignorant behaviour.

He called our office one morning blustering and demanding answers to unasked questions as soon as I'd taken his call. He needed our help in solving a problem that he had regarding his earnings, and I guess, this had resulted in a disagreement with the taxman.

Good as I was at my job, and I was always striving to do it properly, I was not going to make it easy for someone behaving in such a rude manner, as he shouted and ranted. Most telephones at this time were of a shape and design that had been standard for years, with a receiver sitting on top of the main body of the phone with a dial and finger holes for each number. As old Dayo ranted and, presumably got redder in the face as he became more flustered and angry, I listened patiently, whilst casually dialling zero … this resulted in a series of loud clicks over-riding his manic rants. "I'm very sorry Mr Day, but we do have a bad line, I'm afraid I can't hear you very well at all", I said calmly while oozing buckets full of charm. "What, what, what are you saying I can't hear you …" he blustered. I let him continue for some time until he slammed the phone down, which prompted me to leave the office for a break; I was sure someone else would eventually help him to solve his financial query, but it certainly wasn't going to be me.

Another caller from the Sir. Robin Day school of courtesy was a man, who I found out later, was quite a well-known actor. As he blustered down the phone, he demanded to know if I knew who he was. Always keen to reply truthfully, I told him that I was afraid I'd never heard of him, and he rang off.

Fortunately, most of our callers seemed to be reasonably pleasant and normal, and went away happy.

*****

It was August 5th,1971, and our local newspaper, *The Maldon & Burnham Standard*, printed a story on the front page about a guy who had a radio studio in his back bedroom. The headline read: *'Painter Doug's Dream, Radio Maldon.'*

Doug King was a painter and decorator and a wedding photographer at weekends. He'd wanted to be a disc jockey and, like many at the time, would have welcomed the chance of being on the radio anywhere, but sensing that would probably not happen he realised his dream by setting up his own station, Radio K.I.N.G. at home. He had the studio, the records, the jingles, and friends who were also attracted to the idea of being on the radio.

Maldon and Burnham

THURSDAY, AUGUST 5, 1971

PAINTER DOUG'S DREAM— RADIO MALDON

PAINTER and decorator Douglas King is planning to give Maldon its own local radio station.

And if the Government refuse him a licence, he said intended to beam out music and news programmes from a pirate ship in the North Sea.

● Mr King in the studio at his home.

Draught men are hit by a drought

DRAUGHT beer drinkers in the Maldon and Burnham area have been hit by a drought, due to a strike by brewery workers at Romford.

Some Ind Coope public

Painter Doug's Dream, Radio K.I.N.G –
The Monarch of The Airwaves

I wrote to him immediately, asking if I could visit his radio station. I couldn't believe that someone else, living relatively close by, held the same interest and passion as I did. But I was just seventeen, I'd only had two driving lessons, so I was dependent on the family trip to the nearest supermarket every Thursday for a lift to Doug's radio station. Once there, I would spend a couple of hours 'doing radio' with a lift home once the weekly shop was completed.

It was great to sit at a proper radio control panel, cueing records and jingles. Doug had a good selection of records, including the latest new releases and the best of the Top 10. I recall playing 'Nathan Jones,' by The Supremes, a great song, but it also featured phasing, so it just had to be a favourite. The magic of introducing a record over the intro and then seamlessly fading into the next record, then another announcement followed by a jingle - I was in my element. I became a regular visitor to Doug's Radio King for about three weeks… and then I discovered girls and that, for the time being, was the end of my craving for anything radio related.

I only ever met Doug again once. He was taking photographs at a wedding that I was attending. Regrettably we did little more than acknowledge each other. Doug was working and the speeches were underway. I regret not sidling away from the wedding breakfast to reminisce about my short spell on *Maldon's Music Machine*, but the story doesn't end there.

More than thirty years later, sadly after Doug's demise, my early efforts in a radio studio resurfaced. My mother-in-law, Jean, suffered from Multiple Sclerosis and had constant visits from carers throughout the day. One regular carer, Joy, asked if her son-in-law was Ray from the radio and the next day she passed on a CD containing a recording of *The Ray Clark Show* on Radio King from August 15th, 1971.

It seems that Doug had kept the recordings of my early attempts at being a radio hot jock, and there I was, sounding much younger and certainly more 'rural', with my Essex accent, tinged with a hint of Mid-Atlantic drawl, as all DJs had in those days. Also in the package was a framed publicity photograph from more recent days. On reflection, Doug must have seen me as his protégé and enjoyed my relative success in later years. I treasure that recording and my memories of my all too brief spell at Radio K.I.N.G.

I'd also read about Hospital Radio Chelmsford in another newspaper report; it was based in a caravan at St. John's Hospital, not far down the road from the current BBC Essex studio. I wrote to the studio and received a letter inviting me to attend for an initial chat. While my dad waited in the carpark, after driving the 18 miles to the hospital, I entered the office for a very formal interview. I didn't find it welcoming at all, in fact I thought it very pompous. It may have been that I was too keen to be let loose in the radio studio, but it was made very clear that there would be a long wait ahead before that would ever be considered. The man showing myself and a few other potential recruits around set us a few tasks. One was cueing up a record: 'A Never Ending Song Of Love,' by The New Seekers and 'TomTom Turnaround,' by New World. Our guide seemed so surprised that anyone other than himself was able to do such a thing. I know many highly successful radio presenters that have started in hospital radio, and a number with Hospital Radio Chelmsford, but I wasn't to be one of them. I never went back.

*****

The weather over the August Bank Holiday in 1971 was hot and sunny and I spent the Friday night sleeping under the stars in a field in Weeley, near Clacton-on-Sea. The infamous Weeley Pop Festival was supposed to be a small event, attended by no more than 10,000 music fans and organised by the Clacton Round Table. In previous years these charitable-minded gentlemen had organised a donkey derby, but this year they were to hold a pop festival. What could possibly go wrong? Well, as history has shown, just about everything, though for most it was a happy, memorable event from a more innocent time.

However, more than 150,000 youngsters eventually turned up, overwhelming any efforts at organisation. Rod Stewart and The Faces thought they were the stars of the event, but so did Marc Bolan and T. Rex. Status Quo, Mungo Jerry, Lindisfarne, and a whole list of rock bands performed from a home-built wooden stage, constructed in a corn field.

More than a hundred Hells Angels arrived with trouble in mind, they were beaten off by the caterers who planned an ambush, and many of the 'helpers' ran off with most of the profits. Despite the troubles behind the scenes, the music fans and festival goers had a happy and peaceful time, and I was one of them, but only for about 18 hours. I was there with my pal, Alan, but neither of us had a tent or sleeping bags. We had food, but no means of cooking it so, after roughing it overnight, we decided that we weren't really cut out to be festival goers and came home before most of the major groups took to the stage!

Decades later, I wrote a detailed account of what was titled: *The Great British Woodstock. The Incredible Story of the Weeley Festival 1971*, published as my second book.

Where have all those years gone? My chum Alan and I return to Weeley for BBC 1 – 2019

I was in the Curry's store in Basildon in December 1971, buying another tape recorder and even though I was earning a reasonable wage, I still couldn't afford to buy a Philips N4307 four track tape recorder outright. So, way before the days of credit cards, I found myself signing an H.P agreement (hire purchase) with three carbon copies, for more than £40 worth of reel-to-reel tape recorder.

It was a very good machine, one step up from a domestic machine, with push buttons and better still, no big 'clunk' from the mechanism as I started the tape rolling. I still have recordings made on it at the time, including my little sister; she's now over 60, singing the number one song from the previous Christmas, 'Two Little Boys.' Better still, this machine with four tracks enabled me to do all sorts of fun things with jingles and effects, including singing with myself.

Well, nobody else would! I was really quite creative and able to double track and reverse recordings and introduce echo, all the things that Kenny Everett became famous for doing, though I could never hope to be as good as him.

My second year at the BBC started with a pay rise, but I was getting impatient with just working in an office. I noticed an internal job advertisement; they were posted on green sheets of paper on a noticeboard on each floor. There was a vacancy for an assistant in the gramophone library. Quite what an assistant did, or whether the gramophone library looked after the Top 40, or more likely, classical pieces from unknown composers, I had no idea, but I asked for an application form and was told firmly that I was employed within the Finance Division, not the Gramophone Department so I couldn't apply!

The novelty of working in London was starting to wear off, even if it was for the BBC. The daily journey was taking more than five hours and my season ticket was very expensive. The £20.20 a month was a large part of my monthly income. But there was one part of the journey that I often enjoyed, thanks to a guy with a wonderful Caribbean accent, who worked on the Central line platform at Liverpool Street Station. He was great, and would really make my day if he was on duty. His job was to move people from the overcrowded platform onto equally overcrowded trains.

"Take your time, chill out, calm down ... there's another train behind this one ... and yet another one will follow behind that one ... enjoy life ... move down the platform and give yourself some space".

Whenever I hear the 1988 hit song, 'Don't Worry, Be Happy,' sung by Bobby McFerrin, I think of the guy at Liverpool Street Station in 1972. Perhaps Bobby McFerrin travelled on the Central Line, or maybe it was his dad. I handed in my notice in May 1972. I'd decided to leave the BBC and take a job as a bus conductor. Perhaps it was the guy on the public address system at Liverpool Street station who influenced me, who knows, but working on the buses sounded like fun. To be honest, it wasn't likely to help me find that radio job, although it would get me an audience. I'd met a friend who had already started working on the buses and would sing its praises. "It's great fun and all the girls talk to you", he told me, and he was right on both counts.

Working as an 18-year-old 'Jack the lad' bus conductor was indeed great fun, and for most of the following 15 years, I would be involved with the world of passenger transport, as a driver on local bus routes and later touring all over the UK and mainland Europe on the coaches and I had some wonderful adventures. But throughout all this time I was still following music trends, still buying records and avidly following every change and development in the radio world.

Chapter Five

"Playing Music to a Captive Audience"

I've mentioned the excitement of our local carnival when I was a child in the 60s, but because of a confrontation between the Mods and Rockers in 1966, it had all but ceased. However, over the five year period since 'the troubles,' it was slowly returning to its former glory and, after an absence of some years, the funfair also returned to town. I've always been excited by funfairs, the sounds, the lights and the engineering. One of the rides, now commonplace at most funfairs but seen in very few places at the time, was the Twist ride - in fact the fairground family that came to our carnival built them. The ride was fast and smooth as the cars sped across the track, passing diagonally, with each car just inches away from the one from the opposing direction. The lighting effects were great and the sound system loud. One of the effects of the ride moving across the track was the phasing of the music, coming from the huge speaker bins on each side of the machine. 'Walk In The Night,' by Junior Walker was played frequently and is not just a wonderfully memorable song, but to hear it at such an exciting venue was unforgettable. The fair was a great place to hear new music, and still is.

I decided that joining the Carnival Committee was a good thing to do when I was about 17. Given a white coat and placed on the gate of the car park, there was very little for me to do, as most visitors coming to the town just parked on the side of the road. But it did show that I was willing to help, and the next year I was able to offer my services for something far more interesting.

Although the procession had now returned to being held in the evening, several events were arranged throughout the day as visitors started to arrive into the town. Those events were held in the broad High Street, overlooked by a Victorian clock tower. This vantage point, in the heyday of the event in the sixties, had been used as a control point, and the place from where record requests were played throughout the mile long High Street. Unlike those earlier days, we no longer had a chain of loudspeakers relaying the music, but I did have access to just one public address speaker horn, which, powered by a small amplifier and connected to my antique double disco decks put me in a position to offer my services as 'Head of Public Address'.

And so on the last Saturday of September in 1972, with a very basic set up, 'Virginia Plain,' by Roxy Music blasted out across the High Street at 9.00am, and, to be honest, caused shock, stress, and consternation to the elders of the town. But I felt I was broadcasting, or at least playing music to a captive audience.

Frustratingly, it soon became obvious that some of that captive audience weren't ready to appreciate the sound of a Moog synthesiser, as featured in Bryan Ferry's fabulous song, that early in the day. "Have you got anything a little quieter - perhaps you could find some brass band music?" said Stan, the kind, elderly former bass drum player of the town's Salvation Army band.

Over the following 20 years, or so, I continued to hold my lofty position as in time, the event regained its popularity, attracting crowds of many thousands. The Public Address system was again extended throughout the town, playing music and announcements throughout the day and into the evening. We even had commercials which went some way towards paying the not insignificant charges for the hire of a professional PA system.

I was still fixated with radio, but I did very little about trying to get a radio job. The possibilities were extremely limited, there were very few options, and I knew that having no previous experience and a rural accent were not likely to get me into a radio studio. The closest I could get was just to tune in and listen to either Radio 1 or Radio Luxembourg. There was also the offshore Radio North Sea and it was whilst listening one Sunday evening in September 1972, that mention was made of the former Radio Caroline ship, Mi Amigo, being towed past the RNI ship.

I was amazed, and thinking that Radio Caroline might return, I tuned around the medium wave looking to find evidence of broadcasts resuming. Unfortunately, there was none.

During the week between Christmas and New Year, I made a visit to London to meet my former colleagues at the BBC and I enjoyed a couple of hours in their company in the BBC Club and, sadly, I realised that once you leave a place of work the relationship with former workmates is never quite the same when you go back. Making my way home, I took the Central Line tube back to Liverpool Street Station and picked up a discarded copy of the *Evening Standard. 'Pop Ship Mutiny'* read the headline. There, at the station, I learned that Caroline had been back on the air for a few days broadcasting from their unseaworthy radio ship. But, the marine crew had mutinied over lack of pay and the ship had been towed into Amsterdam harbour. However, within days, the ship had returned to sea. Unbelievably, as I started to tune around I rediscovered the radio station that had given me my near fanatical interest, even if it was broadcasting intermittently from a wreck of a ship. Between the constant breakdowns I listened, or tried to listen, as the static on medium wave and interference from more powerful stations obliterated the weak Caroline signal. I remember hearing Paul McCartney and Wings' new double-A-sided single, 'C Moon' and 'Hi Hi Hi,' and then Carly Simon with 'You're So Vain'. Oh, and 10cc's wonderful 'Rubber Bullets.' I was seriously tempted to contact 'The new Radio Caroline' as they were calling themselves, at their address in Holland, and ask for a job, but it seemed such a Mickey Mouse organisation, that I decided against it. Periodically I'd think about applying, but most of those on-board were professional, established disc jockeys, who'd worked on radio ships before and I managed to convince myself that I wasn't good enough and had no chance of a job.

Not for the last time in my career would I interview myself, and not get the job, because I'd decided, without applying, that I wasn't the right candidate. If I had my time again then that trait would certainly change.

*****

My record collection continued to grow. I would regularly buy chart singles, but they were expensive, especially when I needed to spend money on socialising and driving lessons.

Suddenly, a most wonderful product appeared in the Woolworths record departments, allowing anyone to own a great selection of chart songs on one album. What a wonderful day it was when I discovered *K.Tel's 20 Dynamic Hits*. A range of TV advertised compilation albums containing original versions of pop songs and on the market for less than £1. There was now a vast choice of LP compilation records from Ronco, K Tel and Arcade, although the audio quality was lacking. With so many songs squeezed onto one piece of vinyl, after just one play all of the songs were subject to clicks and crackles. But it did mean I had the latest hits by T Rex, Dawn, David Essex, David Cassidy … and even Donny Osmond.

Another of those memorable moments came when I discovered another new innovation. It came about one afternoon as I made my way upstairs on the Number 31 bus to collect the fares. There was a guy reading a magazine and on the front cover was a wonderful full colour photograph of the *Mebo2*, the Radio North Sea ship. I had never seen such a picture in a mainstream magazine and certainly not seen the ship that I listened to in full colour before. "Wow, what's that you're reading?" I asked. I couldn't wait to get my hands on a copy of *DJ and Radio Monthly*.

This fabulous publication survived for less than a year, but a glossy magazine all about radio certainly earned a regular order from me. I still have all of the copies and years later they still make for an interesting read, not least because they gave space to all aspects of popular radio, not just Radio 1, with great features on RNI and the return of Caroline.

Throughout 1973 Caroline had overcome many of their technical problems and their broadcasts were becoming more reliable, or at least until another of their huge, towering masts collapsed. During the summer months it was possible to tune in regularly. Those broadcasts were made even more exciting, as by now, after passing my test, I owned a car with a radio.

My first car was an aged Mini and in August I drove alone to Cornwall, leaving home around 8pm. It was becoming dark as my journey started and Caroline's signal followed me as I headed west. As the night progressed, the signal increased in strength and I have great memories of hearing the station as I followed a makeshift route alongside Dartmoor.

Major construction work was taking place on the main A38 road to Plymouth, replacing small country roads with a dual carriageway and flyovers and intersections along its entire length throughout Devon. Lou Reed's 'Walk On The Wild Side' and Timmy Thomas' 'Why Can't We Live Together,' were two songs that I clearly remember hearing on the journey as I listened on my new Motorola radio, which had cost almost as much as the car. I have fond memories of driving around Cornwall in that car, listening to Radio 1 during the daylight hours. 'Rising Sun,' by Medicine Head, 'Skywriter,' The Jackson Five and the superb, 'Summer, The First Time,' by Bobby Goldsboro, are songs that, even today, take me back to those carefree days: '*It was a hot afternoon, the last day of June and the sun was a demon*'. It's one of my favourite songs – ever. Please don't laugh! Thinking back to those days and listening to that song can almost bring me to tears. Just where have all those years gone? That little Mini gave me very few problems and I sold it back a year later to the guy I'd bought it from, and for the same amount of money.that I'd originally paid. The radio wasn't included in the deal though, that came with me when I bought my next car.

Much was made about the launch of legal commercial radio in October 1973. More than nine years after Radio Caroline had first broadcast commercials on the radio the government had finally granted a handful of licences for radio stations to broadcast from a few major cities.This was not to be called commercial radio, it would be known as public radio with commercials. Music radio fans, still mourning the demise of the pirates from the sixties, weren't expecting too much, which was just as well. LBC, London Broadcasting Company, was first on air - an 'all news service' based in London, followed a week later by the launch of Capital Radio and, certainly in their early days, neither were exciting, or a suitable alternative to the pirates, or even much of a challenge to Radio 1.

My cousin Paul, who was a few years older than me, and I suspect much better paid, suggested forming a mobile disco team. His surname was Mayhew, so at the start of 1974 we became the *MayRay Roadshow*. Paul owned the equipment and most of the records, 'Jambalaya,' by The Carpenters,'Knock Three Times,' by Dawn and 'The Air That I Breathe,' by The Hollies were some of the records that I remember us playing. In truth, I just went along to the few bookings we received to make up the numbers, it wasn't long before Paul realised that he didn't need me onboard, but it got me thinking about starting my own mobile disco... Just not yet I decided.

1974 was another great year for listening to the radio. What a choice we had, RNI continued with both a Dutch service through the day and English at night. Caroline's broadcasts were now far more reliable, the programmes now featuring albums, rather than singles. While Radio 1 was concentrating on playing chart hits, Caroline introduced me and thousands more to albums by Elton John, Rod Stewart, Pink Floyd, Barclay James Harvest and so many other bands who became a must for any self-respecting record collector.

The Caroline ship was also home to an exciting sounding radio station called Radio Mi Amigo which broadcast to Holland and Belgium. They played some great songs, the majority 'Euro hits' but in English and had some really groovy jingles. Sadly, Radio Veronica was no longer audible in the UK as the IBA, Britain's commercial broadcasting authority, had allocated the same frequency to London's Capital Radio. But the lack of Veronica was made up for by, probably my favourite station ever, Radio Atlantis.

This station was relatively low-powered and broadcast from a converted trawler moored off the Belgian coast. Sounding very much like the pirate stations of the 1960s, it was fun and packed with jingles, great songs, presented by upbeat disc jockeys who were obviously enjoying their job.

Radio Atlantis broadcast throughout the night and often included an entire side of an LP, and in particular the *Cruisin* series that I had heard Rosko playing on Radio 1 some years earlier. I would travel into work in the very early hours listening to these fabulous, recreated radio shows from iconic American radio stations on my car radio. At the time, 'W.O.L.D,' by Harry Chapin was also played regularly, '*I am the morning DJ at W.O.L.D'* – well I could dream.

Years later I would become friendly with Steve England, the guy who was playing those albums from that tiny ship. Steve went on to produce and supply most of the jingles heard on the UK's radio stations. Several years later I would spend a couple of days in his company as a jingle package for Breeze AM was recorded in Dallas Texas. Sadly, although the recording session took place in Dallas, it was directed via a telephone link with Steve in charge … from Stockport.

A few of my radio friends did get to make the journey to Dallas, home of the radio jingle, but unfortunately not me. However, Steve and I did spend a long and enjoyable evening chatting over a meal, and just a little wine, about Radio Atlantis and how much I'd enjoyed listening to, while he recalled playing those albums in the middle of the night, wondering if anyone was listening. I could assure him, I was.

The days were numbered for the radio ships off the Dutch coast. As with the British radio stations in the sixties, the Dutch government introduced legislation against the remaining radio stations. Just one week before the closure of Radio Atlantis, the team on board gave listeners a tour of their ship, in between playing simply great songs. It was an amazing insight on a gloriously hot, sunny day. They even broadcast from a small rubber dinghy at the end of a long rope tied to the ship in calm waters, some twelve miles off the coast. So memorable.

I listened avidly, sadly aware that the end was due for Atlantis, wishing, by now far too late, that I'd made contact to ask for a job. Several years later it would be another member of the Atlantis crew who hired me as a disc jockey and became a dear friend. More about that later.

August 31st 1974 arrived and most of the shipborne radio stations closed down. It was very sad to hear Radio North Sea's close down, its short history had been so eventful with boardings, bombings and hijacks - just an ordinary day on the radio. RNI was the station that had reignited my interest in music radio four years earlier and had kept me company through many of my teenage years. The closure of Radio Veronica was even more disappointing for radio listeners in the Netherlands. Veronica had become part of everyday life for the Dutch, having broadcast off the coast of Scheveningen since 1960. But as in 1967, broadcasts would continue from the ageing Mi Amigo radio ship. Radio Caroline, together with the Dutch station, Radio Mi Amigo, remained on air, once again defying a government order to close down. Sad news for fans of the other stations, but good news for Caroline fans, as the Mi Amigo moved back to the English coast and anchored less than 20 miles from my home. Reception from Radio Caroline would be good for years to come.

It was during this time that the radio phone-in format first became popular in the UK. I've always thought the king of this style of broadcasting was Robbie Vincent. He presented a daily phone-in show on BBC Radio London. A series of industrial disputes in the country caused a three-day working week to be introduced as electricity was rationed and, consequently, all television programmes had to close at 10.30pm. The idea was that we could all go to bed early and save electricity. Robbie Vincent presented a late evening phone-in, and it was an excellent listen. It's strange how you remember unusual, sometimes quirky moments that you've heard on the radio and one of those was a call to Robbie from a lady called Sybil, who had married a Mister Dibble, thus making her name…. wait for it … aah, you've already got it, but I'll bet you'll now remember it forever more. Another call was from a girl who said she was 'just a dogsbody in a paint factory in Stratford', she sounded much too smart to be 'just an' anything. I hope her life became more fulfilled and happier after that call.

That's the amazing thing about radio, you can hear just one call or comment and it stays with you forever. It's how good radio works. When you need to remain in your car, outside your house just to listen to the end of a song, or an interview that you've been listening to on the journey home, then that's radio at its best. I discovered a superb double vinyl album, produced by East Anglian Productions, based in Frinton. It was a well-produced three-hour documentary, all about Radio Caroline, telling the station's story to date. Listening to this I became aware that many archive recordings from the sixties had survived, and the inclusion of several interviews made me realise that, much as I loved hearing music on the radio, speech could also be very interesting, planting another seed in my brain for later use. EAP became the source of the best Offshore radio products, with books, and LP documentary records amongst them. It was the go to company for pirate radio fans.

Britain's licensed commercial station network was slowly expanding, but the new radio stations had started their broadcasts at the worst possible time. With a recession and rampant inflation in the country it was hardly the best time to sell radio advertising. Both Capital and LBC struggled to make money and were facing bankruptcy - a good thing for the listeners as they were forced to improve their output to attract a bigger audience. I started listening to Capital Radio, 'in tune with London town,' on 194 metres, as the programming began to appeal more to music fans.

Roger Scott's *Three o'clock Thrill* on Friday afternoon set the standard for a nostalgic 'hits and headlines' feature, that would later be imitated on countless other radio stations and, likewise, the smooth, unflustered Dave Cash, on air every lunch time with his competition, *Cash on Delivery.* Little did I ever imagine that years later I would be working with him, and of course, the wonderfully creative Kenny Everett. Kenny just made it sound oh so easy as he championed some fabulous new records, often before anyone else: 'Bohemian Rhapsody' by Queen was one. I bought the album, *A Night at The Opera*, which contained this amazing song, on the day that I first heard it. I must have had some spare cash at the time as I bought a new music centre on the same day. Music centres were the latest 'must haves'. A record player, radio, and cassette recorder, all in one. My Sharp music centre positioned on my MFI, self-assembled flat-pack furniture music unit looked cool.

A growing number of commercial radio stations began to pop up around the country. The closest to me was Radio Orwell from Ipswich. Listening on FM was difficult, but medium wave reception was reasonable, although being very close on the medium wave band to the powerful Radio Caroline signal caused some interference. Interestingly, Radio Orwell had a team of former pirate disc jockeys: Andy Archer, Greg Bance and Keith Rogers and in the years to come, I would get to work with all three of them.

I remember visiting the Suffolk show, a huge agricultural show held every May, and spending two hours or more sitting in the sun and watching the Radio Orwell outside broadcast, live from a caravan. I would have given anything to be a part of that team. The closest I got to one of the new commercial radio stations was when I won an LP in a phone-in competition on Plymouth Sound while listening during a family visit to the West Country. I was told the prize would be waiting for me at reception. I planned to ask for a tour of the studios as I collected my prize; but by the time I got there I'd already talked myself into believing that they were far too busy to show me around. Yet another missed opportunity to get into a radio studio. I really don't know why I was so reluctant to ask if I could get involved at this time, maybe because I feared rejection, or perhaps I just didn't think it possible that working class lads who grew up in a council house might be thought capable of presenting a radio show.

I'd thought of buying proper disco equipment. It was now easier to obtain. A guy called Roger Squires was offering ready-made double disco decks and lighting effects. His company also advertised disc jockey training courses. 'You can become a top DJ, book now for a crash course, spread over five weeks for just £25"... I thought about signing up, often... but never did!

I was still keen on starting my own mobile discotheque and when the 1976 autumn edition of the Great Universal Stores shopping catalogue, which my mother ran, arrived, there on page 263 was a FAL double disco deck, purpose built with two Garrard SP25 record turntables and a built-in amplifier. The price was still high, but it was available on 12-month terms at £8 a week. Double decks, two sound to light columns and an oil light wheel that projected psychedelic patterns on the wall and the Right Sound Disco was in business!

I now had a substantial record collection, but I decided that I would invest any earnings from my discos into buying every new entry into the Top 40. I would go to Mid Essex Television, the closest record shop to my workplace, and collect up to ten new chart entries each week. So seriously did I take all this that I would buy cardboard covers for each of my records and record the chart history on the sleeve. I still have my collection of vinyl singles, seldom used now, but every record sleeve still has the chart notations on them. I was soon spending every Friday and Saturday providing the music at parties and wedding receptions, remembering the words that my English teacher had told me when I organised the school lunchtime disco, "If you want them to dance you must play songs that they can dance to."

I was no longer working as a bus conductor. Now I was driving the bus, so I had to arrange my work shifts around the disco bookings as my diary was soon filled with dates all around the area.

Throughout the next three years, disco hits swamped the charts: 'Dancing Queen,' by Abba was soon followed by a whole catalogue of dance hits from *Saturday Night Fever* and possibly the best disco song ever: 'I Feel Love' by Donna Summer revolutionised music at the time. I smile at memories of a wedding reception on a hot summer's day in a small village hall. 'I Feel Love' had just been released and everyone, young and old, couldn't get enough of this great song. It was the easiest wedding booking I ever had. I could have got away with playing just this one record over and over, all evening.

A friend told me that the landlord of The Ship Inn had heard about me and would like me to pop in and have a chat about providing a regular Friday evening disco. Jock, the landlord, knew about running pubs. He was very good at it and his was the busiest pub in town. After a successful Friday evening trial, I was now his resident DJ.

The choice of what I played was left to me, just as long as it filled the pub. I decided to veer away from disco as I attempted a sort of radio approach to the presentation and the songs that I played, I based those Friday nights, and later the Saturday nights too, on the style that I, and many of the clientele, were hearing on Radio Caroline, anchored just a few miles away and with a signal that boomed in louder than any other radio station. Caroline had resumed a 24 hour daily English service and the music they were playing was wonderful: The Eagles, 'Hotel California,' Queen, 'Bohemian Rhapsody,' Rod Stewart, 'The Killing of Georgie,' were regularly played, and after any particularly busy and lively evening, we would always finish with 'Riot In Cell Block Number 9,' by a relatively local band,

Dr Feelgood. Pubs were subject to strict closing hours then, but we were usually the last pub in town to empty. These were happy, memorable days.

'Anarchy in the UK' by The Sex Pistols was an addition to my collection at this time, but this was an early pressing on the EMI label, released just before the Sex Pistols caused public outrage after their appearance on tea time television, causing their record company to sack them and withdraw the record from sale. Immediately, the value of my copy increased by a huge amount. I later swapped it for a twelve-inch copy of 'Miss You' by the Rolling Stones on pink vinyl. I don't think that was a very wise deal.

Chapter Six

"A Step Closer To a Dream"

I got to hear about a weekend event celebrating the pirate stations, to be held in London and called Flashback 67. Tickets for the event weren't cheap at £20.00, but included a Saturday evening meal, hotel accommodation and entrance to the two day event which included talks, films and attendance by many of the offshore DJs. I just had to be there. But there was more. Exactly ten years after the closedown of Radio London, a boat trip out to the Knock Deep in the North Sea to view the Mi Amigo, the Caroline ship was also on offer. I bought a ticket for it all without hesitation. Everyone attending this event was sent a quiz sheet with their tickets asking ten questions about the offshore radio stations. From these quiz sheets a dozen of us with correct answers would be selected at random and those chosen would take part in a contest on the Sunday afternoon. The prize was a state-of-the-art mini JVC TV and radio, the big new name in hi-fi at the time.

As my turn to register came, I was told that I would be a contestant in the quiz and that, without a doubt, was the moment that my career in radio started, although I certainly didn't realise it just then.

Flashback 67 was a very enjoyable event. Those who attended were immersed in wall to wall radio and many of the DJs from the sixties were there, together with several current Caroline presenters, surrounded by a small army of like-minded followers. It was a radio anorak's heaven. Films were shown, jingles and archive recordings were played, with numerous presentations, some more interesting than others and trade stalls were selling records and tee-shirts. This was where I wanted to be, and I craved to have a role in this unique and, to be honest, rather strange group of people who were involved in clandestine pirate radio. The evening entertainment promised to be fun: It was certainly memorable. Screaming Lord Sutch and the Savages provided the cabaret in the hotel's huge function room. The man behind the pirate station, Radio Sutch and the leader of The Monster Raving Loony Party, was also known for his repertoire of rock songs and his unusual, but exciting stage show. Lord Sutch had never had a major hit record, but throughout his career his act had become legendary with his regular appearances in pubs and rock clubs, and on this occasion, he certainly made his mark.

As The Savages played, Lord Sutch was carried onto the stage in his coffin, rising from his confined space, dressed in his black cloak and hat and wearing his usual ghoulish stage makeup. He then appeared to pee 'a fiery liquid' into a crucible already set up on stage. The trick was to obscure a small watering can containing the flammable liquid from his audience and as he moved onto the next part of his spectacle, he discarded the can into the crowd. However, on this occasion the can was thrown back onto the stage by a member of the audience, hitting the crucible and knocking it over, causing the still flaming liquid to spread across the stage. As Sutch continued his growling, grunting, and singing, frantic attempts were being made by him, and the Savages to extinguish the flames that by now had caught the curtains alight. The situation was starting to look serious. Fortunately, quick thinking by someone prevented a possible disaster as they pulled the stage curtains from their track. Unperturbed, Sutch just continued with his act, seemingly unaware that he'd nearly burnt the hotel to the ground – with everyone in it!

Several years later I would be the last person to interview Screaming Lord Sutch. Sadly, he was a troubled man and took his own life a few days after our chat.

Day two of the Flashback event continued with even more films (these were the days before video), listening to more presentations and hearing more jingles than I ever thought existed. Then it was time for the Flashback 67 quiz. There were twelve radio fans, including me, assembled on the stage prepared to answer questions about the number of rivets in various ships and what Tony Blackburn had for breakfast in 1964. What serious anoraks we were. The competition was fierce, but eventually one person was victorious, and that was me. Andy Archer was the disc jockey who had asked the questions and he duly presented my prize of the mini-TV/Radio. I was a very happy man.

I travelled home with my prize and a pile of radio related LP records, whilst listening to Caroline on the car radio. That evening a special programme was broadcast, including many historic recordings, interviews, and memories of the station over the years, and celebrating the fact that ten years after the law to ban them was passed, they were still there.

This show also included interviews that purported to be 'live from Flashback 67'. It might have made the authorities a little upset thinking that a pirate broadcast was being made from a hotel in London, but it was obviously a tape that had been created during the dinner, held on the previous evening, and sent out to the ship during the day. The guy responsible for recording the tape, Bill, was also involved with the technical aspect of the offshore radio quiz.

Bill was to become a good friend - he also worked for the guy behind East Anglian Productions. I knew neither of them at that time, but both would influence my route to a radio career.

The weekend had certainly been a celebration of offshore radio, but there was more 'anoraking' to follow. I had tickets for two to travel out to the North Sea to view the Radio Caroline ship, Mi Amigo, and the Thames forts. Sue, my girlfriend at the time, joined me, but I suspect she wasn't particularly excited at the prospect of a long journey out to sea to see some rusty old ship. This was to be the first time I'd ever been to visit a radio ship, it certainly wouldn't be the last.

Sue and I were onboard a Thames tourist boat that normally operated within the Pool of London. We were told that it had special permission to make a voyage to the mouth of the Thames, though I suspect this didn't extend to 18 miles out into open seas.

With around 100 passengers and a disco onboard we set off downstream towards the coast, but I realised what a long journey it was going to be when, nearly two hours after departure, we'd only reached as far as Southend pier. Fortunately, the weather was bright and warm, and the seas very calm, probably just as well as we were on a near flat bottomed boat. Mark Stuart, a former Radio North Sea DJ was onboard, playing records and jingles and keeping the passengers entertained on the long, slow journey out to sea.

After a further hour, the first of the Thames forts came into view, Red Sands fort, the former home of Radio 390 ten years earlier. As we drifted closer, there was a brief commentary about the fort, followed by a request for Ray, the guy who'd won yesterday's quiz, to make contact. Hang on ... that was me!

I was handed a microphone and became part of the 'presentation team' relating the history of the pirate stations that had used both Red Sands and, further out to sea, Shivering Sands Forts. I used my best 'disc jockey' voice, honed by the regular discos. Everyone seemed impressed, nobody complained, and I was happy. Give me a microphone and a topic that I know something about and I'm away. Within hours of winning the Offshore Radio quiz, I was assumed to be an expert on the topic.

Our boat continued onwards, towards the radio ship, or at least in the general direction. We were lost, it was pretty obvious that we were lost, we'd been due to reach the Caroline ship at lunchtime, but as 4pm approached we were still bouncing off sandbanks in the Thames estuary. Eventually the huge radio mast of the ship was spotted and everyone rushed to get a better view. It was a magical and memorable moment. Most of those onboard, including me, had never seen the ship before. The Mi Amigo was much smaller than I'd imagined, very beaten up, very rusty and looking far from cared for, but I'd have given anything to have been invited to join the crew.

All those onboard our boat waved, shouted, and drank in the magic of seeing this plucky little ship that had revolutionised radio and music in the UK. We drifted around for a while, not getting too close for fear of people throwing gifts aboard, which would have been illegal. Then the disco onboard our boat played the Caroline theme – loudly – several times and those onboard both boats waved and cheered even more as we turned for home and started the long, long journey back to Tilbury.

We got off the boat at midnight, it had been a very long, but very enjoyable day and the boat hadn't sunk, although I suspect many first-time mariners, including me, thought there was a good possibility that it might.

So, after a flurry of excitement, it was back to my fulltime job and regular discos, now twice a week in the pub and an assortment of party and wedding bookings playing more great tunes: 'Oxygene IV' by Jean Michel Jarre and any number of disco hits by the Bee Gees, who were huge at the time, 'Night Fever' was just one of them. I always preferred playing the tunes regularly in the pub, rather than playing the songs at parties and wedding receptions. Working in a bar made it possible to play more varied tunes, and although the clientele was mostly friendly and reasonably normal, the occasional drunk could be challenging. But it appeared that my style of presentation, or at least the music that I played, was very popular, and what a choice of music there was in the autumn of 1977. Another big favourite was a track from a newly released album by Ian Dury and The Blockheads', *New Boots and Panties,* 'Billericay Dickie,' which included the line, *'Oh golly, oh gosh, come and lay on the couch, with a nice bit of posh from Burnham-on-Crouch'*. That certainly went down well with the locals as I played all the hits and more at the pub with the biggest hits. One of the presentations at the Flashback event included a short film about The Voice of Peace, a very popular offshore radio station moored off the coast of Israel. They were looking for staff. If successful the deal involved a flight out to the Middle East where you would be expected to work on air from the ship for six months, with regular shore leave included, and then a flight home.

I recorded a demo tape, ready to send off to an address in London ... and then I listened to it again, and again, and again. It just wasn't good enough, well at least that's what I thought, so I made several more attempts, striving for perfection. I never did send my audition tape to The Voice of Peace, but I do still have a copy of it. One day I might listen to it. Who knows, it might have been quite good.

I've since spoken to several friends who were confident enough to send off their tapes and got to enjoy the adventure of working in Israel and learning their radio trade on board The Voice of Peace. I really do wish now that I'd sent that tape off all those years ago, but it was to be yet another missed opportunity.

I was also busy helping a friend with his public address business. Mick Williams was a technical wizard, often seen shimmying up telegraph poles to erect loudspeakers at county shows, sports events and village fetes. He loved the challenge of erecting a system that everyone could hear, but he wasn't so keen on making the announcements, so I became a regular voice at all kinds of outdoor events around the region. It wasn't the same as being on the radio but I suppose it was heading in that direction.

After my success at Flashback 67 I was now in regular contact with Bill, the sound guy at the quiz. He was very much into collecting recordings of radio programmes and jingles. Some people have very strange hobbies and interests! I quickly realised that in the world of jingle collectors, cassette tapes were considered very uncool. "It's got to be reel to reel", I was told. I invested in a brand-new Sony tape recorder and once again I started making and editing radio jingles with special effects. So, not only was my library of vintage radio recordings growing regularly, but, via Bill, I was now collecting studio recordings of the very best quality, many of them originating from the Caroline ship. I was fast becoming a very serious radio anorak indeed.

Then in May 1978 around 200 radio fans made their way along Southend pier to join the preserved paddle steamer, Waverley, for another voyage to the Caroline ship and I was one of them. Also on the ship were several Caroline personnel and a Dutch brother and sister who I didn't know at the time, but would later meet on my next offshore adventure, and in the strange way that life works, form another link in the long route to me working on the radio. At least this time the Captain of our ship knew where he was going, and as on the previous trip out to the Caroline ship everyone on board was eager to get a closer view as we approached Mi Amigo, which was now looking even more of a wreck. We didn't stay alongside for long. As the passengers on the Waverley rushed towards the starboard side to get a better view of the pirate ship. the paddle steamer took on an alarming list. As the Captain struggled to keep control of his ship we steamed past Caroline at a high rate of knots, while frantic announcements were made for those onboard to move away from the starboard side of the ship.

A follow up event to the previous year's Flashback 67 was planned for July 1978. Zeezenders 20 was the name given to this latest offshore radio event, but this time it was held in the Netherlands, a country that I'd wanted to visit since the early seventies when it became the centre of offshore radio activity. The plan was to get a lift to Holland with my new chum Bill, who was to drive via Ipswich as Radio Orwell and former Caroline DJ, Andy Archer, was to be part of the presentation over the weekend and would also be travelling with us.

Zeezenders 20 was another enjoyable event, and as with Flashback there were even more films, talks and presentations, but this time the bar was the most popular venue of the weekend, with like-minded radio fans downing glasses of Heineken beer.

It was during the evening that I met a brother and sister, Hans and Louise who had also been aboard the recent paddle steamer voyage to the Caroline ship. We were soon chatting about our unusual hobby, and enjoying a few drinks that, surprisingly, helped me to speak and understand fluent Dutch, or so it seemed at the time. It's strange to think that mainland Europe seemed 'very foreign' at the time and quite different to Britain. Attitudes and lifestyles have changed beyond recognition in the years that have followed, though sadly I fear in recent times political events mean that our countries are becoming distant once again.

The journey home from Holland was uneventful, although it did give me my first taste of satay from a roadside snack bar on our way to the ferry. Onboard Andy Archer was holding court and recounting stories of life on the Caroline and Radio North Sea ships. Despite some of his unsavoury tales, the lure of the radio ships still appealed. I was convinced that radio was where I wanted to be.

My regular weekly appearances at the pub continued and my reputation as a mobile disco DJ was growing and keeping me busy with bookings. I would single-handedly heave the double disco decks, speakers and light columns from my car into various halls and venues, often upstairs, together with six wooden Britvic orange juice crates as they were the ideal size for holding seven-inch singles and contained at least 100 records in each.

I made a return trip to the Netherlands in October 1978, meeting my newfound friends that I'd met at the radio conference and exploring their country and visiting Amsterdam and the coastal resort of Scheveningen, the port where much offshore radio activity had taken place a few years before. I was also introduced to a friend of theirs: Peter Chicago, the famed chief engineer of Radio Caroline.

The Dutch like their food, though with meatballs as a favourite dish, it's not that sophisticated, but then neither was my choice of cuisine back then. My tastes have certainly evolved over the years. Now I enjoy far more adventurous dishes than I did then. Over meals and drinks, Peter chatted and spoke of life onboard the Caroline ship. Now, you would have thought with my near fanatical wish to get involved I might have asked if he would help me get out to the ship, but on this occasion there was a good reason to avoid asking the question. The radio ship, Mi Amigo was silent. It seemed that the money had run out and whilst the ship was being occupied by a skeleton crew the resumption of broadcasts was unlikely for some time and conditions onboard were bleak. In fact, she was abandoned during the following January and the crew were rescued by lifeboat. It was Peter Chicago who returned to the sinking ship with pumps and single-handedly kept her afloat until others joined him.

While I was in the Netherlands I took the opportunity to visit the record shops in Amsterdam, buying compilation albums from bands that I'd heard on the radio, but which had failed to reach the charts in Britain. One superb band was Earth and Fire, fronted by the lovely Jerney Kaagman, later to become a household name in music and on TV in the Netherlands, but now, sadly, unwell. Their songs such as 'Invitation' and 'Maybe Tomorrow, Maybe Tonight,' were huge hits in the Dutch charts and certainly familiar to offshore radio listeners in Britain. A Dutch band called The Cats had also been very successful with hits such as 'One Way Wind' and 'Lea,' I had heard their records played frequently in the past. Throughout the seventies many great bands from Holland came close to breaking through into the British and American charts but didn't quite make it. There were those that became highly successful, Golden Earing with their rock anthem 'Radar Love', Focus with their fabulous instrumentals and Shocking Blue's 'Venus' certainly enjoyed worldwide success.

Chapter Seven

"Pirate of The Airwaves"

Radio Caroline had been off air for six months, but as always it was always worth checking in occasionally, just to hear if anything was happening on the medium wave band. Caroline's birthday was always celebrated over Easter and tuning in, on Easter Sunday 1979 just after 10am, I heard the familiar sound of the carrier, the audible hum of the powerful transmitter onboard the ageing, unseaworthy Mi Amigo. As I continued to listen, the sound of sea wash and seagulls confirmed that this could only be Caroline, as a simple announcement by disc jockey Tony Allan was made: "It's us, we're back" and programmes resumed without fuss.

By summer it was time to take another voyage out to sea. Together with my Dutch chum Hans and a couple of others, we hired a boat from Brightlingsea to visit the Mi Amigo. On calm seas, and after a smooth three hour journey, the battered and rusting radio ship appeared on the distant horizon. On such a clear day, the huge radio mast could be seen from miles away.

As our boat pulled alongside the radio ship a couple of the crew came out to say hello. "Is Peter up yet, we've come to visit him", said Hans. And as he came out onto the deck, Peter immediately invited us on board. It seemed that my yearning to get onto the ship was about to be fulfilled. "Er, I'd rather you didn't", said our skipper. He was happy to stay alongside to enable us to chat to the crew members and take photographs, but he didn't want us to go onboard from his boat. He feared that he could be prosecuted for taking us out to the ship, although providing we didn't take part in the broadcasts or deliver any supplies then no crime had been committed. It was a memorable day, but it could have been so much better.

While I was still at school, I'd thought of trying to use a boat moored midstream in the River Crouch to broadcast radio programmes to fellow river users and those walking along the seawall, via loudspeakers. I'm not sure how popular I would have been, breaking the tranquillity of our peaceful riverside town with distorted records playing at full blast. Thankfully that idea never got beyond a daydream.

In the pub where I presented my weekly discos I was befriended by a local character called John. He was a regular at The Ship who somehow seemed to survive without having a job. It didn't seem to worry him, and he always had enough money for his beer, but he was a wizard when it came to understanding electronics, and in particular radio and how it worked.

"Can you make me some radio station tapes so I can broadcast them on my low powered transmitter?", he asked. The idea seemed fun and harmless enough, so I recorded an hour-long programme, announcing test transmissions for a fictional Radio Sunshine and included the post box address of my Dutch friends.

"This is a test transmission from Radio Sunshine – if you can hear this test broadcast, please write to ..."

I heard nothing for a few weeks, until I received a call from John.

"Take a listen to 220 metres", he said. As I turned the radio on, I could hear my voice booming out. This was no low powered bedroom broadcast, the signal was huge, far louder than anything else on the dial. After an hour or so John turned his transmitter off, which was probably just as well because the strength of the signal was sure to attract the attention of the Post Office broadcast engineers whose job it was to locate radio pirates. They already had their suspicions about John and had tracked him down before, although on their previous visit to his home they'd found no physical evidence of an illicit transmitter. John had cleverly built it into the ice box of his fridge freezer.

A couple of weeks later the proof of the signal strength was evident. I received a Jiffy bag packed full of reception reports sent over from Holland. There were more than fifty and the locations were from places all over South Essex and Kent, including Deal, Margate and Whitstable. Radio Sunshine had certainly been sending out quite a signal on that Sunday afternoon.

Another guy who occasionally drank in the pub was involved with Radio Basildon. This was a cable station in the new town that broadcast regularly and had quite an audience, long before proper local radio started in the county. I was invited to go along and sit in on his show. So, I did just that on a couple of occasions, but nobody asked me to join them - and, of course, I didn't ask if I could.

My next adventure was Radio Barracuda. I was asked to record regular programmes for broadcast in Belgium on a land-based pirate radio station broadcasting from Wevelgem, a few miles from the coast. I supplied programme tapes for a while and the response was always good. I tried to include a few words in pidgin French and Dutch, I'm not sure that they were proper words, but nobody complained. Many years later I was invited to attend a radio nostalgia event in Wevelgem and met the guy behind Radio Barracuda and he certainly didn't look like a pirate to me.

I'm older and possibly wiser now and I realise just how slow I had been at taking advantage of numerous opportunities that were presented to me in my quest to get on the radio. Probably the craziest was not taking up an invitation to join Radio Caroline immediately. I was again visiting my friends in Holland, and engineer Peter Chicago joined us for a meal and several drinks. After dropping plenty of hints about how exciting I imagined life on the ship could be, Chicago made the offer "Well, Why don't you come out to the ship then?"

I was actually being invited to join Radio Caroline! But again I was thwarted. The radio ship sank just a few weeks after Peter's invitation. At the time it really seemed that Caroline was finished, and with it my dream of being on the radio. I was convinced Caroline would never return and, without any radio experience, I'd told myself that no radio station would offer me a job. Thankfully, I would prove to be wrong on both counts.

*****

I would spend hours of my spare time making my own recordings and generally playing around with pieces of tape, the sort of thing that radio wizard Kenny Everett was renowned for doing. I got great pleasure from producing something that often only I would get to hear. So I decided it was time to enter the world of big boys toys and get myself a professional tape recorder. German built Revox machines were the best, but the cost in 1980 was more than £1,000 for a two speed Revox B77, complete with 'NAB adapters' - these were the real flash looking things that held the large 10.5-inch metal reels onto the machine. You could buy cheaper plastic reels, but they weren't cool. I could barely afford a reel of tape, let alone the cost of the machine to put it on, so, off to the bank I went to get a loan of £1,500 – the price of a decent second-hand car at the time.

Now I wasn't used to having much money in my bank account, I was still paid weekly and was usually counting the days until the next payday, but with the bank crediting my account with the borrowed money I was rich, at least for a couple of days. Conveniently, I happened to be spending a day in London with my coach driving job, so after dropping off my passengers and parking up, I made my way to Soho. Walking past the strip clubs and dodgy book shops, hidden in these back streets were a few remaining 'wireless' shops that still sold things like valves, old ex-military radio gear, reels of tape and quality Revox tape recorders. A shop in Frith Street was my destination. I walked in confidently: "I'd like a Revox B77 today please, but only if you can get my cheque cleared this morning."

The two guys in the shop couldn't believe their luck, a sale worth more than £1,000 on a Wednesday morning and I didn't even try to haggle and get the price down. "I think we can do that, of course you'll want metal reels .. and a full reel of quality tape … and the NAB adapters?" "But of course", I replied, "I'll be back at 12"…and I was, to the minute.

There on the floor of the shop was the biggest box I'd ever seen tied with string. I hadn't realised that it would be so big or so heavy. I'd not given any thought as to how I would get my purchase to the coach, which was parked near Lambeth Bridge. It was a fair distance to walk, even without carrying such a huge weight. So, leaving the box on the shop floor I stood on the corner of Frith Street looking to beckon a black cab. The cabbie had to help me lift the heavy box into the boot: "Be careful with that, it's worth a lot of money", I urged him, then we spent a good half hour, going the long way round, talking about my tape recorder and me telling him that, although I was a coach driver, I was going to work on the radio one day.

Eventually we arrived at the coach and the cabbie helped me unload my precious Revox. He'd charged a large fare and, prompted by my generous tip, he said: "I think your boss pays you too much" and drove off. He might have been referring to the taxi fare rather than the cost of the tape recorder!

I loved that tape recorder. I experimented - producing creative audio masterpieces, recording radio shows, and producing spoof commercials for local businesses, and soon I was earning some money with it. Somehow the sales manager at Perry's, Southend's major car dealer, got to hear of my abilities and asked if I could produce advertisements for various products on sale in the showroom - no, not the cars, but sponges, jump leads etc.

I enlisted the help of an old school friend to help me. Martin had a band which included his dad, his sister and a couple of their friends. They were quite good and leaned heavily towards country and gospel music. Understandable really, as he went on to become a vicar and a missionary. Anyway, I came up with a snappy little jingle for the garage: *'Perrys of Southend, the people who care for the motorist, Perrys of Southend, the people who care for your car.'* It wasn't bad, the tune was very memorable and the sales manager at the garage loved it. So my Revox recorded Martin and his band and every week I would supply new cassettes to Perrys advertising their high mark-up goods and collect £30 a month.

Martin's band were very popular locally and held regular sell out concerts to an audience of middle-aged church goers. Between us we decided that I would record one of these concerts and we'd market the cassette. I don't know how many were sold, I don't think we made a profit, but the cassette case did bear the legend: *Sound Engineer, Ray Clark.*

Although technology has left that old Revox tape recorder way behind, I still have it and switch it on every time I enter my home studio. Professionally serviced several times since it was new, it would still go for a good price online, but I don't plan on ever selling.

On yet another holiday to Holland I went to Hilversum, a place that once appeared on every wireless dial and the Dutch radio capital. My visit was to the studios of Hilversum 3, the national pop radio station. My friend Hans and I were invited in as the country's pop chart, *The Nederlandse 40*, was being broadcast. Songs in that chart included, 'Shine Silently,' by Nils Lofgren, 'The Devil Went Down To Georgia,' by The Charlie Daniels Band, and 'Money' by the Flying Lizards. The regular presenter of the national chart was former offshore DJ Lex Harding, the guy I'd listened to years earlier on Radio Veronica. It was the first time I'd ever been into a real radio studio whilst it was on air. It was fascinating to watch the show in progress and my dream of getting involved was rekindled yet again.

Chapter Eight

"'Psst … Wanna Buy a Jingle?'…
Ahoy, Anoraks Aboard!"

The next wave of local commercial radio stations were coming on air at the start of the eighties and Essex Radio was one of them. It was to be my local radio station so I sent them a demo tape. I didn't get a job, or even a reply, but I do still have the tape that I sent. Several years later I was able to retrieve the very tape from a huge supply of used cassette tapes in Radio House, the home of Essex Radio. I suspect that it hadn't been listened to since I'd checked the recording before sending it off. Essex Radio came on the air in September 1981 with 'Wired for Sound,' by Cliff Richard as their opening song. Those lyrics date the song more than the style nowadays… *needles to plastic, cassettes,* even *AM* were on the way out. Besides singing in his band, my chum Martin worked by day in a local estate agent. This is the guy who went on to become a vicar! I'm not sure how those two careers married up, but back in 1982, a national housebuilder, Broseley homes, was building a number of developments in Suffolk and Essex. One of these estates was in my hometown, and a representative of the company visited the estate agents where Martin worked. The conversation going something like this:

"Would you sell my new homes?"

"Yes of course, will you be advertising them?"

"Yes, in the local newspaper"

"Have you thought about radio advertising?"

"Well, no, I don't really know anything about radio advertising"

"Well, my chum Ray and I are experts in the field; would you like us to make you a commercial?"

The outcome was that I composed their jingle *"Broseley makes more of a home ..."* and the company paid us £200 to record the commercial with Martin and his band performing it. The voice, encouraging people to buy a new house, was mine. The whole thing was recorded in Frinton on Sea, at East Anglia Productions. Through my friend Bill, I'd got to know Ray, the guy who owned the recording studio. At the time he had secured several commercial recording deals for the new Essex Radio, so we did a 'mates rates' deal with Ray and recorded there.

It resulted in my first appearance on a proper radio station, in fact two of them. Our ad was booked to rotate between two different versions twice an hour, every hour, and every day for a month on both Essex Radio and Suffolk's Radio Orwell. It was just so exciting listening to the ad on the radio. "That's me" I would say to anyone who was anywhere near the radio. "Yes, of course it is" they would reply, with a disbelieving look.

Studio boss Ray had invested a lot of money into building a superb studio to record commercials, although it was extremely over engineered for its task and more suited to recording major music productions. But, following all the recent successful radio commercial recordings he was planning to expand. He assumed that, as I'd sold a radio commercial to a national house builder, I was obviously destined to become a top radio ad salesman, so he offered me a job as *EAP's* travelling sales executive. The plan was for me to travel around the country servicing the new wave of commercial radio stations, now broadcasting in most major towns and counties. I would visit each radio station every two weeks in my company car and take orders to produce commercials and radio jingles back in our Frinton studios, with the finished product being sent out to the radio station, almost by return.

There was, however, a problem with this great empire building idea: the new radio stations quickly discovered that, rather than go to an outside recording company, they could produce their ads 'in house' and make more money from their clients by charging them for production costs. The commercial production teams at the radio stations then realised that as their bosses were making money through selling their services, they could start their own independent production companies themselves, so they could really cash in. Anyway, before I, or my new boss became aware of this major flaw in our plan, I was prepared to join the company and waited with anticipation for my company car. "Aah", I was told, "bit of a problem, I have ordered a car for you, but cash flow is a bit tight at the moment, I wonder, would you mind signing the HP agreement for the car and I'll make the monthly payments". Unfortunately, I failed to receive one payment from Ray in the three months that I worked for him, but I did become the owner of a year-old Ford Fiesta with no synchromesh on third gear. The idea of a travelling jingle salesman was a good one, in theory, except I soon discovered that I was a rubbish salesman, and there wasn't enough money to pay the petrol bill or accommodation while I was travelling the country. I only ever did one national tour of commercial radio stations and only sold one voice over for £75.

I almost sold a commercial to Radio Trent, for a garden centre, but by the time the original brief had been passed between the client to the radio station sales team, then onto the radio station production team, who passed it to me, then onto studio boss Ray, Kevin the jingle writer, Bill the studio engineer and the voice over artist, it bore absolutely no resemblance to what the client wanted. "No thank you" was the client's reaction; I can't say that I blamed him. Now this wasn't to say that the product was lacking, Ray and his team were keen and eager to produce quality commercials, and given the chance, did well on several occasions, but just not enough of them.

On a visit to the newly opened Wiltshire Radio studios in Wootton Bassett, I thought I'd cracked it. Having only been on air for a couple of days, I walked in before they'd got around to setting up a commercial production team. I sat with a rather pompous guy who was Head of something or other and was bullsh**ing me even more than I was him. "Try this" he said as he handed me a pot of locally produced mustard from a prospective client who had given him some samples. Even though my tastes have become more adventurous over the years I still don't like mustard, but rather than decline, thinking it might help to clinch a deal I dipped a finger into the pot, and placed a huge dollop of the stuff into my mouth. It was the most unpleasant thing I'd ever tasted, unbelievably hot and full of uncrushed peppers. I was close to throwing up as my eyes watered and I gasped for water. I didn't sell any commercials to Wiltshire Radio that day and, as I journeyed home to Essex, I was very aware that I was unlikely to be a salesman for much longer.

Ray, though, still believed in the idea, "We'll give it a bit longer" he said, so I became a Frinton based telephone salesman. I doubted the wisdom of the idea. If I couldn't sell jingles face to face, I was unlikely to sell them down the phone, but now Ray had another idea, sales videos – but they didn't sell either!

We booked a stand at a sales exhibition in Southend over a weekend. Every stand was displaying and selling white goods: fridges, washing machines, cookers etc. Every stand except ours, "What are you selling?" asked the many families attending. "Jingles" I replied. It was obvious that the end was near, but not before one final payday.

Pay day was always the last day of the month, and the three of us working at the studio were anticipating a pay cheque, which we were usually given around 11am. But we all knew there was very little money available to cover the cost of three employees, so as lunchtime approached, me, Bill and jingle writer Kevin made a rush for the door so as to be the first to pass their cheque over the counter of Lloyds bank in Frinton's posh Connaught Avenue. Whoever got their cheque over the counter first had a chance of getting paid.

I enjoyed my short but hardly productive time at the studio.

Ray had good ideas and produced very good products, but things just didn't work out for him at the time. They didn't work out for me cither, as I was soon back to driving coaches around the country. But at least I was able to listen to the increasing number of ILR radio stations up and down the country: Devonair, Plymouth Sound, BRMB, Victory, Metro, and all of them had their own sound and qualities and perhaps all of them were waiting for me to send my audition tape. I'll do it later, tomorrow, next week, and besides I'm not good enough: I always had an excuse. If there's one thing I now know after successfully working in radio for nearly forty years it's always believe in yourself and your abilities and don't take no for an answer. I wish I'd told myself that all those years ago, and I wish I'd practised that belief since – but I've still not learned it.

*****

Since the sinking of the Radio Caroline ship there had been regular rumours of the radio station's return with the imminent arrival of a new, replacement ship returning to the English coast. Like most supporters I'd tired of hearing different variations of the same story, but throughout the summer of 1983 the rumours became more persistent.

I was often working away from home, driving around Europe, spending most of my time taking people on coach holidays to Spain, France and Germany. But I was in the UK during August and happened to see a news report on Channel 4, filmed aboard a fabulous new radio ship with an amazing 300-foot high mast… Radio Caroline certainly had a new ship and it was about to go on air.

The next few days I spent tuning around the medium wave band, searching for the new Radio Caroline, when suddenly, wow, what a signal. Even to this day I don't think I've ever heard such a superb quality signal from a radio station, either on AM or FM. Caroline was back and meant business this time. The ship was superb, a former Icelandic trawler, pumping out this amazing signal. Disappointingly, the Caroline sound had returned to an album music format, left over from the 70s. The music they were playing veered between songs destined to become timeless gems to boring, non-melodic dirges. The good songs played at this time included 'Wouldn't It Be Good,' Nik Kershaw, 'High on Emotion' by Chris de Burgh, 'Atmospherics' by Tom Robinson and Carly Simon, 'Hello Big Man,' which was played hourly. Once again my interest was captured by radio broadcasting from a ship, and, yet again awoke my dream of getting involved. Perhaps, I thought, I'll send a tape… tomorrow, maybe.

Then, a few months later, there was a new, loud signal. It's funny how radio anoraks always found them. I stayed listening to the Beatles track that was playing, followed by another. This was getting interesting, no 'regular' radio station would play back-to-back Beatles, especially on a Sunday afternoon – and then the recognisable sound of what could only be an offshore broadcast and the voice of former Caroline DJ Johnny Lewis.

I was listening to one of the first test broadcasts from a radio station that would go on to shake up the entire UK music radio scene. This was Laser, eventually to become Laser 558, and listened to by millions. These tests only lasted for a couple of hours and much work had to be done behind the scenes. It would be three months before the station came on air with regular, high-powered programmes and with a crew of experienced American disc jockeys, and it was unlike anything we'd heard in Britain since the 'All American' programmes of Swinging Radio England in 1966.

'This is Laser 558 where you're never more than a minute away from music,' and it was absolutely true. 'When Doves Cry,' Prince, 'Dr Beat,' Gloria Estefan, 'Time After Time,' Cyndi Lauper, 'Talking Loud And Clear' by OMD were amongst the fabulous songs played on high rotation with a minimum of chat.

'You're tuned to Laser 558, home of the hits,' punctuated by *Star Wars*-style audio zaps with disc jockeys Jessie Brandon,

Tommy Rivers, David Lee Stone and Charlie Wolf. It was no wonder that Laser was pummelling all the staid local stations into submission and even Caroline became a poor relation to Laser which had quickly caught the attention of younger radio listeners.

As 1985 dawned, so did my desire to return to the North Sea. I'd not been out to visit Radio Caroline in the Knock Deep since 1979, but now there were two ships to investigate.

A couple living in landlocked Hertfordshire, Albert and Georgena, had been organising clandestine boat trips out to Caroline since 1977, for those radio fans, like me, who were interested in seeing the radio ships close up. They had no boat of their own, they took to hiring one. Paying for it out of their own pocket, purely to support Caroline. Larger boats took supplies of fuel to the radio ships, usually from France or Belgium, but it was small fishing boats chartered by Albert and Georgena that supplemented these visits, taking up to ten 'anoraks' on each trip and passing on urgent messages and delivering records and smaller supplies.

Most countries had outlawed the offshore radio stations over the years, in their efforts to close them down. Spain was now the only European country that could legally be used for supplying the offshore radio ships. So, our clandestine boat trips would usually depart from the 'Spanish port' of Brightlingsea, on the Essex coast.

I drove to Brightlingsea on April 5th, 1985, ready to renew my relationship with the grey, unwelcoming North Sea. Although the trips could be cancelled if the forecast was really bad, there was never a guarantee of a comfortable journey out to the Knock Deep, the channel where the ships were anchored. Even on a summer's day passengers could experience lively conditions. Occasionally though the sea could be flat calm and Caribbean blue, but that didn't happen too often with the North Sea off the Essex coast. On this occasion, I joined a small group, mostly unknown to each other, already congregating outside the Anchor Hotel in Brightlingsea. Bookings were arranged by telephone, or letter, this was way before the internet, and it was suggested that we didn't attract attention to ourselves. But a group of strangers in Brightlingsea at 6am on a Saturday morning would certainly catch my eye. We were told to wait for someone to arrive with instructions, but timing was important because of the state of the tide which dictated both our departure and the return times. Our trip started with four of us at a time being transferred from the quay in a small dinghy with an outboard motor. We were taken out to the slightly larger launch that would take us 18 miles out to sea. Once all were aboard, we'd slowly chug out to sea, usually losing sight of land after about an hour. Brightlingsea church tower and Bradwell nuclear power station were usually the last signs of land that we would see, assuming we had good visibility.

By leaving on a rising tide, we were usually able to sail over several of the large sand banks off the coast, in particular The Long Sand, making the journey just a little shorter. If the tides were wrong, the journey to the ships would take much longer, as the route involved a diversion to avoid these notorious sands – worse still, if the skipper got the times and heights wrong when taking the shortcut across the sands, it could result in running aground and waiting, potentially hours for the tide to rise before enough water to float the boat had washed over them.

If visibility was reasonable, and the skipper was travelling in the right direction, which wasn't always the case, all on board would vie with each other to be the first to spot the huge 300-foot-high mast of Radio Caroline; it could often be seen for an hour or more before our eventual arrival. "There it is", someone would shout, only to be told, usually by those who'd travelled out before and considered themselves experienced sailors, that what had been seen was one of the numerous beacons, tall wooden structures placed as basic signposts for mariners who relied more on local knowledge than sophisticated marine navigation equipment.

Ross Revenge with 300-foot tower

These ageing structures were only twenty feet tall, just twigs when compared to the amazing structure fixed to the deck of Ross Revenge, the home of Caroline. When the radio mast was eventually spotted, it was impossible to turn away from it, nobody had ever seen anything like it on a ship at sea, it was impossible to forget that first sight of the tallest structure ever fitted to a ship.

As our boat came closer towards the Caroline ship, the smaller Laser ship, anchored nearby, also came into view. The radio station was off the air temporarily following a recent gale that had damaged their frail aerial system which was strung between two relatively flimsy masts, each about 100 foot high and positioned at the bow and stern of the scruffy, ungainly former coaster. The Communicator was about half the size of the Caroline ship, her hull painted a washed out orange colour with a white superstructure, streaked with rust.

We passed closely by and only one person could be seen, high up in the front mast, working on repairs, ready for the most-listened-to radio station in the UK to return to the air. If only the millions of listeners on land could see the very basic conditions that those involved with the radio station had to endure while keeping them entertained. We shouted our greetings to the guy up the mast and he shouted back to us, though his words were lost in the breeze that was blowing. The repairs to the aerial were successful as Laser had returned to the air before we got back to shore later that day, and was again entertaining millions of listeners, though sadly, by the end of the year money had run out and Laser was forced to give up the battle and close.

Our boat was now less than a mile from Ross Revenge and the size of her incredible mast and the beautiful lines of this former deep water fishing vessel, the largest ever of her type, became evident.

It was an amazing sight that just had to be photographed, and we did, everyone on board taking countless snaps from every angle, while attempting to hold our balance as the swell rocked our small boat vigorously once we drew closer to the radio ship towering above us.

Years later, the sight of this same ship, Ross Revenge, still excites me. There really is something breathtaking about approaching a ship at sea, approaching at night is even more magical, and approaching this ship in particular is still very special to me. The roar of the powerful generators could be heard above the engine of our boat as we drew alongside the bright red painted hull, the bridge and superstructure high above us. Our arrival had been spotted by those onboard who gathered on deck, waving to those visitors that they recognised and reaching out to assist our skipper, taking hold of the ropes he offered and securing our boat, which seemed tiny in comparison to this huge radio ship.

We made our way up the flimsy rope ladder and clambered over the gunnels to the deck way below, a drop of four feet, quite a step. For many of us, it was our first time aboard and I don't think I'd met any of the DJ's before. They included Jay Jackson, now sadly deceased - his real name was Howard Rose and he'd spent most of his adult life as a pirate. He was also known as Crispian St John having previously worked on Radio North Sea, Radio Atlantis and the Voice of Peace. I chatted with disc jockey David Andrews, who went on to work in London for Capital Radio, and found that he'd gone to the same school as me, though a year or two after. We were given a brief tour around the ship, but were then allowed to just wander around on our own.

Just to be onboard the most famous radio station in the world was quite special and for a radio fanatic like me, almost overwhelming, though I tried to contain my excitement and act as the cool dude I imagined I was.To hear the songs that Caroline was playing regularly at this time, played live in the studio and to see the discs they were played from was a special experience: 'Industrial Disease,' Dire Straits, 'Jack & Diane,' John Cougar Mellancamp. 'Easy Lover,' Phil Bailey and Phil Collins and 'A Good Heart,'by Fergal Sharkey. My first visit aboard a radio ship was both exciting and memorable. It had been a wonderful day and it wouldn't be long before I returned.

*****

There are important events that happen when you can always remember where you were at the time, and one of those was the Live Aid concert held on 13th July 1985. I was still driving coaches, usually on tour and living out of a suitcase. It was a job that I loved, and my travels took me to such a variety of places, many I would never have visited had it not been for the job I did. On the day of Live Aid, I was due to pick up a party of pensioners in Stevenage and take them to a holiday camp on the Isle of Wight.

As 12 noon approached, I was parked in a layby and tuned in to Radio 1, listening on an old medium wave radio, as the opening announcement was made and Status Quo kicked off the concert. Minutes later, I arrived at the pick-up point for my passengers. Sadly, they were unlikely to have been appreciative of the artists performing, so, as we travelled south to the ferry terminal in Portsmouth, all of us on the coach were listening to a Max Bygraves tape. Several hours later we arrived at our destination, the Isle of Wight holiday camp and my passengers made their way to their accommodation while I unloaded their cases and later joined them in the restaurant for our evening meal. I was one of the first to leave the room after the meal, making my way to the television lounge. Unbelievable now, but we were staying in a place with just one television for the entire camp. As I settled down to watch at least some of the Live Aid concert, one of the old guys from the party came out and promptly turned the TV over, "We don't want that noise; *Play Your Cards Right* is on the other side", he announced. I got up and left the room, giving him my very best death stare as he settled down to watch his stupid quiz show.

I made my way back towards my chalet, resigning myself to missing the event, but, as I passed through the car park, there were four guys sitting in their car and listening, with the volume high, to Live Aid in stereo – they were members of the band who were later to entertain the old folks that I'd delivered to the camp. "Is that The Who just starting?" I asked, "Yeah, get in," they said, and, as darkness fell and the rain started to fall, I rocked to 'Won't Get Fooled Again' played full blast on the car radio while huddled up next to four blokes from the local dance band. It would be thirty-five years later, in 2020, before I got to see that performance by The Who as the entire concert was shown again on TV.

There is an interesting follow up to this story. Many years later I would meet and interview the nurse, Dame Claire Berschinger, who was caring for the sick and dying in Ethiopia and brought the story to the world when she was interviewed by the newsman, Michael Buerk, who I would also interview. I'd also speak to Midge Ure, who together with Bob Geldoff made the whole Live Aid thing happen and I'd work with Trevor Dann, the guy responsible for the television coverage. Oh, and I would also get to interview several of those artists that were performing on that amazing day…life can be strange - who'd have known at the time of the event how my life would change, certainly not me.

Through a mutual friend I'd met another fan of Caroline, Kevin Turner. He had radio experience with a number of land based pirate stations, both in London and Ireland and had recently joined Caroline for his first tour of duty in February 1986.

Within hours of his arrival, the ship lost her anchor in very rough seas – a major problem at any time and potentially very dangerous. The crew on Ross Revenge were waiting for a replacement anchor and chain to be delivered from land by a large tender. The radio ship had now been held in place by a much smaller, temporary anchor for a week or so, and this was prone to dragging, so their exact position couldn't be guaranteed. Supplies of food and drink were running very short and it was vital that a few basic food supplies got out to sustain those aboard. As a result, a small boat was organised by Albert and Georgena to make a quick run out to the ship and I was asked if I wanted to go to make up the numbers. It was a bitterly cold Sunday in February and there was snow on the ground, but the chance to go out in unusual circumstances appealed to me.

I paid my £15 contribution towards the boat costs and felt quite the adventurer, setting off to give my chum on board moral support and to make sure that at least a few loaves of bread made it out to the crew. We left from Brightlingsea on course for the Knock Deep channel, with a slight swell forecast, but during our voyage the wind and seas were starting to pick up. It was a clear day and the huge 300-foot-high mast had been in view for more than an hour as we bobbed, weaved, and ducked into breaking waves that were starting to spray over the bow of our small boat, the saltwater stinging the faces of those standing on the open rear deck.

As we came close to the one thousand-ton radio ship we could see that even she was rolling in the confused seas, although not as much as our little fishing boat which was now bouncing around like a cork in an unpredictable manner as the waves buffeted between us and the much larger Ross Revenge. Our small boat rose and fell several feet on the waves, and it soon became obvious that we wouldn't be tying up alongside and going aboard the radio ship for even the slightest respite from the ice cold waters of the North Sea. So, after enduring three hours of increasingly rough seas, we were now facing an immediate return to land, with no refuge from the weather. As our boat wallowed and rolled in the heavy swell, repeated efforts were made to transfer the few essential supplies that were in a plastic crate onto the ship. It was eventually hauled aboard after several attempts to throw the rope attached to it over to crew members on the radio ship, while the skipper of our boat juggled with the engine's throttle, revving the engine, and backing off to keep us close enough alongside to pass the items, but not close enough to risk crashing into the much larger ship. After messages for us to take back to land were shouted across between the two boats, we turned and started to make our way back towards port, we faced a very uncomfortable voyage ahead of us.

Conditions in the southern North Sea on that cold February Sunday were far from ideal as the winds continued to increase. As the route back to land was dependent upon the height of the tide, our skipper had to make a difficult decision. Take the longer route home, avoiding the sandbanks, or take a chance and head in a straight line for Brightlingsea. Misjudge the tide heights, and we could run aground, putting boat and passengers in an extremely precarious and dangerous situation several miles offshore, having to wait until the tide started to rise before freeing the boat from the grip of the rock hard sands.

We took a chance, and cleared the notorious Long Sand, just, with very little water underneath our boat, making the journey even more uncomfortable in the shallow, confused sea. As the weather worsened our skipper opened the throttle fully and we slowly made headway, spiralling against the winds and seas with the engine screaming away. We'd crossed the sands and it was now a case of heading directly for home, each of us onboard keen to get back to dry land. Suddenly a rogue wave was spotted, a large swell with a deep trough behind it. Our skipper lurched towards the throttle to reduce our speed, but he wasn't fast enough.

As our small boat smashed into this huge wave it tipped alarmingly to starboard. Everything in the wheelhouse and the small cabin down below crashed to the floor: cups, kettle, the small gas cooker, torch, fuel cans, life jackets – all the normal detritus found on small boats. The passengers grappled to keep some sort of balance to avoid a very real chance of being thrown overboard. Despite the cold, most of us were out on deck and fell as the boat tipped, fortunately we all managed to grab hold of a secure bit of boat and each other and stayed onboard and dry. It was a close-run thing as the gunwales dipped into the cold and grey North Sea. I was praying for calmer waters, until at last, after more than six hours at sea, we eventually approached Brightlingsea.

The snow started falling again as we came ashore, it was freezing cold as I made my way to my car, clearing the ice and snow from the windows. I turned the key in the ignition, but it had a dodgy starter motor and would often refuse to start without a hefty hammer blow to encourage it, as was the case on this day. I wished that I had a different interest, other than pirate radio that day, as I eventually got to drive home on those icy roads.

On another occasion two boats, with around 30 visitors aboard left Brightlingsea early on a calm Sunday morning to visit the Caroline ship. The journey out was enjoyable and without incident – until the first boat had just tied up alongside Ross Revenge. The passengers, including me, had just climbed onto the radio ship when the Essex police launch Alert was spotted speeding through the haze. Now, in theory there was nothing illegal in a boatman taking visitors out to the ship, and Essex police had no jurisdiction in international waters, however, both boat skippers took fright and ran back to Brightlingsea, one with their passengers still aboard.

Those of us on the Caroline ship were marooned with no way back to shore. We spent a wonderful day onboard whilst coded messages were sent back to land via the CB radio from the ship, trying to arrange our rescue.

By now, I'd visited the ship several times and got to know a few of the guys involved including disc jockey Johnny Lewis, who, knowing my interest in the station, asked if I wanted to stay. The temptation to become a member of the crew was huge and my heart came close to overruling my sensible head. Here was the chance that I'd dreamed of for years. If I said yes then I would be on the radio tomorrow morning – but I couldn't let my family know where I was, I had a job that paid for my mortgage, I didn't have my passport with me and I hadn't even got a toothbrush, so, reluctantly I declined the offer to stay.

Eventually contact was made with a regular Caroline skipper out of Ramsgate who came to collect us, arriving more than twelve hours later. "This is going to cost someone a lot of money", he said as he tied up alongside Ross Revenge. I don't know if he ever got paid, but I do remember leaving from the floodlit radio ship at midnight. The boat that was taking us home was bedecked with flags and bunting and coloured lights above the deck. It looked, and sounded, just like a Thames disco boat, with a fully stocked bar and Caroline's broadcasts blaring out from a huge loud speaker on deck. Not a sight that you would expect to see, 20 miles off the coast at any time, not least at midnight.

There is something magical about leaving, or approaching a ship at night, and the atmosphere on that night in June was very special and a memory that will stay with me. We eventually arrived back on land in Ramsgate at 4am and the sight of more than a dozen weary but happy 'anoraks' walking around the harbour must surely have raised suspicions, but nobody challenged us as we made our way towards three cars that had been driven down from Essex to collect us. Eventually, I arrived home, more than 24 hours after the start of a real adventure, just in time to call in sick to my job, which at this time was with the Department of Transport. I don't think they'd have believed me even if I had tried to explain.

On yet another occasion I was invited to join a private trip out to the ship that my chum DJ Kevin Turner had arranged. It was a glorious summer's day in late August and the sea was Caribbean blue in colour with the sun blazing down. We left from the Kent coast and the journey out was so enjoyable, sea conditions were flat calm, it was idyllic. As we approached Ross Revenge, she was perfectly reflected in the North Sea. It was amazing to see these waters could be so placid, and yet change within hours to become a seething cauldron of saline anger. It was on this visit that I decided I really should sign up to become a pirate - or forget the idea altogether.

The music that was played on Caroline during this period

were songs that weren't really promoted by the ILR and BBC stations; 'Radio Africa' by Latin Quarter, 'More Than I Can Bear.' Matt Bianco,' Human to Human', Adu, 'Hot In The City' by Billy Idol, 'Ain't Nobody', Rufus & Chaka Khan. Even the commercials during this period were memorable: '*Get the tan of the islands with Hawaiian Tropic*', Arabian Sands holidays: '*Call Epsom double four double four one*' '*Visit The 1986 world's fair* in Vancouver' and of course, the incessant promotion for the Canadian National Lottery, Lotto 6/49: '*Pick six numbers between one and forty nine, send your entry to Bet Canada and you could be a millionaire…*'

Chapter Nine

"I'm Cosmic, Get In Quick!"

As 1987 dawned I decided that if I was ever going to have a stint onboard Radio Caroline, I should make it happen now. I was 32, positively ancient, but I just wanted that one go at doing what I'd dreamed of doing for so many years. I recorded yet another demo tape, but this time, rather than putting it into a box and forgetting it, I passed it on, via my chum Bill, who was by now heavily involved with the land-based team. Knowing that my tape would be heard and was likely to be accepted, I arranged a loan to ensure my mortgage was paid for a couple of months and resigned from my job, working for a government department, though I was sensible enough to arrange a return to my old job of coach driving whenever I returned to shore.

I was told to expect a phone call soon. It came a few days later at 10pm, and not surprisingly it was quite bizarre: "Is that Ray? Bill told me that you might be interested in joining us at the weekend, you do know Bill don't you, and do you understand what I'm talking about?"

"Yes," I replied. "OK, be at the Army and Navy pub in Chelmsford at 8.30 on Saturday morning, bring your passport," and the line went dead before I could ask any questions. Be careful what you wish for, I thought, I was about to become a pirate.

Saturday 4th April 1987 started as a fine spring day. I was up by 6am and listening to Steve Conway read the news on Caroline and I remember thinking: I'll be out there and meeting this guy soon. A friend had offered to take me to the pre-arranged meeting point and there I was, complete with my suitcase by 8am, just in case my lift was early.

The agreed meeting time came and went, as did 9am, 9.30,

9.45 and I was at the point of making my way back home when a dirty, noisy, battered faded green coloured Volvo estate roared into the car park, coming to a halt with a screech of tyres. The aroma of hot, burning oil and the cloud of black smoke coming from the exhaust confirmed my observation: - here was a car that really worked for a living and probably wouldn't be working for much longer. "Ray?", asked the driver as the car rolled to a halt, "I'm Cosmic, get in quick".

I was still closing the door as we roared off onto the roundabout, our destination Felixstowe, about 60 miles away. We were hoping to catch the next ferry to Zeebrugge, due to leave in little over two hours. Just about possible, providing the Volvo's engine lasted that long, or we didn't get stopped on the A12 by the police, either for speeding or pollution. Cosmic I'd met before on one of my 'anorak' boat trips, though he didn't seem to remember me. He looked just as you'd expect someone called Cosmic to look. Thick, black swarthy hair, a beard and moustache to match and wearing a faded denim jacket and jeans.

Sitting next to Cosmic was another new recruit, Captain Keith, from Bristol – not a proper captain, but a nice guy who knew a bit about boats and engines and all things marine. Keith, with a lovely Bristolian accent was dressed in faded green overalls and had long hair halfway down his back. I knew the third of my new colleagues, my friend disc jockey Kevin Turner, dressed, as usual, in a casual jacket and ironed jeans. Kevin looked normal, almost too neat and tidy. If we'd been looking for a table in a restaurant Kevin was the one we'd have sent to ask. I fear we'd have gone hungry had Cosmic or Keith tried to make a reservation.

The Volvo continued to race along the dual carriageway towards Felixstowe, leaving a cloud of black acrid smoke whenever Cosmic pumped the accelerator as he weaved in and out of the other vehicles. The car's performance was not helped by being down on the back axle, due to the weight of boxes of records and tapes for the God service (paid for religious programmes to be broadcast in the evening after the Dutch, Radio Monique service had closed for the day) and various lumps of ship, including chains and at least one life jacket.

On arrival at the port check-in, Cosmic made little effort to reduce his speed, racing up to the first checkpoint: "Sorry we're late," he said as we continued to drive past the surprised ferry official, then we were waved through with just a cursory check of our passports which we held up at the windows and after stuffing the ferry ticket into the hand of the man counting us on, we came to a halt on the car deck of the ferry. "Always works, don't stop, just keep on going" said Cosmic, with a contended grin. Then he added in a stage whisper: "We'll wait till everyone has cleared the car deck before we go up. So while everyone else was eager to find a comfortable seat in the lounge four decks above us, we just sat in the car.

Cosmic was the fixer for the land side organisation of Radio Caroline. Charged with arranging supplies, booking tenders to sail to and from the radio ship and finding staff. By now I'd realised he was taking the dream of life as an outlaw to heart. "We've got to break cover now and mix with the other passengers" he said, "And try not to look conspicuous". The four of us, dressed as we were, couldn't have looked more conspicuous if we had tried, as we made our way up the stairs to join the other passengers.

The North Sea crossing to Belgium took around six hours and as our ferry approached Zeebrugge many of the passengers lined the railings on the port side as we sailed past the poignant sight of the crane ships alongside the wreck of The Herald of Free Enterprise, the ferry that had capsized just three weeks earlier with the loss of 193 lives. Everyone onboard, I'm sure, taking a moment to grasp that none of us knows just what fate has in store.

At Zeebrugge we were waved through customs – nothing to declare, although our cargo might have taken some explaining had we been stopped.

"I'll take the back roads" said Cosmic as we sped away. "The

'Feds' won't be watching there." He really was living the dream. The next part of our journey saw us bouncing through huge potholes along narrow back roads, avoiding the border post between Belgium and France on the main autoroute – the same border post that had been unmanned for several years after European border checks had been abolished!

Our destination was the French port of Dunkirk. The supply ship Bellatrix operated from here, servicing both Ross Revenge, home of Radio Caroline and The Communicator, the Laser ship. Owned by the Dutch owners of Radio Monique, she had been making the journey out to the Knock Deep, off the English coast, for some time with large supplies of fuel, water, food, and personnel. Although the offshore radio stations had long since been outlawed by nearly every European country, including France, a blind eye was turned towards her activities by the local Dunkirk authorities, so the ship, crew and passengers were free to travel in and out of the French port. There were a couple of reasons for their free passage at that time. Margaret Thatcher was the British Prime Minister and, in general, the French weren't her biggest fans. Perhaps more relevant was the purchase of many tons of fuel oil and ships' provisions from local Dunkirk businesses - the Mayor of Dunkirk and the Chamber of Commerce, if not listeners, were certainly fans of the pirate radio stations spending money in their town.

Despite the best efforts of Cosmic to drive us off the road, we arrived, intact, alongside the still and lifeless Bellatrix, tied up in a quiet corner of the docks in Dunkirk. There was no sign of the crew or any of the Dutch radio team from Radio Monique who shared the Caroline ship and were due to journey into the North Sea with us. We decided to head off in search of a bar and after a couple of hours returned to the ship.

The dockside was now a hive of activity with many differently sized boxes and crates of supplies being loaded onto the Bellatrix. The crew of three and a couple of Dutch presenters had arrived and were working hard. Our arrival, just as they had finished loading supplies destined for the Caroline ship, was met with a few choice Dutch comments. You always recognise uncomplimentary phrases, even if your knowledge of the language is poor. The ship's engine was throbbing and even without moving the ship was vibrating. The sea beyond the harbour breakwater some way in the distance was still quite rough, with waves breaking over the stone built protective harbour wall, and either side of the harbour entrance a high surf formed as the breakers broke across the wide, flat Dunkirk beaches. "We wait", said a Dutch seaman, "still rough," as the strong wind continued to blow. I was happy to go along with this plan.

Those who were returning to Ross Revenge had found a bunk or a quiet corner of the Bellatrix to while away the forthcoming voyage, but for me and two other new recruits who we'd met on the quayside, disc jockey Dave Foster and the would be cook Gary, it was the start of what we hoped would be a great adventure. I have always, and still do, enjoy 'an adventure' and this was the start of, possibly the best one of all.

The crew of Bellatrix were becoming bored, waiting for the wind to drop and the seas to calm. I remember slumping in an uncomfortable seat in the mess room, unaware that there was probably a bunk that I could have rested in and, although by now it was late evening and I'd been travelling for much of the day, I found it difficult to sleep. This was not helped by the loud soundtrack of a porn video that was playing in the lounge and the Dutch crew noisily enjoying a few beers. The thought that within a few hours I would be a disc jockey on Radio Caroline – the most famous 'pirate radio station' in the world, was also stopping me from sleeping.

After an uncomfortable night just waiting around, the decision was made to sail, despite little change in the sea conditions. "Keep out of the way and don't go on deck," was the order, as we passed through the narrow lock leading to the outer harbour and the North Sea. It seemed that whilst the French authorities were reasonably OK with the supply of the radio ships from Dunkirk, they were not too keen on the movement of people, especially the odd-looking collection who seemed to be attracted to this adventure. So we were told not to be seen so the crew of the ship wouldn't be questioned.

As we left the shelter of the last breakwater, Bellatrix lurched with the heavy sea that we were now ploughing into. I was already aware that I wasn't the best sailor in the world and had, in the past, discovered the joys of seasickness. I quickly eyed up the quickest route to the toilet, or 'the heads' - I was already learning the nautical terms. Fortunately, the call of 'Huey' wasn't heard, well not from me, at least not on this occasion.

The journey out to the Caroline ship was long and slow. Although I'd journeyed several trips to both Mi Amigo and Ross Revenge, I'd only been out from the English coast and this time our voyage from France was much longer and involved following the Northern French coast before making our passage across the major shipping lanes in the Channel. I think I had a meal of some sort during the crossing - I have vague memories of a huge pan of stew that was simmering on the hob in the galley. I remember the smell of it rather than the taste and neither were particularly pleasant.

After what seemed hours, the novelty of standing on the deck searching for a glimpse of the Ross Revenge was wearing thin. I remember spending more time in the mess room with nobody really saying anything as we all wanted to be at our destination. Even the Dutch porno film playing on the TV had, by now, failed to attract anyone's attention. Then suddenly a shout went up, our destination was in sight. We rushed back onto the deck of Bellatrix and ahead of us was Ross Revenge, a fine-looking ship that looked strong enough to take on any sea. However, this time I was seeing her from a ship that was almost the same size, rather than a small fishing boat, and she seemed so much smaller from my current viewing position.

The amazing 300-foot-high mast was always an unbelievable sight, pointing towards the sky with the astonishing array of steel cables fixed to all parts of the ship's hull, holding it tall and sturdy as the Revenge rode the still high waves. They caused the solid ship to buck and pull on her anchor chain but the storm that had prevented us from leaving earlier was starting to calm. The clouds were scudding along at a seemingly fast speed, but every so often the sun would break through, causing the bright red painted hull of the radio ship to be reflected in the grey, green sea. It was a wonderful, memorable, and unique vision and one that I feel so privileged to have witnessed, I will never forget it.

Our ship, Bellatrix, was allowed to drift around from our position about half a mile away from Ross Revenge as the crew waited for the sea to calm further. It was taking it's time and although there was no need to supply diesel and water on this run, as the tanks on Caroline contained enough to last another couple of weeks, there was a desire to offload food and drink and general ships supplies; as well as disc jockeys, and it would be far easier to do this with both ships tied to each other. The normal procedure in calm seas was for Bellatrix to tie up directly to the stern of Ross Revenge and the boxes and crates of supplies passed from ship to ship. However, the seas had decided that this would not be the case on this April afternoon.

After drifting around for an hour or so, the decision was made to supply the radio ship by transferring everything by rubber dinghy - that meant personnel as well as supplies.The ship's crane lowered the small rubber 'rib' with its outboard motor into the North Sea. Cosmic, already on-board, gave V for victory signs as the boat started bucking and rolling as soon as it touched the waves.

Cosmic and Kevin Turner, both with business to be sorted on board, were first to journey across between the two ships, with one of the Dutch sailors taking charge of the outboard motor steering the tiny craft as it bounced over the waves on its way to Caroline.

Twenty minutes later the small launch was back, ready for the next two passengers and one of them would be me. I'd decided that, rather than watch with growing concern, I would put myself forward for the next crossing.

Gary the cook and I made our way down the scramble net on the side of Bellatrix towards the cold, grey and uninviting North Sea, the waves now enjoying their final chance to dance wildly before the arrival of the fine weather, forecast for two days' time. Neither of us had life jackets, we weren't given the option, and I certainly don't remember seeing any, but I was saying my prayers, I hoped that they might keep me safe.

As soon as we were aboard the small rubber boat, we sped off towards Caroline with the spray already doing its best to drench us. Gary looked petrified, I tried to look cool and calm, but I was more than a little concerned as we kept our heads down against the spray and the wind. We held on for dear life to a grab rope running the length of our 'ferry boat' as it bucked, swerved, and bounced across the choppy waters. Whereas the one thousand tons of Ross Revenge had looked quite small from the deck of Bellatrix, she was now towering above our tiny craft. The waves would take us up, almost to deck level and then suddenly we were plummeting way down to below her waterline, rising and falling at least ten feet with each wave. Our skipper, Willy, an experienced boatman, aimed the rubber boat towards the radio ship. Although we were on the leeward side the wind was still whipping up the sea as Willy grabbed hold of a rope attached to one of the many protective tractor tyres chained to the side of Ross Revenge, there to protect her from damage when bigger boats than ours came alongside. Despite Willy's ability, it was impossible for him to manoeuvre our boat to a position where it was safe to transfer to the bigger ship. As we lurched towards the ship for the third time, I was already soaked and just a little worried as I became more aware of the precarious position that all three of us were in. Gary was even more concerned and he was off at the first opportunity, throwing himself towards the radio ship, with no apparent idea of where he was going or how he was going to get aboard.

I helped to hold our boat steady, gripping the rope, and ducking as we crashed into yet another wave, while Skipper Willy attempted to control our boat and avoid taking on the huge waves that had the potential to capsize us. Somehow Gary had scrambled up the side of the ship and was being helped aboard by the radio crew. Now it was my turn to board the ship. The remains of a once sturdy rope ladder trailed down the ship's side, but by now the rope had frayed and many of the wooden steps were missing - the remaining ones just hung limply. I made a move towards it and held on for dear life while planning my next move, which would be upwards towards the ship's rail high above me. That was the plan, but the sea had other ideas as a wave caused our dinghy to drop some five feet from the crest of the wave that it had been sitting on just a split second before. As the boat dropped away, I was still holding onto the near useless rope ladder. Willy the boatman held onto me, trying to drag me back to the relative safety of our craft, but I wasn't letting go of that rope for anyone. Three times the 'rib' rose and fell and three times the waves came up to my chest as I dangled halfway up the side of the ship in the icy cold waters. It was at this point that my instinct for survival came into play. I became aware that the situation I was in was serious. Here I was 18 miles from land, a non-swimmer with no life jacket, hanging precariously to a one-sided frayed rope ladder whilst being swamped by icy cold waves that were attempting to smash me into the side of a steel ship, or worse, wash me away, never to be seen again. I remember thinking: *I might be about to drown here* – a conscious thought…. and then suddenly I was up the rope and being rolled over the side of the ship to safety.

I boarded my new home upside down, soaked to the skin and in a puddle of sea water, I'd made my way up the final few feet, but it was Dutch disc jockey Ad Roberts who helped me to my feet. "Good afternoon" I said, brushing myself down and desperate to appear in control of my actions, Ad grinned and welcomed me on board.

Nearly 40 hours after I'd left my home on the Essex coast, I was on the ship, anchored just a few miles away from where my journey had started. There was no going back, I'd already become part of this strange world.

I was already familiar with the layout of the ship from previous visits and made my way to the mess room where I sat hugging a radiator attempting to warm myself and dry out. Ignored by everyone, I watched as they went about the hectic business of packing to leave the ship on the returning tender or moving new stores around, which were piled high on the deck and along the main companionway running throughout the length of the accommodation area of the ship.

I was now seriously doubting my decision to join the radio station, my mood wasn't helped by one of the Dutch guys having a sarcastic dig about me not helping to stow away the new stores onboard. I can't remember who it was, but he obviously wasn't impressed with me, but equally, a little compassion for the new guy who was soaked to the skin wouldn't have hurt.

Eventually the supplies had been stashed safely onboard. Those crew members who were heading home had left the ship and a calmer mood descended on the messroom. As I was beginning to thaw out, I went off in search of someone who could help me to find a place to change from my damp clothes.

Radio Caroline's Programme Controller was Peter Philips, a tall, slim guy with a very distinctive voice. Those onboard referred to him as '*The World Service*' because of his diction and pronunciation. He had even more of a BBC accent than most broadcasters on the BBC - surprising on a so-called 'pirate' radio station.

With covering programmes for the next few weeks uppermost in his mind he had seen an influx of new faces coming onto the ship and was hopeful of a first-class line-up to allow the radio station to continue with 24-hour programming. We passed each other in the passageway inside the ship. "Hello, I'm Graham" (everyone had two names, their own name and their 'radio name' to avoid possible prosecution), "What radio experience have you got then?" Rather than explain the lengthy route that I'd taken to get this far on my radio journey, I thought it prudent to just reply "None." "F***ing marvellous" he said as he stormed off to the galley.

Eventually I was allocated a cabin and dripped my way down the stairs to the accommodation area and changed out of my wet clothes. I took a few minutes to take in my new surroundings. The cabin, directly at the bottom of the stairs was about ten feet square, I had a small table and a sink. "Best not use that because of the plumbing," I was warned. Ahead of me in the wood veneer-lined cabin was my bunk, interestingly some five feet above the floor and reached via a bench midway between the floor and bunk. The bunk was also 'walled' in, to prevent the occupant falling to the floor in rough weather, so effectively my sleeping place was within a cupboard. It turned out to be warm and dry and quite cosy. It was to be my home for the next six weeks.

The daily procedure onboard the ship was for everyone, apart from the on-air DJ, to sit at the large table in the mess room for one meal a day, usually around 6pm. It gave everyone a chance to introduce themselves and I realised that I was quite fortunate here, because I already knew one of those onboard, and he was the deputy programme controller. I wondered if this might play into my favour when the decision of who did what on-air shift was made later in the evening.

Our crew comprised of Captain Keith, who was on his first visit to the ship, three Dutch/Flemish disc jockeys - Ad Roberts, Dick Verhoel and Jan Veldkamp, and the English presenters: Programme Controller, Peter Philips who I'd briefly met and who had now become much friendlier towards me, Deputy Programme Controller Kevin Turner, Mark Matthews, Dave James, and the new guys, me, Dave Foster, and Gary who'd come out as the new cook. I'd already figured out that the two on-air shifts needing to be covered were the afternoon show, 1pm-5pm, and the midnight till 6am shift. I rather hoped that

I wouldn't be put on overnight, I'd told a few friends where I was going and I hoped that they would have the opportunity to hear my efforts, at least once. I received the briefest of instructions on how to work the equipment in the studio, and was asked if I was happy 'doing afternoons' - "no, no, no, that's fine with me," I replied.

It was now many hours since I was last in my bed, I needed to sleep and I was quite keen to retire to my bunk and the privacy of my cabin, but even going to bed was a novel experience. I had to climb up to my bunk, at least five feet off the floor, and then manoeuvre into a sleeping bag without hitting my head, bumping my knee, or falling back to the floor. It was quite difficult, and this first occasion was on a calm sea.

As I lay in my bunk, inside that small box, I realised that the accommodation on the ship was just below the waterline and although you could hear the throb of the huge, powerful generators running all the time throughout the ship, the cabin area was reasonably quiet with the sound of waves lapping just inches from my head and the scraping of the chains holding the old truck and tractor tyres in place along the ship's sides to protect them when other ships came alongside. I spent a while just laying still, listening to the sounds, feeling the motion of the ship and trying to take in everything that had happened throughout the previous two days, and that within the next few hours I would be broadcasting to millions across the UK, Holland, Belgium and Northern France.

I smiled to myself as I drifted off to sleep, I was about to become a pirate disc jockey on the iconic Radio Caroline.

Chapter Ten

"Mick Williams Follows The News"

Monday April 6th, 1987 was a fine day, and as I climbed the wooden staircase from the cabins and turned left into the galley, the bright sunshine blazed through the port holes filling the room with light. I made a cup of tea and a slice of toast and wandered around the deck taking in the sights, not that there was too much to see. We were surrounded by sea and more sea. Land could only be seen on exceptionally clear days. In the far distance a few ships were visible as they passed through the deep-water channels, making their way to or from the English Channel or in or out of the Thames estuary.

Our only neighbour - the Communicator, the Laser ship, was anchored about a mile away. After the close down of Laser 558 in 1985, the ship had returned to sea at the end of 1986 and relaunched as Laser Hot Hits. Sadly, a ferocious storm in January had wrecked their radio masts and aerial system, and since then they had returned to the air with a very small team on board. But money was scarce, and it was obvious to all that the radio station's days were numbered.

The crew of Ross Revenge went about their daily business, a mixture of doing nothing, taking it easy or gathering in small groups in the messroom, on the bridge or in the record library. Jobs like presenting programmes and show preparation, engineering, cooking, and washing up were the only essential tasks, for most of the time. But all this could change if an emergency or unplanned event occurred, and then it was all hands to the deck.

The record library on the ship contained thousands of vinyl treasures; remember, this was in pre-CD and digital days. We had a strict format that included classic hits from the previous 20 years, interspersed with newer recordings, some of which were obvious chart hits and others which were songs that fitted the Caroline sound.

There were also certain records that were on quite high rotation. These were songs that had come to the radio station with a cash donation from the record company or producer, several of them recorded by big, familiar names. In effect these were 'plug' records which provided a bit of cash to help with the survival of the operation. For what was to be my first show, I was presented with a neatly typed list of songs to be selected from the ship's record library.

Now, I consider myself a fine, upstanding law-abiding citizen, but if the worst thing I do in my life is to play a Bruce Springsteen record from a rusty ship, then my conscience is pretty clear. But as one o'clock approached, I was about to break the Marine etc. Broadcasting (Offences) Act 1967.

I admit I was a little nervous. Avoiding the use of your own name, the sensible precaution of a second name was employed to scupper any awkward questions back on dry land. Ahead of my first broadcast, the Caroline studio was occupied by Peter Philips, who was presenting the morning show and he asked me what name I would be using on air. I'd already been quizzed about my 'on-air name' by my good friend Mick Williams before going out to the ship. Mick was the guy who I'd worked with at public address events on many occasions. "I might just use your name" had been my jokey reply, and I gave a similar reply to Peter Philips, who then announced my new name to the Caroline audience. "Mick Williams will be with you after the one o'clock news here on Caroline 558…"

In the newsroom, positioned on the upper deck and behind the ship's bridge, Steve Conway was updating the huge Caroline audience with the latest news events around Europe as I settled myself into the studio chair in front of the large Gates mixing desk – or board, as it would have been called in the U.S, where it originated thirty years earlier. All of the studio equipment on board was extremely well made and reliable, but it was all very dated with rotary knobs rather than sliding faders and it had already been operated for many years in the States before Radio Caroline acquired it.

Nervously, with my arm shaking, I cued up my first record on turntable one situated to my right hand side. I placed the tape cartridge labelled 'News Out' into one of the three cart machines and I was ready to go. Mentally checking the order in which I had to push the buttons in front of me to remotely start the various pieces of equipment, I noticed that the remote-control buttons had come from a redundant fruit machine, ideal for constant use because of their strong construction. I had a choice of Twist, Stick, Hold or Gamble. Steve finished the news: "*For Caroline 558 I'm Steve Conway*", and we were off.

I pushed the Twist button firmly and the 'click' was reassuring. The remote cart machine on a shelf above the turntables made a clunking noise as the instant start motor came into play, followed by a soft whirring noise as the recording tape ran over the tape heads: '*That was Radio Caroline News brought to you by Newsweek magazine.*" There was another click as I pushed the Gamble button and Paul Simon's recent hit 'You Can Call Me Al' started to play and I was on the air without any disaster.

Peter Philips started to leave the studio as I prepared to cue the next record, and then Paul Simon suddenly stopped in his tracks: I'd pushed the wrong button, causing my first record to grind to an unscheduled halt. ... *You can ..... c a ...l...l m......e......A.........l.*

Realising my mistake, I quickly pressed the button again, allowing Paul Simon to continue his tale. I was mortified. "Anyone who has ever been out to this ship and been any good has done exactly the same thing" said Peter as he left the studio, chuckling, while I continued my programme, becoming the latest to join a long list of Radio Caroline disc jockeys that had been heard cutting their broadcasting teeth over many years since Easter 1964.

That afternoon zoomed by with four hours of great music

and my occasional 'witty link' between the songs. It all went very smoothly, and I was feeling very pleased with myself. At last I was doing the job that I had dreamed of and on the radio station that I had grown up with. Five o'clock came and I handed over to Dave James who would follow my programme. *"For the last four hours I've been Mick Williams, and I shall be Mick Williams again tomorrow…"*

I struggled back to the record library with my huge pile of records and filed them away, a job that took a surprisingly long time, and then I made my way down to the mess room. I was expecting, perhaps, a huge round of applause or cries of *'Bravo, well done … so good on his first attempt'*, but I had none of those. However, I did have a cup of tea waiting for me – and I soon realised that this was a simple sign of acceptance as one of the Caroline team - I was very happy.

'Mick Williams' arrives onboard Ross Revenge (photo: Francois L'hote, Offshore Echoes Magazine)

The next day's programme went just as well, though this time there was a different greeting waiting for me in the messroom. Whilst I'd been on air a small rubber dinghy had arrived from the Laser ship anchored nearby. A couple of their crew had come to visit us and one of them was Paul, a tall imposing guy with a full dark beard and a great American broadcasters voice. He was one of the small on-air team from Laser Hot Hits. He'd already enjoyed a successful career in American radio and had journeyed to Europe for the adventure of working for a pirate radio station. As I entered the mess room he shook my hand. "Hi" he said, "I've been listening to you, you're sounding good – how long have you been in the business?"

"Oh, about 24 hours now" I replied smugly... I felt so pleased with myself.

I quickly settled into life on board the radio ship. Every afternoon I would play a selection of great oldies and songs that were current at the time. Played frequently were: 'Let My People Go Go', by The Rainmakers, 'Living In a Box' by the band called Living in a Box, 'La Isla Bonita' by Madonna, Paul Simon's 'Graceland,' 'With or Without You' by U2 and 'Nothings Gonna Stop Us Now' by Starship. I have only to hear the opening notes of any of those songs all these years later, and my mind is transported back to my early days on the radio. We were playing the very best. *'Best of The Old, Best Of The New, This is Caroline 558.'* There's a line in 'The In Crowd' by Dobie Gray that I remember heartily singing along to on a beautifully sunny afternoon - *'Other guys imitate us, but the original's still the greatest',* and here I was playing the song on Britain's original music station.

With every show I became more confident, and the discipline of the strict format taught me very quickly how to present music radio properly:

Keep the music flowing.

If you can't say what you have to say over the run up to the vocals don't say anything.

Station name every link.

Avoid back announcing.

Keep up the pace.

Keep to time.

Don't crash the vocals.

Don't fade a story song.

Never 'diss' a song on air, even if you dislike it - as far as your listener is concerned every song you play must always be one of your favourites.

Progress forward all the time.

Fun links are fine.

Avoid cheesy jokes.

Always be positive.

Give an insight into life onboard, but don't give away the secrets.

Forward promote but don't list songs.

Always make it sound as if you are talking to just one person.

It's as simple as that!

I lived, slept and ate radio. Stuck on a ship several miles from land, there was little else to do. And I still try to put all that I learnt back in 1987 into practice whenever I'm on the radio today – what an apprenticeship.

I had no thoughts of being able to make radio my career at this time. I still thought that this was to be my only stint on the radio and so I decided to get as much experience as possible by volunteering to read the news bulletins for a few days, as well as presenting my daily show.

Working on the breakfast show, which was presented by Kevin, I would get up at 5.30am, and head straight to the newsroom which was the former chart room from the ship's deep sea fishing days. It was situated behind the bridge and one floor up from the main studio and perhaps calling it a newsroom was an exaggeration. It contained a chair, a small desk, an ancient typewriter and a small portable television, fixed to the wall. Our news came via Teletext and Ceefax. I would decide the news stories of the day, taken from what the

BBC and ITV were reporting, then re-write the news copy ready for the first bulletin at six o'clock. Between bulletins I would update the stories, keep an eye on the weather forecast and keep Kevin, who was playing the music, supplied with tea from the galley. It was just possible to visit the galley from the studio, make tea from the constantly simmering tea urn and return back upstairs. But if you did all this during a song lasting less than four minutes you'd be cutting it fine. So having a newsreader who could make tea for the breakfast presenter was a bonus.

Everything's fine on Caroline

During those early days of April 1987, we had early-summer-like conditions, flat calm seas, and warm sunny days. The forecast for Easter was great and being on air on a sunny day was a wonderful experience. The anniversary of the launch of Radio Caroline is always marked over Easter, and here we were celebrating the station's 23rd birthday on board. There had been plenty of times in the past when Caroline had struggled for survival, but right now this world-famous offshore radio station was riding on the crest of a wave. We had a fantastic signal that travelled several hundred miles with a huge audience tuning in daily, our tanks were full of diesel and water, food cupboards and freezers full of food and there was a full complement of disc jockeys onboard. As one of the radio stations jingles from the 1960s went: '*Everything's fine on Caroline',* and it was.

Being on board the ship as an integral part of the team was just so exciting, yet at the same time, ordinary. Wherever you went the sound of the generators, deep in the bowels of the ship far below the main deck, could be heard, and felt, as they vibrated everywhere. The throb of the generators could also be heard in the background every time the microphone was opened in the studio. It was one of the ways you knew that you were listening to Radio Caroline. Ever present was that lovely smell of over warm, almost burning electrics, mixed with a hint of warm engine oil. There were cooking smells too, not always so pleasant, emanating from the galley.

The crew of 15 all had the same purpose, to broadcast to Caroline's loyal listeners and keep the station on the air. It was one of the most exciting experiences that I had ever encountered and I loved it.

Since the arrival of the last tender there was now the luxury of a dedicated cook onboard, replacing the need for various disc jockeys having to cook the meals. But it soon became obvious that our new cook wasn't very good. Gary really wanted to be a disc jockey, but sadly, he didn't appear to have much of an idea about how to do that either. His expertise in the galley soon revealed itself when he attempted to make an apple pie. What he thought was a catering size tin of apple slices in the ship's stores, labelled in Dutch, actually contained not slices but *appelmousse* – applesauce, eaten by the Dutch as a refresher between courses. As Gary proudly presented his masterpiece with an exaggerated, even for him, camp flourish, to a hungry crew the sloppy contents slowly broke through the soggy pastry and slid, like an oil slick across the table. Several choice words followed, both in English and Dutch and the probationary cook was demoted to cleaning and rust chipping duties.

*****

My sleep was interrupted by the loud alarm bell that could be heard throughout the ship. It was 4am on Easter Sunday and the tender was approaching. I quickly got dressed and went up on deck, joining the rest of the crew in time to greet those coming aboard, and there was certainly a surprise in store for all of us.

Standing on the deck of the tender was Ronan O'Rahilly, the elusive, charismatic founder and the man behind Radio Caroline. It was extremely unusual for Ronan to visit the ship, he'd probably not been onboard since the return of the radio station back in 1983, and yet here he was together with his small entourage of friends. Also on the tender was Fred, the Dutch Radio Monique boss. Any suggestion that money was scarce, and times were hard could certainly be dismissed as preparations were made for many tons of fuel and fresh water to be pumped aboard through thick hoses running across the decks between Bellatrix, the supply tender, and Ross Revenge. The deck of the radio ship became cluttered with crates, boxes and trays of fresh food and supplies.

With the appearance onboard of 'the big guns' it was obvious that something important was going on as a group of people made their way to the record library for a meeting held behind closed doors. Being a newcomer, I kept out of the way, I felt that whatever was being discussed wasn't for my ears, although I was itching to know what was going on. So I went out on deck and enjoyed the sunshine. It was while I was daydreaming and gazing out to sea that an 'anorak' boat became visible in the distance, heading for Ross Revenge. I could see those onboard taking photographs and waving, much as I'd done on my 'anorak' visits to the ship in the past. It seemed strange to be waving back from the radio ship. I was soon joined by other crew members, and we presented a wall of reasonably friendly faces to the 'anoraks' on board the small boat that had left Brightlingsea three hours earlier.

The boat, organised by Caroline stalwarts Albert and his wife Georgena, would normally have been allowed to tie up alongside, but not this time. And rather than allow our visitors on board, they were given a story about work taking place that prevented access to the ship. Obviously, this was a huge disappointment to those who had paid their £15 to see the pirates, but we were protecting Ronan from being mobbed by a dozen 'anoraks'. As the small boat circled Ross Revenge, Albert's eye caught mine, "How did you get out here then?" he shouted across the water, with his broad East Anglian accent, having recognised me from previous trips that he'd organised. "It's a secret Albert!" I yelled back.

Whatever was being discussed behind the closed record library door was still going on. I would soon have a show to present and I had yet to select my records, so I needed to enter the room. I knocked and walked in, trying to make myself inconspicuous as Ronan held court in the corner with what could loosely be called the Management team.

As I started pulling my records from the complex filing system, I heard a whisper from Ronan to the others, "What's the guy's real name?" My new colleagues told him: "Hey, Ray, it's great to meet you, you're going down very well in London" he said. I smiled and thanked him and carried on with my record selection, aware that I was yet another to be charmed by this smooth-talking Irishman. Many people before me had spent time working for the radio station and had never met the boss and he seemed quite happy with the latest on-air recruit.

I would get to meet Ronan on several other occasions after I left the ship, and he was always very pleasant and always appeared to remember me. His business methods may have left much to be desired, and I'm certain that there are many who were financially less well off after meeting him, but by keeping an awareness that he wasn't always the angel that many thought, I decided he was an OK guy.

As I would soon learn, the big onboard conference was about an imminent change to the territorial waters boundary of the UK, which meant that, in order to stay outside British law, and legally safe, Ross Revenge would have to move further out to sea.

A few days later I was part of a conversation in the chart room as to where the ship should be moved. There were only two options, either the sea area known as The Galloper Sands, which was much further north than the Knock Deep, off the Suffolk coast and much further from the important London audience, or The South Falls Head, which was further south and closer to the French coast. It would make supplying the ship easier and send an even stronger radio signal into the London area. But this position was in much deeper and more open waters, and would also place the ship closer to the Goodwin sands.They were directly to the southwest of the proposed new position, which meant that should the anchor chain break during one of the frequent north easterly gales, and the ship drifted - something Caroline ships had a history of doing - the first stop would be the notorious ships graveyard. Unfortunately, this scenario became a reality four years later.

The supply tender and our visitors stayed for nearly eight hours and those of us remaining aboard Ross Revenge were lucky enough to witness yet another memorable sight from the back deck.

The Bellatrix slowly moved away with Ronan and a couple of presenters returning to shore on board. With a blast of the shrill horn from the supply ship the shimmering reflection of both ships became visible on the unusually smooth surface of the North Sea, as those onboard both ships waved and exchanged friendly banter until out of earshot. As the tender made its way back to Dunkirk, via the Laser ship, we were once again alone, 18 miles out, and enjoying the calm conditions, at least for a few more days.

Working on the Chain Gang, Ross Revenge, 1987

You can tell when a storm at sea is brewing, you notice little things at first: the colour of the sea and the sky slowly turn to increasingly dark shades of grey, there is an absolute stillness before an increasingly fresh breeze becomes a strengthening wind, and you become aware of less shipping passing by. For a few days several Dutch and Belgian fishing boats had been trawling in our area and a couple of larger sand dredgers regularly passed by, but now, as the skies darkened, they were gone. Sitting in the on-air studio, the sea was visible in three directions, by looking to the right and beyond the Dutch studio, which was separated by a large glass window, you could see the sky, then the sea, then the sky, then the sea, and so it continued as the ship rolled in the increasing swell. Looking straight ahead you could see the back deck of the ship rising and falling on the increasingly bigger waves. The same waves that were getting higher all the time and rolling just inches from the top of the gunwales as you looked through the square porthole to the left of the studio. There was no doubt that a large storm was heading our way.

The records continued to play. Only in extremely heavy seas would the DJs resort to playing pre-recorded 'storm tapes'. Whilst the ship rolled, it did so gradually, allowing the pick up arm to remain in the grooves of the vinyl records, but with each wave the microphone moved from left to right, with the DJ following it during a link. Having a studio chair with castors, it stopped being fun after a while as you held yourself into position by grabbing the underside of the desk and wedging your knees beneath it just to stop yourself from rolling to the other side of the studio. Working in the newsroom was slightly less demanding as the microphone was attached to a rope, so if the ship happened to roll during a news bulletin the reader could draw it closer to his mouth, simply by tugging at the rope.

I knew conditions could be bad in a storm, particularly in this part of the North Sea and especially if the winds were from the northeast, but just how bad the storm would be was the unknown factor: how bad is bad? I wanted to get an idea of what was brewing, and while trying to appear unperturbed, I casually remarked to one of the seasoned Dutch guys, "It's getting a bit wild, isn't it?" The reply wasn't what I wanted to hear, "Oh yes, it'll be heavy… but it will be over by the end of the week." The end of the week? ..But it was only Sunday!

When I was packing for my spell at sea the possibility of rough weather had been on my mind and as a precaution, I'd packed a couple of plastic bags for emergency use in case of seasickness. One of the bags was constantly in my pocket, just in case, though I'm sure I wouldn't have been the first Radio Caroline disc jockey to throw up over the broadcast desk. However, I didn't think it would have done my popularity any good at all had I been the next one.

I walked around the ship trying to appear unconcerned and watched, spellbound, as the ship dipped and rose into the huge waves that were now breaking over the bow, seemingly in slow motion, and onto the deck. Sea spray frequently reached up the mast, causing the tremendous electrical power from the aerial to arc around the ceramic insulators that were spaced all the way along the many metal stays holding this amazing 300-foot tall structure steady, while the ship kicked and bucked in the near white sea with the wind screaming through the rigging. Watching the waves and the electrical sparks was mesmerising, especially once the salt laden spray had deposited crystals on those same insulators, causing them to glow and appear to dance in time to the music. If you were brave enough to go out on deck in such a storm you could even hear the radio station's output in the air, the sound just seeping from the aerial mast.

Amazingly, even through the roughest of weather, the huge transmitters anchored down by strong steel beams on the floor of the former fish room, now the ship's transmitter hall, continued to pump out the music from both Radio Caroline and Radio Monique without missing a beat. The large blue *RCA* transmitter cabinets, already more than 25 years old when Caroline acquired them, housed giant glowing valves. Huge when compared to domestic valves that were once commonplace in televisions and radios at home, these monsters were at least two feet high and nearly as wide and glowed brightly. Dials, and numerous mysterious electrical components surrounded them behind the closed doors and cages, set to instantly trip out the electronics should an attempt be made to open the doors to access the huge voltages, especially by those that had no understanding of the technology. Touch the wrong part of the transmission system and it was quite capable of killing you, either by frying you alive with the great heat generated or by electric shock. I kept a respectful distance from the whole set up. Though I loved to gaze at the flickering lights and dials and listen to the air cooling fans. These were quiet by comparison to the monster *M.A.N* diesel generators powering the whole ship, screaming away on the other side of a partition wall that separated them, keeping the transmitters free from sooty, oily smuts from the generators.

As the ship bucked and kicked you could feel all one thousand tons of Ross Revenge climb up the anchor chain as far as it would allow, as she pounded into the angry waves, and then crash down through the white crests as the waves just kept rolling incessantly. The swell would push first to port and then to starboard as the ship violently tugged back into the next giant wave. It was comforting to feel that regular tug and shudder from the ship, at least we knew we were still at anchor.

In her days as a working fishing vessel, the ship had every possible navigational aid available. But now, at anchor, we just had a limited version of a Decca navigator, more suited to a small pleasure boat. It worked by defining a parameter and an alarm would sound if the ship moved outside of it. One bleep was fine, two was OK, but three gave cause for concern, especially if it continued to bleep three or more times in succession. I would often climb up to the bridge, in as casual a manner as I could, just to check that all was well. The problem was in a rough sea the radar signal was cluttered by the waves and frequently caused the alarm to sound, often during the news bulletins, giving those listening on land a cause for concern as they thought the ship might be in distress. I almost survived the storm unscathed, but on May Day Bank Holiday, a day you'd expect to be warm, calm and sunny, the storm threw everything at us. It was a force 10 North Easterly, the worst possible direction in our position, and I was on the breakfast show. Although I'd had no need to use my emergency plastic bag, as Kevin Turner popped into the studio to check all was well I asked him if he fancied starting his programme half an hour early as I made my way down to my cabin via the galley where I borrowed a large saucepan, just in case the plastic bag wasn't up to the job.

As I lay in my bunk, I listened with concern as crashes and bangs could be heard from all over the ship, echoing down below as the chains holding the fender tyres rattled loudly and chaffed on the ship's side, competing with the sound of breaking waves and the screaming winds outside.. One huge crash from somewhere upstairs puzzled me, but I wasn't prepared to leave my bunk to investigate. I later learned that it was a spare cooker that had crashed to the floor from its storage place – a spare cooker that would never again be used.

Later in the day, I ventured up to the galley, as the wind howled outside and all the external hatches were securely closed. The temperature inside the ship was very warm, too warm. I passed by the gas cooking range with two full pans of stew bubbling and spitting while the contents overflowed onto the gas jets every time the ship rolled. I quickly returned to my bunk and my own standby saucepan, thankfully unused - but it was a close run thing. The storm continued to rage through the night and into the following day. I was due on air for the afternoon show, so staying in my bunk wasn't an option, though fortunately, I was now feeling less queasy and made my way to the mess room for a breakfast of tea and toast, the best antidote to potential sea sickness.

The large crew table in the mess room was surrounded by

several permanently moored but swivelling seats that enabled the occupant to move with the unpredictable motion of the ship. To counteract this, the fiddles had been put into place. These raised rims or ledges came out in times of rough seas and clipped to the edge of the table to prevent tea mugs and dinner plates and their contents from falling onto the floor, or worse, into your lap. The record library was also designed with rough seas in mind. Each shelf had a small lip to prevent the hundreds of vinyl albums, filed in numerical order, from cascading onto the floor, although with each roll of the ship they constantly tipped from side to side. But whatever the weather everyone on board was aware that this was the world famous Radio Caroline, where the music continues... most of the time.

And then suddenly, four days later, the storm was all over. The sun started to shine again, the sea became calm, and life returned to normal, or as normal as life on a pirate radio ship could ever be.

All was good, I was back on air playing the hits, when suddenly I heard a loud bang from down below. The lights dimmed and the domestic 60-watt light bulb in the corner of the studio started to glow, as did the corresponding bulb in the next-door studio. I exchanged glances with my Dutch colleague. The light bulbs were a basic warning that the huge 50 kilowatt transmitters were both off the air. A fault in the transmitter hold had caused both high-powered transmitters to trip out and putting them back on air was a specialist job for someone who knew what they were doing. And the one person that we didn't have onboard at the time was a transmitter engineer. The ship seemed strangely quiet. Although the powerful generators continued to roar away, the radio in the galley was silent. We had a daily link up with shore via a clandestine CB radio later in the day, but we needed to get an urgent message ashore asking for technical assistance as soon as possible.

Long-serving, legendary radio engineer Peter Chicago was

ashore and desperate measures were needed to contact him. In a room behind the bridge, packed with short wave radio equipment that was used during the days when Ross Revenge was fishing in distant waters off the Russian, Greenland and Canadian coasts, was a telex machine, now only used in emergencies, together with a secret code list. Most of the communication between the ship and land was by using pre-arranged coded numbers and on this occasion the message was to read '*TX off air, needs attention*', not that the silence from the ship wasn't a clue. We later learnt that we'd sent the wrong code, which, when translated, said: '*Man coming ashore in rubber boat.*' This must have been somewhat alarming for those on land as at that time we had no rubber boat, so our simple request for assistance caused considerable alarm to the office.

The message had obviously got through. As I strolled around the deck next morning, enjoying my first cup of tea of the day, I heard the distinctive *putt putt putt* sound of an outboard motor. Over the side of the ship I saw the tiniest rubber dinghy with three men aboard, and one of them I had met before - it was engineer Peter Chicago.

Within a couple of hours Peter had fixed the problem and turned the transmitter back on. Eager to get back on air, I returned to the studio, where thankfully, I'd already picked my records for the afternoon and, as I entered the studio, Kevin Turner, equally keen to get back on air, had already fired off the tape cartridge that was now playing the station's theme tune, 'Caroline' by The Fortunes. Countless times as a listener I'd heard it played, heralding the return of the station after a breakdown, but this time it would be me that was to be the first voice heard on its return. Now the thing with Caroline has always been not to give away too much detail on air about problems and play down any unusual events. As the theme faded out, almost 24 hours after the breakdown and knowing that an audience of millions was tuned in eagerly awaiting our return, I opened the microphone and casually announced "*All*

I said was, what does this button here do?" as I pushed the red *gamble* button to remotely start the next record.

Through all the years of listening to Radio Caroline I had loved hearing the station start up for the day or returning after a breakdown with that wonderful drum roll at the start of the theme tune cutting through the ether. We were back on air, playing music across much of the UK and mainland Europe, and I was the guy playing it.

Chicago Pete, so named many years earlier when he was on Radio North Sea because he loved the band Chicago, was tall and imposing. You wouldn't choose to argue with him, although there was nothing he enjoyed more than a heated discussion. I already knew Peter and got on well with him, although I suspect others onboard, including some of the regulars, feared him, possibly because of his reputation for not suffering fools gladly. Peter certainly had a very dry sense of humour and would revel in starting a discussion in the mess room, throwing in an explosive comment before leaving the room on urgent engineering business, while the heated debate that he had started continued.

After a couple of weeks onboard I was asked to present the weekend breakfast show, which entailed a 5am start.

Dave Foster, later to become a Caroline stalwart, had been on air throughout the night and kindly woke me, by tapping gently on my cabin door at around 4.30am. Ten minutes later he was back, but this time hammering on my door and in a voice that must surely have woken the whole crew, calling me again. I'd just sort of half-dozed off, but on hearing this commotion I jumped up from my bunk and then, still half-asleep, fell almost five feet to the floor below, via the bench below my bunk – a very painful start to the day. More than thirty years on and I am still working with Dave on board Ross Revenge during the monthly Radio Caroline North broadcasts.

Another seafaring hazard were fishing vessels. One day a couple of Belgian fishing boats approached us causing concern. Were they friendly? Even as 'pirates' ourselves we were vulnerable to piracy, either from rival stations, or, as was shown a couple of years later, the authorities. This time the boats came in peace. The Belgian fishermen wanted a look around and moored on either side of the radio ship while I was on-air. Not only did they supply us with freshly caught fish for dinner, but offered a lift over to the Laser ship, Communicator. Several of my Caroline colleagues accepted and went for a visit to the neighbours, while I and a few others manned Ross Revenge.

My time as part of the shipborne Radio Caroline team was one of the best adventures I have ever had. I learnt so much about broadcasting, the weather, ships and the sea, and all things marine. I was even shown how to start the engine on a one thousand ton former Icelandic trawler - no easy task. It involved starting compressors, pumps and even a smaller engine … and all in a certain order. The whole procedure took at least an hour, but it's a handy thing to know. You never know when that knowledge might be needed!

I'd been fortunate enough to work with people who accepted me and would remain friends from that point on, but the time ultimately came to return to shore – I had a mortgage to pay and had to go back to a more conventional job. I'd had a wonderful time aboard Ross Revenge. In the future, others would fare less well, telling tales of hardship and animosity, but I'd enjoyed adventure and plenty of laughs. It really was like being a part of an Enid Blyton *Secret Seven* story.

Time to leave and the tender, Bellatrix, arrived around midday on a Saturday, several weeks after I'd first joined the ship. There was no certainty that there would be a tender of any description, but by now I was concerned that if it didn't arrive at some point over the weekend, then I would have to stay for a further week. I needed to be back home by Monday, ready to start a new job.

Onboard the tender were plenty of fresh supplies, but no replacements for the two DJs, one of whom was me, that were leaving to return to land. I felt very guilty knowing that the on-air crew would now be reduced to just three to cover all the programmes, it would mean that the previous period of 24 hour a day programmes would be reduced. Our journey back to Dunkirk took us via the now, sadly, silent Laser ship. It was interesting to walk around the ship that had once housed Laser 558, the radio station that had challenged and ultimately changed British music radio. Much like Caroline had in the 1960s, Laser had been listened to by millions just a couple of years earlier.

On arrival in Dunkirk, the two departing pirates, myself and disc jockey Dave James, joined the ferry for Ramsgate. Using prepaid tickets, supplied by Radio Caroline, we sailed home without mishap. No-one stopped us or questioned us about our journey. It must have been obvious that, with our scruffy dress and the strong smell of diesel that followed us everywhere, we hadn't just spent time relaxing on a beach in the south of France. Twenty-four hours after leaving the ship, I was home, and after the previous six weeks my life would return to some sort of normality as I prepared to leave home again within hours. I was returning to coach driving and was booked to take a school party away for a week to York.

Back on dry land, I still maintained a link of sorts with my former shipmates. During my time on Ross Revenge a few of us had spent a pleasant afternoon going through the *Guinness Book of British Hit Singles,* noting several missing classics from the Caroline library. At home I had a large collection of singles from the 60s and 70s and was able to fill in many missing gaps by recording them onto a cassette tape which eventually found its way to the ship. 'Quick Joey Small' by Kasenetz Katz Singing Orchestral Circus was just one of the songs that Caroline was now able to play. It was quite amusing just a few weeks later to hear copies of my records being played on the radio.

I was already starting to miss life on board, although I knew there was no way that I could become a regular presenter, much as I would have liked to. Although it was made clear to me that

I'd be welcomed back at any time I needed to have a regular income, something that Radio Caroline couldn't guarantee. I did get paid for my spell on board, a sign that I was considered useful as not everyone received a wage. The grand sum of £75 eventually found its way to me, passed via Kevin Turner from Ronan who retrieved the cash from his sock, transferring it under the table in a Kings Road coffee bar as he held an audience with those regulars returning from the ship.

*****

Another radio convention for fans of Caroline was held at a hotel in Bloomsbury during the summer of 1987 and many of the Caroline team were there, representing different time periods of the station's life. I went along with my Dutch friend Hans and met up with a few of the team that I knew from my stint onboard. We joined a table of presenters and fans of the station. As we chatted there was a sudden flurry of excitement as Caroline boss Ronan O'Rahilly walked in, joining those sitting at our table, nodding a greeting to those sitting there. "Hey Ray, have you been 'Bellarixing' lately - when are you coming back?" he asked, with a reference to the large continental tender boat. It surprised me that he'd remembered me and associated me with the Bellatrix, and now he was asking when I'd be going back to Caroline. I told him that as much as I'd love to return, I just couldn't afford to spend regular stints at sea. "Aah, you don't need money" he drawled with his soft Irish lilt, "Go back out, you could be the next Johnnie Walker".

Praise indeed, but I was sure he'd used a similar line to many others over the years. Hugely charismatic, if he wanted anything he could instantly turn on the charm, but it thrilled me to be asked. I kept in touch with events on the ship and was regularly asked if I was available, but I was kept busy driving until the coach season ended. Then came yet another message from Caroline on my answerphone: "Would you be OK from mid-November?"

I considered the request, I could spare a couple of weeks,

but not on the date that they wanted me to go out as I still had work commitments for the weekend of the tender's planned departure. But I confirmed that I'd be free to go out a week later.

However, on the 24th November 1987, at around 2am, in the middle of a howling gale and very rough seas, the 300-foot-high mast was torn from its supports and crashed over the side of the ship, causing Ross Revenge to list alarmingly. As the rugged steel mast toppled over the starboard side, many of the numerous steel cables holding the structure in place whipped away from their mountings, though some remained attached, causing the wreckage to crash into the ship's side with every huge wave. It was the strength of the ship and the bravery of engineers Ernie Stevenson and Peter Chicago, who went out on deck in horrendous weather conditions to cut away the floundering mast that saved the crew, who, although safe could now do nothing except sit on the mastless, silent radio ship, unable to broadcast, waiting for the seas to die down. It was to be a further week before the weather calmed enough to enable the tender to take them home.

Had I been available to go out, I would have been part of the crew at the time but I certainly wouldn't have been much of an asset to the situation had I been on board. I considered myself very lucky not to have been there under such horrifying circumstances. I did offer to go out as part of the crew on the next tender, but I think my lack of engineering ability had been recognised. Engineers were needed to get the station back on air, not coach driving disc jockeys - thank goodness!

Chapter Eleven

"Fings Ain't What They Used To Be"

And that was it, my five minutes of fame had come to an end. I was a coach driver again and continued to travel throughout Europe and the UK, driving my passengers to various resorts and hotels. And so, at the start of July 1988, I found myself in Bournemouth. Having offloaded my passengers and their cases, before driving towards the coach park, I tuned around on the radio and found Ocean Sound, the Independent Local Radio station based in Fareham. The most recent addition to their personnel line-up was on air; former Radio Caroline disc jockey Kevin Turner. As I listened, Kevin mentioned a phone number for a competition to win a CD. Quickly scribbling the number down as I manoeuvred the coach, I continued my journey to the coach park, locked up and found a telephone box and called the number, which was eventually answered by Kevin.

"I'm in the area, fancy meeting up for lunch tomorrow?" I asked. We agreed to meet after his Sunday morning show; my next challenge was to find a garage in Bournemouth that was still open and able to hire me a car. The logistics of getting around weren't easy when the only vehicle available was a 53-seater coach.

Sunday morning found me, complete with hire car, driving east to the studios of Ocean Sound, the Lite FM in Fareham where Kevin was now employed. It was good to meet up with him again and we chatted about events on the ship since the mast had fallen. Kevin had now decided that working for a legal, land-based radio station offered more financial security, although it was certainly less adventurous than Caroline. Over lunch we continued to discuss radio in general with Kevin suggesting I should investigate joining a land-based radio station: "You weren't half bad, you were one of the better ones on the old tub," he added. His words sank in immediately and from that moment I became determined to go off in search of work on the radio once more.

My first port of call was a letter to Kevin's boss at Ocean Sound. No, I wasn't after his job, but they were operating three different radio services from the same building, so I reasoned they were probably looking for relief presenters, although I gave no thought as to where I would live – it would certainly be too far from home to commute, but I wasn't averse to sleeping on a floor.

Nevertheless, things were looking good, with a reply by return, no offer of work, but an invitation to pop in next time I was in the area. I decided that I would engineer a visit to the area sooner, rather than later. But now I was on a roll, with a little encouragement from one radio station, there might possibly be openings at other radio stations, I reasoned, perhaps closer to home and this time I was determined not to talk myself out of making contact. Which is how Max Bygraves managed to get me a job on Independent Local Radio.

Roger Day was a Caroline DJ in the 60s and one of those who stayed with the station after August 14th. He'd done the rounds in commercial radio, appearing on several different radio stations around the country including Piccadilly in Manchester and BRMB, the radio station for Birmingham, but now he was Programme Controller at Invicta Radio, based in Kent, his home county, and the other side of the Thames to where I lived. Invicta Radio had initially struggled to attract listeners and its survival had been in jeopardy, mainly because of the worthy and wordy format that it had followed, together with competition from the offshore pirate stations, Caroline and Laser. But with a necessary change in direction, almost in desperation, it had quickly become very popular throughout Kent and Essex by taking on the pirates at their own game and playing as much music as the controlling Radio Authority would allow, and more if they could get away with it. Invicta had also become the radio home to Johnny Lewis and Peter Philips following their departure from Caroline and Laser. In a Sunday newspaper article Invicta was described as 'Caroline on Land,' at one time employing more than a dozen former pirates, and I was about to be one of them.

Roger presented a Sunday morning show that included a feature that he called *'The A to Z of pop music'* and as I listened he had reached the letter B, and was playing a Max Bygraves song 'Tulips from Amsterdam.' As he introduced it he said that he'd rather be playing 'Fings Ain't What They Used To Be,' also by Max, but he hadn't got a copy… But I had. Although it wasn't something that I would boast about, that single was part of my family's vinyl collection that I'd taken charge of. I sat down there and then, wrote a short note and packaged it up with my copy of the record. "Hi Roger, borrow this, let me have it back," I wrote. "Oh, and by the way I was on Caroline a few months ago". I also enclosed a tape of one of my Caroline shows. I really didn't think of asking for a job, and naively I just assumed he might like to listen to my tape. Monday came and I sent the package off, thinking little more about it, but just two days later I received a letter from Invicta, 'Roger Day would like to see you in Canterbury on Thursday' it said - Thursday was tomorrow.

Immediately calling my boss and arranging to take the day off, I then sat down and shed a tear of joy whilst reading the letter several times. I'd desperately wanted a job on the radio for much of my life, and here at least was a chance to talk my way onto a top local radio station.

I had a great chat with Roger in his sparse office in the former Canterbury warehouse home of Invicta."I'd like to have you on the station", that's what he said, "Unfortunately we've no vacancies at present, but in the New Year we're starting a new service and I'd like to have you onboard."

As I walked through the reception area and out of the building I was barely able to contain a huge grin. I had a job offer, sort of, and I'd retrieved my Max Bygraves record, but

as I drove home, I analysed exactly what Roger had said…
'a job in the New Year,' but that was months away. I already
knew enough about radio stations to appreciate that the job of
Programme Controller, the guy who hires and fires, was almost
as precarious as a football manager. Would Roger still be there
in the New Year? Would he remember me? More importantly,
would he remember offering me a job?

"It's someone called Roger" - I was back at work the
following day, washing a coach in the depot when I was called
to take a phone call in the office.

"Ray, it's Roger Day here, what are you doing tonight, can
you do the overnight shift?"

Result! I was in, and that's how I became an ILR presenter.
That night I drove to the Maidstone studio of Invicta Radio.
I'd never been there before, and I was following directions
on my scribbled note. I had so many questions. How did the
studio work? How do I put it to air?

I parked in the street outside the studio building, it was after
midnight and the building was in complete darkness. A couple
of late-night drinkers staggered past, but took no notice of me
as I struggled to enter the building using the door code that I
had also written on my scrap of paper.

I sat down at the impressive looking MBI broadcast desk,
like all similar pieces of equipment it had loads of knobs and
buttons and did stuff that I didn't know about, but it did have
faders – I'd only used 'pots' potentiometers, on the Caroline
desk. The show before mine was coming from the Canterbury
studio, I would be taking over from former Caroline colleague,
Peter Philips, but before then I had to fathom out how to put
the desk to air. The studio needed to be connected to the
transmitter on a hill several miles away, so that my upcoming
words of wisdom and fine choice of music would be heard by
an audience across Kent who, for whatever reason were up
and about and tuned in through the night. As 2am approached
I was still not sure that I'd pushed all the right buttons in the
right order…

'Independent Radio News, it's three-minutes past two':

I pushed the button on the tape cartridge machine and the jingle that I'd heard a hundred times before as a listener played out: *'You've got it right across the county, Invicta Radio'*, and into the first record, Yazz and The Plastic Population, 'The Only Way Is Up'. Well, this was the 80s, and it seemed to sum up my situation. It was all going well, and continued that way for the next four hours, with each record I played and each link I made I was becoming more at ease with the equipment which was quite different to what I'd used on Caroline more than a year earlier. It was certainly newer, but you could debate as to whether it was technically better. The early hours of the morning and I was solely responsible for the output of local radio in Kent. Me, just me, no engineer, no producer. I was also the only person in the building and as the radio station had an outside toilet, no, it's true, my major concern was not locking myself out of the building when I wanted to pay a visit. How embarrassing would that have been, especially during my first programme. With only the length of a record to do what had to be done, I figured this was not the time to be grappling with door security codes so I propped the door open with a waste paper bin, just in case.

The telephone switchboard in the studio was flashing continuously, there were six lights showing, all had been waiting to be answered since I started the programme, but as yet, I'd taken no calls. Nobody had explained how the system worked. As I became more confident with the equipment, I decided to go for it. "Hello Invicta Radio", it may well have been the middle of the night, but Kent was certainly awake.

"Can you say hi to the supermarket bakers in Maidstone?" - *"Hi Ray, we're working down at Shakespeare Cliffs on the Channel tunnel"* - *"Give a shout out for everyone at Dover docks"* ... and so on. Calls kept coming. Invicta Radio had a huge audience in the daytime, and it seemed to be reasonably healthy through the night.

My first programme had gone well, although I don't think

anyone from the station was listening, least of all Roger, the programme controller, but I was booked for two shifts initially. I was back on air the following night, but, on the strength of those two shows I was offered the job as regular weekend overnight presenter.

I needed to have a regular income, I had a mortgage to pay and the extra money from my new radio job would certainly help me through the winter months. But now I was faced with a dilemma, "Can you cover every night, seven days a week for the next two months, but I can't guarantee anything after that?" said Roger on the phone.

"I'll do it," I answered. Sometimes in life you must take a gamble, and, as I'd waited so long to get on the radio, this wasn't the time to hesitate, this was the job I'd always really wanted. So, although I'd no longer be driving for a living this wasn't to be the end of my life on the road. It was 50 miles each way from home to the radio station, leaving home at midnight and arriving home at 8am.

The first week had passed, and with a total lack of communication from anyone in management. I guessed they were happy with my efforts. Then came the offer that really got me excited, "Will you cover the Olympic Games for us?"

Well, how amazing was this, I'd been there for less than a month, and they were going to send me to South Korea, or so I thought – I can't believe I was that naïve. Covering the Olympics, for which I was paid an extra £25 a week, involved checking all the results from Ceefax. So it wasn't just Caroline that ripped off the news from the TV then? The Olympic report, sponsored by a local estate agent, consisted of me selecting what I considered to be the most glamorous sports and reading out the names of the medal winners during two bulletins on the breakfast show. I was learning quickly; my reports concentrated on the Brits and a small selection of names from other countries that I could pronounce.

As October came then so did the end of my contract, although I'd never had one, nor did I ever receive one during my stay with Invicta. I still had my weekend overnights and the suggestion that there might be another spell of regular work in the New Year, but for the moment nothing during the week and I needed the money, so I went off to the job centre for the first time in my life and saw a van driving job locally.

"Look, I was a bus and coach driver for more than ten years and I know my way all around the country, including London, so I'll look after your van, but I'm really a radio presenter and I might not stay with you after Christmas" was my opening gambit at the interview. But I got the job because of my honesty … and because they desperately needed a van driver who knew his way about!

As I drove my Transit van around London, I listened to the city's radio stations; I particularly liked GLR, the new BBC radio station for London, it was surprisingly music intensive for a BBC local radio station, with some big radio names working for it. Johnnie Walker was one of them and he presented *The News Hour*, great music mixed with current news developments and interviews. *'Wouldn't mind doing that,'* I thought as I delivered boxes of a plastic substance for laminating machines to newspaper and printing companies throughout the day. Then, as I drove back to the depot I'd tune to Roger Day on Invicta, waiting to hear my name on air: *'Ray can you make contact'* that translated to *'Can you do the overnight shift tonight?'* and off to Kent I'd go after sleeping until midnight, then back to driving the van the next day. *"Are you available over Christmas? "Can you cover overnights next week?"* and then at last: *"Can you start regularly, Monday to Friday, and will you take care of the travel news on the breakfast show."*

I was invited to spend Christmas Day with 'the lads' living just a few miles from the radio station's Canterbury base. I drove to Peter Philip's house for a few hours sleep after my overnight show and then teamed up with quite a crew from Invicta including Peter, Johnny Lewis, and another former Caroline guy, Mark Matthews.

The plan was to congregate at the home of one of the Invicta sales team, Hugh, who had a house in Ash in Kent, conveniently situated across the road from the Chinese restaurant. Hugh was a good guy, but, like most salesmen that I've met, didn't like spending money unnecessarily. Consequently, when the cooker door had fallen off in his kitchen it had never been repaired. Which went some way to explain why the planned turkey dinner for the Invicta disc jockeys never materialised and why, at 8pm on Christmas Day we knocked on the door of the closed Chinese restaurant and asked if they'd cook something for us. No turkey that year, but the festive King Prawn and cashew nuts was wonderful.

I was now officially the overnight disc jockey on Invicta FM. I even had my name printed in the radio listings in the local newspapers. My nightly show from 2am until 6am was broadcast from the Canterbury studio, too far from home for a regular, daily commute. Fortunately, salesman Hugh offered lodgings in his house in Ash, just a few miles away.

"So, it'll be £25 a week and you can have a bed every day" was the offer, "Oh, and although I haven't got a spare bed at the moment, I'm getting one soon, but I have a spare mattress on the floor you can use, and you'll have the room to yourself". The new bed never did appear, but I used the spare mattress throughout the time I spent with Invicta. I lodged in Ash from Monday to Friday, returning home to Essex for the weekend and the arrangements worked quite well. After a daily double shift at the radio station I would drive to my mattress and sleep until 5pm, then 'the lads' would congregate for food and drink, often spending part of the evening at *The Blushing Bovine,* better known in Sandwich as The Red Cow pub. Of course my colleagues, who had been working during the day, could enjoy a pint,, but I was on fizzy soft drinks before driving off to Invicta after midnight.

The shows were enjoyable, with regular callers throughout the early hours, not all of them being put to air. I remember two girls who would regularly call from their place of work – I never found where that was, or what they did, but they would call frequently, and their conversation often became very saucy and suggestive. I guess they liked the sound of my voice and, whilst working throughout the night, they'd built up a picture of this handsome hulk with the deep voice, 'seducing' them with his words each night on the air.

I also became the regular DJ in a large pub in Maidstone on Saturday nights. I can't remember how I got the gig, I suspect they wanted an 'Invicta name' but didn't want to pay the full rate, so they got the overnight guy. Anyway, there I was doing my stuff in the corner of the bar and earning enough to make a return journey from Essex to Maidstone every Saturday night worthwhile.

"We're coming to the pub on Saturday night to meet you", those saucy girl's giggled during a mid-week call. Whether they did or not I'll never know, the calls stopped, they never called again. They obviously saw that I was so popular with the other female pub goers that they were frightened off, or, more likely, the guy they saw playing the records in the pub looked very different to the person they'd imagined during their saucy calls.

I was quickly learning the quirks of the radio industry, and behind the scenes it was not all as smooth and professional as it sounded on air. Pay cheques arrived 'as and when', usually when there was a reasonable chance that the company cheques wouldn't bounce. I was summoned to attend an important meeting for all presenters and the sales team. The radio station wasn't earning enough money to pay the bills, and something had to be done to rectify this. The on-air team were feeling reasonably secure as we were doing our job and Jicrar (the audience survey organisation) listening figures for the station were good. Invicta was very popular throughout Kent, and beyond but jobs were on the line. The sales team went on the attack to protect their own position, and their main target was wacky disc jockey Caesar the Boogieman. Caesar, or Chris, was a big Greek guy who presented the popular evening phone-in show. He was a larger than life character, very good at what he did, and he certainly believed in his own popularity. He made a point of picking up on the vulnerability of some of his on-air callers by convincing them that they needed help, and then he would steer the conversation to the point where they believed he was the only person that could possibly rescue them from their situation, all done with his best intentions of helping, even when they didn't need it. He certainly entertained his work colleagues. Often after returning from an evening in the pub various presenters and journalists would call him up posing as some poor soul and begging him to rescue them from some awful predicament, while Caesar, unaware that he was the victim of a wind-up would go into overdrive with his concern for the wellbeing of the caller.

Caesar had an audience, but not the type of listeners that the sales team wanted. They needed to get big spending advertisers onto the show - car dealers, exclusive furnishers, and expensive clothing stores. But listening to Caesar, it was obvious that very few of his listeners were ABC1 listeners from the highest socio-economic group just about to buy a new BMW or an haute couture gown. As the meeting became more heated Caesar the Boogieman, aware that he was the target of the sales team, banged his large fist on the table, kicked his chair back, knocking it to the floor and, glaring at the sales team, declared that he had hundreds of DC3's listening to his programme. There was a silent pause until someone calmly said, "Sit down Chris, a DC3 is an aeroplane."

*****

I used every minute of my time at Invicta to create the sort of production pieces that I had yearned to do for years, and there was nobody to stop me from doing what I wanted. Every morning after my overnight show I became a member of the breakfast team as the studio voice of travel, working with *Julie Jambuster* as she flew over the county reporting on travel queues and we made a good team.

The air to ground audio link from Julie in the small aircraft was permanently 'live' to the studio, but she was only on air at the relevant time during the travel bulletins. Not only could I hear her singing along, always ever so slightly out of tune, as the songs were playing on the radio, but I could also record her. With the addition of a few sound effects, we were able to promote '*Julie Jambuster's Greatest Hits*', with clips of her singing at her least tuneful. We had great fun every morning and the listeners loved it.

For some unexplained reason, Kent police suddenly became quite uncooperative when I made my regular calls to them for traffic updates, something that they'd previously been happy to help us with. The problem was soon rectified after a morning travel report: "Kent police say that traffic is moving freely this morning around Maidstone, what can you see Julie?" I asked as we crossed to the Jambuster plane, "They obviously have no idea of what's happening, Maidstone is grid locked this morning, with nothing moving anywhere" Julie reported. Good relations resumed the next day when they realised that we were there to help.

The regular sponsored flight report was recorded as 'live from Gatwick' and in every report a squeaky trolley would always pass by as the delays were listed. When we eventually confessed that we were playing a sound effect we had numerous calls from listeners who told us they'd been searching for the source of the squeak in their car for ages.

It was really a case of too much time on my hands between the half hourly travel bulletins. I had an empty radio studio, a reel of tape and years of ideas that I'd always wanted to put to good use on the radio. One morning, however, I thought I'd overstepped the mark and was about to be shown the door.

A lightning strike had been called on the railways resulting in numerous cancellations, the list of non-running trains filled a whole teleprinter page as the information was delivered to us and as Kent was a serious commuter county, we needed to get the information on air. Aware that listing loads of cancelled trains was necessary, though hardly entertaining, I decided to add a little humour to the situation, by announcing the times and destinations in the style of Alan Freeman's *Pick of the Pops* countdown, together with the appropriate tune, 'At The Sign Of The Swinging Cymbal'. It worked brilliantly and sounded great on air.

All was well until the Head of Sales burst into the on-air studio just a little later. Eddie, a Scottish guy and lifelong salesman had been involved in numerous ILR radio stations and certainly knew the business, and he'd been listening in the car on his way into the office. "Who was responsible for that train report this morning? I've got a sales meeting with Network Southeast [the train operator] later today!" he yelled. I shuddered, thinking this was the end of my radio career. I was already picking up my coat as I owned up to it: "It was bloody brilliant", beamed Eddie, "I loved it, can I take a tape of it for the meeting?"...Phew!

We had so many features on the Invicta breakfast show, all of them sponsored and all should have been bringing in good money. Each morning we called up the cross-channel ferry captain to record a report on the state of the sea crossings between Dover and Calais. The information they gave was always a bit suspect as they couldn't make conditions sound too rough, or they'd frighten off the many sail and booze passengers that the ferries relied on in the mid to late 1980s. Most of the captains played their part well. They enjoyed making the announcements to our listeners and a couple became notable characters, but one of their team was so dour he sounded decidedly miserable, and it was my job to record him and make his report sound, well... happy.

There was a facility on our professional tape recorders called vari-speed. I would edit out most of the huge gaps in his report and then speed up the recording. It seemed to do the job and I made him sound quite jolly. Nobody complained but I often wondered if he heard himself and realised what we'd done.

Much as I loved the chance to record production pieces, it

was playing the tunes and saying stuff in between the songs that I really enjoyed. Being on the radio while presenting an overnight shift was certainly the place to learn the trade. The night time audience were very loyal, and their comments mostly complimentary, although there were occasional exceptions. Fortunately, I didn't get too many of them, but one of the first still sticks in my mind and makes me chuckle to this day. It was around 3am on a cold and snowy February Sunday night and I took a call from a guy, luckily not on-air, who'd obviously had too much to drink: "I'm listening to you on f**king Radio Invicta and I think you're a w**ker."

For a second or two it hurt, then as I pondered the call, I realised that he was the guy out in the cold who'd had to find a telephone box, put his 10 pence in the slot just to pass on his observations. My only concern was if he still had the same thoughts in the morning when he sobered up.

As the overnight presenter I was the only person on the premises for four hours. The studio was housed in a former Victorian warehouse opposite Canterbury East station. The upper floor was home to a nightclub until around 2am, but for the next few hours, the spooky looking building was eerily quiet. Sitting in my small, compact, studio I felt warm and secure, and comfortable with my own company, but early one spring morning, just as day was breaking, I was convinced that I had company. As I glanced up during a link I saw an apparition, an outline of a person, looking like a grey cloud, and I could see through it. I still remember it vividly all these years later. I was midway through a link…

Here on Invicta it's ten past four – I paused… and I've just seen a ghost…

As I pushed the remote start for the record deck to start the next song, I rubbed my eyes and looked again into the corner. Had I really seen someone from beyond our world? My listeners certainly thought I had, the switchboard erupted with calls asking if I was alright and just as many saying, "Hey Ray I'm on my own here and that's just spooked me out."

After the initial shock of 'seeing a something' I carried on with my show, waiting for the breakfast team to arrive. First Stuart the engineer, and later a couple of the office staff, quietly took me aside and independently told me their stories about the Invicta ghost. They too had seen something unusual and took my report quite seriously. As we compared notes, each of us described a similar apparition. This was fine until the early hours of the next morning, when once again I was alone in this creaky old building.

I settled down for the next four hours of playing the hits and talking to the many night shift workers and insomniacs of Kent. But naturally the time came when I needed to visit the toilets, and they were some distance from my studio, through the newsroom, into the large front reception and then around the side of the building.

Unlike the Maidstone studio, the toilets were inside - just. But when the building was fitted out as a radio station the toilets were an afterthought, and as money was short the facilities were basic. I fired off a record that lasted around four minutes which was enough time for a quick return visit to the Gents. Still with the preceding night's occurrence in mind I moved swiftly through the newsroom with the route feeling spookier with every step. Constantly looking over my shoulder, as I stood taking a pee, I was frightening myself with scary thoughts. I ran back to the safety of the studio, through reception and into the newsroom. Now the newsroom could best be described as rustic, and as I let the door slam and ran across the bouncy wooden floor a large ten-inch reel of tape fell from a shelf with a crash and rolled across the floor behind me.

I screamed, but nobody could hear me. It was just me, the rolling tape reel … and who knows what? I rushed into the sanctuary of the studio and hoped that the early breakfast team would arrive soon.

There were some memorable songs around at this time in 1989 - a good mixture of different genres: 'Real Gone Kid' by

Deacon Blue, 'Beds Are Burning' by Midnight Oil, 'Waiting For a Star To Fall' by Boy meets Girl, Donna Summer, 'This Time I Know It's For Real', 'Man Child' by Nena Cherry and the wonderful 'Belfast Child' by Simple Minds. Most songs were still being played from vinyl, but CDs were just starting to appear, and the playlist box of current songs would include a couple in this new format. I even had a personalised jingle included in the new jingle package that had been delivered to the station: *Hottest hits and golden memories, with Ray Clark, Invicta Radio.* And very catchy it was too!

Chapter Twelve

"Coming Home"

W orking with a great team at Invicta was fun, but it was time to move on. I'd covered a few daytime shifts and got the taste for a bigger audience, but I was still the overnight guy, and I didn't want to spend the rest of my radio days locked away in the studio at night and sleeping on a mattress in Ash through the daytime. I was ready for a change, preferably to somewhere closer to home and with the chance to see a bit of daylight. Then I spotted this in *Radio Magazine*, a photocopied journal put together by former Radio Caroline presenter Howard Rose, aka Crispian St. John, aka Jay Jackson, who was a bit of a legend in offshore radio circles:

Essex Radio is splitting their AM and FM services and are looking for presenters for a new radio station aimed at a more mature audience.

This was one snippet of news gossip that I'm glad Howard had picked up on. I don't think Essex Radio had paid for an advertisement, news of most radio jobs was spread by word of mouth. It wasn't FM and it wasn't playing the hits of the day, but it was a radio station based much closer to home, in Southend. I quickly scribbled a handwritten note, there was no time for a properly typed letter of introduction, and sent a tape of my last show to Keith Rogers, the programme controller for this new service, to be known as Breeze AM. I'd been a fan of Keith's, with his laid-back style of presentation and his deep North Devon accent, since his Radio Atlantis days. He had an obvious love of music from the 60s and 70s, so now, as I was approaching my 35th birthday, I was prepared to accept that I would be playing 'Gold Hits', rather than 'Hot Hits'. But first I had to get the job.

When Essex Radio started broadcasting in 1981 I'd been in awe of it. Although I'd sent them a demo tape, I'd heard nothing back. It seemed a very professional organisation and not one that would entertain a coach driver who desperately wanted to play records and talk on the radio. I would walk past their building whenever I was in Southend. The former newspaper office in Clifftown Road was just across the way from the town's Central Station and looked imposing with its wide, inviting reception and the tall communications mast on the roof with guy wires to all sides of the building. To me it looked exciting, perhaps a little like a radio ship at sea, and I would have given anything to be a part of it. I wanted to be working inside Radio House, Clifftown Road, Southend-on-Sea.

I got a call during the week: "When can you come in for a chat with Keith Rogers?" I was asked. This sounded promising, and I now had an appointment to get beyond the door and into the flash reception for a meeting on the following Saturday afternoon. However, there was to be no grand entrance through the large front glass doors for me: "Can you come to the back door and Keith will let you in?" I was told.

Keith is a lovely man, and I'm pleased to say we soon became good friends. But we all have our strange ways. 'Radio people' are certainly a bit quirky, and there's no doubt that Keith scores quite highly on the quirky scale. Any idea I'd had about Essex Radio being a bit posh and proper went straight out of the window as I was interviewed for a job while sitting on a disintegrating cardboard box full of tee shirts in a back corridor. Keith had put the keys to his office somewhere and had no idea where they were.

Our chat was one of the easiest going interviews for a job I'd ever had. From the start Keith was apologetic: "I'm really sorry, but all we have left is the overnight show", he told me. Keith has since told me how my face dropped at the thought of more nights without sleep, but I replied immediately. "That'll have to do then", was the gist of my reply. "OK then" said

Keith, and that was it. I was working for Essex Radio. Once again, I would be presenting the overnight shift from 2am daily, but at least I could sleep in my own bed, and I would be finished at 6am on a brand new radio service. '*Lite and Easy Breeze AM*' was to appeal to the over 40s, as competition for the BBC's Radio 2, which back in 1989 was a much older sounding radio station than it is today.

During the preparations for the station's launch I travelled into the Southend studio daily. Breeze was to have its own music library, playing music either using the new CD technology or on tape cartridges. A small team of us spent several days recording songs from vinyl onto the carts which were to be played on a relatively fast rotation. The order of songs was dictated by computer, and the vinyl records wouldn't have stood up to such frequent plays. I was hearing many songs that were new to me. Our format included big band favourites and songs dating back to the forties. Our playlist certainly wasn't made up of too many current chart hits, though we did feature a sprinkling of recent 'lite and easy' tunes. Surprisingly, 'Kayleigh' by Marilion and 'Golden Brown' by The Stranglers merged seamlessly with 'Moonlight Serenade' by The Glenn Miller Orchestra and classics by Ella Fitzgerald and the like.

As the launch day approached, I met up with the other Breeze presenters. I would again be working with Peter Philips and David Baker, who was another former Caroline guy, though he'd only spent a few days on the ship.

The station would feature regular celebrity interviews and my first was set up by David with Gerry Marsden from Gerry and The Pacemakers. We were pre-recording several interviews ready for day one, and as I walked into the studio David got out of the studio chair and opened the microphone: "I think you're doing this one Ray, here's Gerry." To say I was surprised was an understatement. Until that moment I had no idea that I was interviewing anybody, and it took me a while to even work out which 'Gerry' I was speaking to. A little warning and time for preparation might have helped, but with some quick thinking it was an OK interview which was to be the first of thousands that I've done since.

The Essex Radio company had spent quite a lot of money on pre-publicity; we had a TV commercial on Anglia Television and a surprising amount of advance newspaper publicity throughout the county. We also had presenter photographs. I'd missed out on getting one printed at Invicta, but now I was to be a proper radio presenter with a picture card to sign should any listener ask for one. We were all told to attend a photo shoot in a professional studio and asked to pose for our individual photographs. "Try to look old" I was told, as we were aiming at a mature audience. Sadly, I can now look old with very little effort!

Day one for Breeze AM came in July 1989 on a beautiful summer's day, and a barbeque was held in the car park of Radio House in Southend. Bill Rennells, the major signing from the BBC, had started the programmes at 10am, followed by David Baker and I was due on at 2pm. My opening song was 'Light And Easy Does It' by Frank Sinatra and there I was, on the radio broadcasting legally to Essex. The afternoon went well, apart from a little unfortunate confusion with the telephone system.

One of my telephone guests was Lennie Peters, the blind guy from Peters and Lee. 'Welcome Home' was their biggest hit. I called him five times and each time he answered the phone I cut him off. Eventually we got to speak, fortunately he didn't appear to be annoyed.

Light 'n' Easy Breeze AM enjoyed a very successful start. Since the advent of ILR (Independent Local Radio) every radio station had broadcast the same service on both AM and FM frequencies, but now the Radio Authority expected new radio services to be provided by each licensee, so Essex Radio continued on FM, as Essex FM with Breeze AM for an older audience on medium wave.

In the first Jicrar (audience survey report) Breeze had a 19% reach or share of the 1.25 million possible listeners in Essex.

I can't do the sums, but this was a very healthy audience, or should I say a very good audience, as sadly, not all our ageing listeners enjoyed good health. Certainly, through the night I was playing songs for some elderly insomniacs, many of them were very lonely and continually calling the nice young man at the radio station for a chat.

Looking on the bright side, I was on the radio, it was my job and it was in my home county, but it was becoming quite difficult to get too excited about playing yet another Mantovani track at three in the morning.

After being on air for six months, there was movement within the lineup of presenters. Experienced afternoon presenter, John Hayes, who had worked on numerous radio stations, including UBN, United Biscuit Network (playing music for the workers on the production lines in the nation's biscuit factories) was off to join BBC Essex, and with John's departure I was now to become the afternoon guy. This was what I'd always wanted, a daytime shift on a commercial radio station, shame it wasn't on FM and shame about the format, but we had a large audience and a good boss in Keith, who gave me a free hand to experiment with different features. I was keen and he was happy.

Many radio stations had a daily 'hits and headlines' feature, an excuse to play records from a certain month or year. I loved the idea of playing those great songs from the sixties and seventies that I'd grown up listening to, but I wanted to make the feature an important part of the programme, so I would visit Chelmsford library regularly and spend hours researching stories from the microfiche copies of old local newspapers. I found it fascinating, and I still have many index cards from those days packed with reports of newsworthy and sometimes quirky events that happened years earlier in Essex.

I loved researching a story for a radio feature and because I knew the geography of the county like the back of my hand, the daily *'Magic Moments on Breeze AM'* was a must listen for many.

On The Air – Breeze AM, Clifftown Road, Southend

The biggest success of the afternoon show was something that nobody else had thought of before, yet it seemed such an obvious idea. Now, more than thirty years on from those early Breeze days, local BBC radio stations are enjoying good listening figures with a form of a weekly treasure hunt style programme where listeners are asked to solve clues leading to a geographical location.

Back in early 1990 we began a feature called *'Old John'* and the Essex audience loved him. My afternoon show started at mid-day, but at 1pm, traditionally lunch time, audience figures showed that thousands across the county wanted to know where *Old John* was.

Old John sounded like an old country yokel but the voice that listeners heard was 100% genuine. *Old John* was in his seventies and had grown up in a very different Essex to the one he now lived in, but he had retained his wonderful rural Essex accent, unlike me, who had spent years trying to lose it. Better still I didn't have to go too far to find him, John had known me all my life, having worked on the farm with my dad years earlier. The response to John's daily appearance was amazing, and the old fella took to it effortlessly. Although the words he uttered were mine, the accent and the way he spoke them was his and it worked a treat.

'Hello together, Old John here again – well where d'ya think I am today?'

Whenever I was out and about in my car, I would scribble down the name of a pub or feature in every town or village that I passed through, although, knowing the county so well I already had much of the information. Then, once a week, John and I would park in the car park of remote Althorne railway station, giving us a rural background of bird song. I would dictate the words line by line and *Old John* would repeat them whilst adding his own, often humorous, witty comments.

'Well, let me tell you, there's a big old duck pond in the middle of this little village and just over there is a tiny church with a spire…'

We'd then include a cryptic clue to the place name and John would always finish by giving the name of a local pub.

"I'm off now for a half in the Flying Horse, so where d'ya think I am today then?"

It was a much smarter piece of audience building than anyone, including me, had ever imagined. From the moment John's pre-recorded clue was broadcast the telephone switchboard would erupt with listeners of all ages, male and female, trying to outdo each other with the correct answer, everyone eager to show their prowess at solving the clue and their knowledge of the county. It had the added advantage that the clues were always local to someone, so there were always callers eager to join in.

I have never seen such a huge response to any radio feature since, even when a valuable prize has been on offer in some competition or other – and solving *Old John's* whereabouts gave no reward, it was all for fun.

"Hello Together".
Old John wows them

Old John was the feature that kept on giving. The imagination of our listeners was captured by this character who appeared daily on the radio. Is he real? Does he really talk like that? Where does he come from? Is he an actor? What does he look like? The interest was such that we took *Old John* out to meet his public, organising coach trips around some of the picturesque Essex villages that he described every day. The response was huge, with every trip selling out. The driver would welcome the passengers onboard and drive for some distance before stopping the coach to point out a beautiful view to the right. While the passengers were taking in the sight, *Old John* would suddenly appear on board the vehicle, shouting loudly *'Hello Together,"* apparently having appeared out of a hedge. The passengers, all Breeze listeners, loved it as John appeared looking just as they'd imagined, dressed in a smock, his jacket tied up with binder twine and carrying his old walking stick. And the coach driver? Me of course… I still had my bus licence.

Old John passed away several years ago and if I were to listen to the recordings today, I would be the one struggling to identify his whereabouts as I never wrote down the answer to the clues. Sadly, many of the pubs have long since closed. It's unlikely that a radio feature such as this would be broadcast now, times change and the feature would take far too much time to prepare, but at the time it was spot on for the audience and the radio station.

*****

As a presenter on commercial radio I was in complete control of the studio and apart from presenting my show I was expected to answer listeners' telephone calls as well. I was on air one day, just a few weeks after starting my afternoon show, and took a most unexpected call: "When you come off air, could you call this number, I'd like to chat with you".

I scribbled the number down and as soon as my show had finished I found a quiet corner ready to return the call - but not before I'd checked the phone code, 0191, which was Newcastle upon Tyne. I was intrigued. Calling the number, I got straight through to a guy who made it clear that he wanted me on his radio station: "I'm calling from Metro Radio in Newcastle, would you come up and have a chat with us on Saturday? I'll book a room at The Holiday Inn next to the Metro Centre for Friday night".

I was excited as I set off for Newcastle straight after work on Friday, my mind racing with the possibilities of where this journey might take me, while driving north on a gloriously warm midsummer evening.

On Saturday morning, after a relaxed breakfast, I strolled across the huge Metro shopping centre car park from my hotel to the Metro Radio building in Swalwell, on the south side of the Tyne, across the water from the city and next to the biggest scrap yard you've ever seen. The immediate surroundings might not have been particularly beautiful, but this was Metro, one of the biggest radio stations in the country.

"Here's our canteen and this is our concert hall," said the Programme Controller who'd invited me 'up north'. At Essex Radio we just had a tea machine in the corner of the newsroom, certainly nothing on this scale. We were talking about Great North Radio, another radio service that had split from the original station, but in the North East it wasn't serving just one radio market. This was a radio station with a huge audience broadcasting throughout Tyne and Wear, including the cities of Newcastle and Sunderland, an area of more than three million potential listeners – and, as our chat continued, it was made clear that they wanted me to present the breakfast show, and they were prepared to pay me £25,000 a year. My salary at Essex Radio was just £9,000. How could I say no?

I loved the area, the people, and their accent. The city, the moors and the coast were beautiful. Newcastle had always felt comfortable to me during my coach driving days and I would often stay overnight in the city on my way to Scotland. Now, the biggest radio station in the North East was offering me a salary almost three times what I was getting in Essex, to present a daily show on the radio. The thought of an entire city, in fact two entire cities waking up with me was very exciting. I was so tempted to say yes there and then. But Newcastle was 300 miles from home. I'd worked away from home on Caroline and Invicta and for several years before that, but I'd recently re-met (another long story) my wife to be, would she want to move north?

As I drove home I was still buzzing about this exciting job offer, but unsure of what to do. By Monday I was no nearer deciding.

It should have been obvious, take the offer, take the money, take the opportunity, but the job was on a one year rolling contract - at Essex I was on a staff contract. I went straight to see my boss: "I've been offered another job," I said. This was not the way Programme Controller Keith wanted to start his week.

"Ahh, let's go out for a chat," he replied, and we took a stroll in the park around the corner from the radio station, overlooking the River Thames and Southend seafront. Keith made it clear that he didn't want me to leave, but when I told him how much I'd been offered he was about to admit defeat there and then. A very long pause followed before he replied, "I'll try to get you more, but I don't know if the board will agree to anything even close to that."

We sauntered back to the radio station, I went on air at midday, loving my job even more than usual. I felt great: I was in a good place with two radio groups wanting me to work for them.

Coming off air four hours later, I was £12,000 a year better off. Although Essex Radio didn't quite match the Metro offer, I chose to stay put. Essex Radio were a decent company to work for and I'd just got the biggest one day pay rise I was ever likely to get. I said thank you to Metro for asking, but sorry, I won't be joining you. Interestingly, a few months later, two colleagues on the FM service of Essex Radio made their way up north to work on Great North Radio, but it was nice to know that I had been their first choice. I've often wondered how my life might have changed had I gone north. On reflection I made the right decision, but I was certainly pleased to have been asked.

As a footnote, two of my grandchildren are growing up on the outskirts of Newcastle and have those lovely North East accents. When we travel up to visit, we usually travel across the Tyne, alongside the site of the now demolished Metro Radio building.

Chapter Thirteen

"'New York, New York' and Celebrity Guests"

As the 90s got underway, I was now part of the daytime lineup on Breeze and very much involved in the larger team at Essex Radio, going into work every day in the same building that I'd walked past in awe just a few years earlier. Whilst Breeze didn't have as big an audience as 'Greatest Memories, Latest Hits Essex FM', we were doing well when compared to nearly every other 'split' service on medium wave.

However, we had a problem. To put it bluntly, our listeners were dying. We had successfully tapped into a mature audience but through natural wastage the numbers were reducing. But my listening figures were good, and the bosses were enjoying it too. As I'd been working with a largely mature audience when I was driving coaches, I knew what I could get away with. I wasn't about to change my persona of 'local cheeky chappie'. That, as it would turn out, was literally a winner on air.

I was nominated for an international award at the *New York Festivals for Best Radio Show* - it would be the first of more than 20 industry awards I would go on to win. But the best thing about my first was that I had to fly to New York to collect it.

Going to the States had long been a dream. Until now, I'd only flown once before, to Jersey, and had been petrified aboard an ancient propeller driven aircraft. Now I would be jetting across the Atlantic, with paid-for-tickets and accommodation, for my wife and I. However, in the days leading up to our flight I was thinking of an excuse not to go. The thought of flying scared me silly and I came very close to saying no thank you, but sensibly, I didn't.

We approached JFK airport late in the afternoon on a beautifully clear midsummer's day. As our aircraft banked for final approach off the coast of New Jersey, the view was spectacular - well that's what my wife Shelley told me. I was holding on for dear life with my eyes shut tight. Once clear of customs and immigration we were taken into Manhattan by a great yellow cab driver. He was an Indian guy who'd grown up in Shepherd's Bush before moving to America. He was as interested in us as we were in the view outside the cab as we passed notable landmarks like The Shea stadium and crossed the Williamsburg bridge with the amazing vista of Manhattan island ahead of us. As he dropped us off at our hotel in the heart of the city he wished us well: "You enjoy my Big Apple," he said. We intended to.

The weather throughout our four day stay was glorious. In extremely high temperatures we set out to explore the Manhattan tourist trail, travelling on an open top double-decker bus with hats made from an old newspaper as we were unprepared for such strong sunshine. Surprisingly, so it seems were many of the other passengers, mostly from various U.S. States. They'd never seen a newspaper hat before and asked Shelley to make them one, which she did, until she ran out of paper. The hats were a huge success, protecting at least half a dozen passengers from the heat of the sun, until we turned a corner near the World Trade Centre and a strong breeze whisked them away. "Yee Haw," cried a rather large lady as she almost left her seat when the bus hit a huge bump in the road. I think she was probably from Texas.

The awards presentation took place aboard a boat cruising the Hudson River, underneath Brooklyn Bridge and out towards Ellis Island, with fabulous views of the Statue of Liberty. It was a memorable evening and receiving the top award whilst dressed in all our finery perfected what was the first of many Atlantic crossings I would make, and hope to make in future.

I'd 'heard' New York in the past by listening to recordings of the city's wonderful Top 40 radio stations from the sixties, now most of those iconic callsigns had changed from non stop music to all speech, but it was still exciting to tune into WABC and WMCA. I'd finally got to hear American Radio. What I didn't know then was that I would soon be a regular on the American airwaves myself.

Light 'n' Easy Breeze AM – 5TH anniversary

No radio station lineup stays the same for long and I was now the Breeze mid-morning presenter. Besides the features that had been so successful during the afternoon, I now had daily guests talking about so many different topics. I enjoyed interviewing people with a tale to tell. I am a naturally inquisitive nosey parker and I love a good chat.

Many of my guests were those who'd recorded the hits that I'd played on our record player whilst I was growing up, and there were regular visitors from the world of television and theatre.

In this mix were also some stars that were just starting out: Ronan Keating, Francis Rossi & Rick Parfitt, Bobby

Vee, Ray Davies, Des O'Connor, Nick Mason,Tony Hadley, David Essex, Edwin Starr, Joan Armatrading, Barrington Pheloung, Jack Bruce, Gene Pitney, Valerie Singleton, Cliff Richard, Gerry Marsden, Graham Gouldman, Michael Aspel, Bill Wyman, Michael Palin, William Roache, Lulu, Peter Frampton, Martha Reeves, Paul Jones, Mike D'abo and Steve Harley are just a few who come to mind. Every day I was able to announce yet another household name as my morning guest.

Celebrity guests were always good to speak to but it was the interviews with less well known characters that often provided unexpected highlights.

Morse was the big new TV detective show – it was certainly different to any other 'cop' show with its complex storylines set in Oxford. An important part of the programme highlighted the love of classical music that Inspector Morse enjoyed. The musical breaks and intermittent pieces were composed by Barrington Pheloung who happened to be living in Westcliff on Sea, just a short walk from the radio station. *Morse* was obviously popular with our audience and an interview with the *Morse* music composer was certain to appeal to many of our listeners. I think I found Barrington via directory enquiries. He was quite happy to be interviewed and invited me round to his house. I knocked on his door and was welcomed by an instantly likeable Australian… "Come in mate. Would yer like an omelette?"

Our chat started over a tasty lunch, with the conversation turning to the evocative *Morse* theme tune and the morse code notes that can be heard throughout.

"Ahh… those notes spell M.O.R.S.E." he revealed. I had an idea that it might just be useful to have the spelling of Breeze in morse to hand, so before leaving the radio station to visit Barrington, I asked Don, the station's engineer, if he could translate Breeze into morse dots and dashes. Moving from the kitchen to Barrington's studio he started to play the haunting tune, I presented him with the slip of paper containing the morse code spelling and grabbing a cassette tape he then started to play the famous tune, but with the notes spelling B.R.E.E.Z.E.

I walked back to the radio station clutching the tape containing my unique recording. But next day engineer Don came searching for me: "Sorry Ray," he said, "I think I got one of the letters wrong yesterday." I still have that tape amongst my 'treasures'. It contains the only recording in the world of the *Morse* theme, complete with the morse code spelling B.R.E.E.X.E.

That wasn't to be my only link with Inspector Morse. Several years later whilst at the BBC I had the opportunity to interview Colin Dexter, the author and creator of the *Morse* stories. As an aside I mentioned that we had a feature on the show where listeners were invited to add their short contribution to a story. My wife, the Story Lady, would write the first paragraph on Monday and by the end of the week, we would have produced a short story with an outcome that nobody could predict. It was a good idea, but very cumbersome to maintain. I think the project would have been more suited to Radio 4 than BBC local radio breakfast, but some you win etc. However, on hearing about it the man who created *Morse*, Colin Dexter offered to join in and started one of the stories. Somewhere I must have a Colin Dexter story, or at least the start of one.

On the theme of less famous people making good radio, it's hard to recall a more humbling experience than the interviews conducted with survivors of the horrendous Essex floods 40 years earlier. A colleague in the newsroom was working on the documentary about the tragic event and I offered to help him source and record the interviews.

The disaster had taken the lives of many residents as their homes were overwhelmed by the terrible flood waters. I was very moved by many of the stories from around the county. The interviews that stood out most in my mind were with a man who lost his little son in the floodwaters. His description of the little boy's tiny feet as his limp body was pulled from the waters would bring tears to anyone's eyes. Another story told of a whole family in a rowing dinghy with a horse tethered behind, swimming to safety. A most humbling interview I was particularly proud of was with a retired police officer. Shortly before his death, he described the part he played in the rescue mission on that awful night. Later we heard how important the interview had been for his widow and family, and that the detail of his bravery had at last been made public.

The radio station often co-promoted concerts at the Brentwood Centre and Southend's Cliffs Pavilion and many of the big stars from the sixties and seventies were touring with shows such as *The Solid Gold Sixties show*. A Breeze presenter would usually host the show, appearing on stage and introducing the guest: "Ladies and Gentlemen welcome Billie Joe Spears, Lindisfarne, Barclay James Harvest, Brenda Lee, Dr. Hook, Chris Montez, Chubby Checker, Bobby Vee, Chris Farlowe, even Freddie and The Dreamers," although Freddie was, by now, on the third generation of Dreamers.

I got to meet, introduce and sometimes chat with so many household names. Most were very pleasant, though some could be difficult. Len Barry was interesting, he'd had a couple of hits in the sixties with '1,2,3' and 'Like a Baby' and then, several years later he'd written a hit song for Fat Larry's Band called 'Zoom'.

"What are you going to say about me?" Barry demanded. Unlike anyone else I'd ever introduced, his manner was odd, almost threatening.

"I don't know yet," I replied with a smile. He wasn't too impressed, at least until he heard my introduction. I think he might have been struggling with his ego. Yes, I'd heard of him and was aware of his two UK Top 10 hits, and I surprised him when I casually mentioned his song 'Zoom', but he was far from being top of the bill that evening. Perhaps he thought he was a bigger star in Brentwood than he actually was.

I've been lucky to have never broken any bones, but I must surely have come very close to it one evening at The Brentwood Centre.

Bobby Vee and Me

I was to introduce a concert and the stage manager told me to just walk out to the front when the band was ready to start, it was all very straightforward, he told me.

As always, the stage was dark, but on this occasion part of the stage had been lowered, as I walked forward, looking out towards the audience the floor just wasn't there. I must have fallen five feet at least and the audience gasped. Stumbling for my footing, I miraculously managed to remain upright. It was frightening, and I wanted to cry out in shock, but I was aware that more than a thousand people were witnessing my acrobatics.

As I regained my composure I smiled: "Good evening, I'm

Ray from Breeze AM, I just thought I'd drop in to ask you to welcome, live on stage Gerry and The Pacemakers."

Whenever that evening comes to mind I shudder and have a vision of being treated by an ambulance crew as the audience were sent home and the band left waiting without a job to do. It truly was a very near miss.

Another near miss involved an interview with daredevil steeplejack Fred Dibnah who spent his days climbing huge chimneys and church spires, either to repair or demolish them. Fred was one of those characters that television discovers occasionally and overnight becomes a household name. Watching his TV programme was a guilty pleasure of mine. I looked forward to viewing his antics as he appeared to show no fear whilst working hundreds of feet above the ground, but I never dreamed that he'd nearly kill me, not that it was his intention.

I discovered that he was working locally, demolishing a 300-foot-tall chimney on Canvey Island. It was part of an unwanted oil refinery, built in the seventies but never used after the price of oil rocketed in 1974. I drove to the site and soon found Fred, working alone.

"Where d'ya want to chat then?" he asked.

"What about inside that chimney, it'll sound great and give listeners an idea of the size of the thing," I replied. So, the interview took place inside the, soon to be demolished, gigantic structure, towering way above our heads. Work had already started on its demolition; a large area of concrete had been knocked out of the chimney wall just a few feet from its base and the entire chimney was now supported by thick wooden blocks. The method Fred used was to build a huge bonfire inside, which would eventually burn the supporting blocks and put an impossible strain on the existing structure, causing it to collapse in a controlled manner.

During the interview I asked if any of his jobs ever went wrong: "Not often," he replied with his characteristic nervous laugh and wave of his hand. Fred was a fascinating man, just as he appeared to be on his TV programmes. I enjoyed meeting him and we chatted further after finishing the interview. As I drove back to the radio station, I listened to the tape. It would make a great feature to be played out a few days later, when the chimney was due to fall. I was very pleased with what I'd got, a good chat with an interesting guest, and it needed very few edits.

Arriving back at the Essex Radio building in Clifftown Road, Southend, I made my way to the newsroom. Flicking the cassette towards the news desk I said, "Here's Fred Dibnah, I'm running the full interview later, but if you'd like to use a clip from it for an afternoon bulletin that's fine".

"Oh, that's great," came the reply, "We'll use it on the main evening news bulletin… That chimney on Canvey that he's working on has just collapsed!"

Less than one hour earlier I'd been standing, chatting with Fred beneath the thousands of tons of concrete and masonry that had just crashed down to the ground, three days earlier than planned. If I'd stayed just a few minutes longer we would both have been running for our lives.

*****

Besides interviewing guests who visited the radio station, I was often invited to press sessions, usually held in prestigious London hotels, to interview visiting stars from the States. Walking into swanky hotel receptions for my rendezvous with these big name stars was quite special: "Neil Sedaka is expecting me."

"Oh yes sir, Room 748".

"I have a meeting with Frankie Valli?"

"Certainly sir, I'll get someone to take you to his room."

I enjoyed scores of interviews with people that I would never have dreamed of meeting in hotels that I would never have dreamed of visiting until I started on the radio. A visit to the rather grand Langham Hotel, opposite Broadcasting House led to a very special afternoon. I chuckled to myself as I strolled from Oxford Circus tube station to the hotel via Cavendish Square and Chandos Street, past the very offices that I'd visited daily as a 16-year-old junior clerk when I first started work for the BBC. I could never have imagined walking into what was then a BBC building but was now a prestigious hotel.

"Hello, the Bee Gees are expecting me," I said.

"Of course, Mr Clark?"

Wow! I was meeting the Bee Gees; they were expecting me, and they even knew my name! What a wonderful afternoon I spent in the company of one of the most successful groups of all time. Sadly, just an ageing Barry Gibb survives, but together with Robin and Maurice, I drank tea, ate biscuits and cake and spoke with them about their entire career. Starting with life on the Isle of Man, moving to Manchester, emigrating as kids to Australia, their first hits, returning to the UK, becoming huge world stars, *Saturday Night Fever*, writing songs for Diana Ross, Barbara Streisand and Dolly Parton - what an amazing story. I recalled sitting by my tape recorder waiting for their first hit to be played on the radio, hoping to record it without the disc jockey talking all over it: '*Here's a new group now from Australia called The Bee Gees, and this is their hit song 'New York Mining Disaster 1942.*"

I liked the Bee Gees; they were just three ordinary, but very talented guys who had worked hard and struck lucky. They were totally relaxed, I knew my stuff, asking all the right questions, and they appreciated that, all of us enjoying a very friendly, informal chat and cracking jokes. I came away with more than enough tales to create a great one-hour 'special' radio show, and a wonderful memory of my afternoon with the Bee Gees. "Do you take sugar in your tea Ray?" asked Barry as he filled the delicate china cup in the small serving area of their plush suite. Amazing!

The annual Chelsea Flower Show in May was always a magnet for celebrities. Getting interviews on press day was like picking plums from a tree with so many star names invited to attend by the organisers on the first day of the show. Many of the stars were 'attached' to various products or displays, and obviously that's what they wanted to promote, so they were always keen to talk on the radio. The knack was to leave questions about the product they were promoting until the end of the interview … and then edit most of that bit out before the interview was broadcast.

The bigger stars were there because of their love of gardening. Cliff Richard was always good value, and celebrities like Barbara Windsor, Alan Titchmarsh and Damon Hill, were all regulars. June Whitfield was lovely and would always find time for a chat. So, perhaps surprisingly, was Ringo Starr: I never pushed for an interview, and I was always polite when I asked, "Ringo, can we have a chat?"

"No, sorry," would invariably be this reply. But then simply asking if he was having a good day would prompt him to start chatting away.

It's 'bloomin' Cliff Richard at The Flower Show

Two of the best interviews I *never* had were at Chelsea …
and with the two Georges - Martin and Harrison. I had long
wanted to interview the Beatles producer George Martin,
and there he was, heading for a marquee entrance at Chelsea
and there I was with my cassette recorder; I walked briskly
to the opposite entrance and into the huge, flower-filled tent.
We met halfway, Sir George was happy to chat and away he
went, responding readily to my questions. I contained my
excitement at chatting with the fifth Beatle as I glanced down
at my recorder and realised that it wasn't recording – I'd
been so excited at 'catching' the world's most famous record
producer, I'd forgotten to push the record button. It was far too
late to suggest starting all over again, so I continued with the
interview in the hope that this recording genius hadn't noticed
that the microphone he was talking into would never record
his words. I don't know if he was aware of what I'd done – he
didn't say, and I wasn't about to tell one of the world's best
music producers that I'd forgotten to turn the tape recorder on.

The following year, same marquee, and there was Jules
Holland sitting on a trestle table chatting to two scruffy looking
guys dressed in their gardening clothes. As I walked towards
them and having interviewed Jules in the past, I smiled and
walked on. The next morning, on the front page of *The Daily
Telegraph* was a photograph of Jules Holland talking to the
same two scruffy guys – Eric Clapton and George Harrison.
Oh well. Some you win…

Some interviews could be quite sad and would expose human
weaknesses that we all have to a lesser or greater degree.
Nat King Cole's daughter, Natalie, had a well-documented
history of drug use and was very much on her guard when I
spoke to her and she was reluctant to answer even the most
straightforward questions. I gently pushed her.

"I have to beware of everything I say to you journalists," she
said. "Gosh, it's only me, I'm just Ray," I replied.

She relaxed immediately and what followed was a lovely
chat and an insight into her childhood with her famous father

and the challenges he and his family faced at a time when race issues threatened even the greatest of talents.

I was particularly cautious with live interviews and especially with those that had the potential to head off in an unexpected direction. Not that I couldn't steer an interviewee in the direction that I was comfortable with if I needed to. It was part of the necessary skill of an interviewer, of course - the ability to listen was essential.

Peter Green, founder of Fleetwood Mac was a musical genius who had suffered with mental issues for many years. I was surprised that he was available for interviews, but his management assured us that he'd be comfortable with that. I started by playing a classic song that he'd written, 'Man of the World' by Fleetwood Mac.

"That must be one of the most beautiful songs ever written," I said, "It's alright I s'pose," he grunted. It wasn't one of my most successful interviews.

Screaming Lord 'David' Sutch appeared to be care-free and I was a fan. He was a character who liked to stir things up a bit. A true rock 'n' roller, one of the original pirate radio station operators, and leader of The Monster Raving Loony Party. His policies at the time appeared 'loony' but many of them were anything but, with some eventually becoming law: Votes for teenagers, 24 hour licensing laws, commercial radio, passports for pets. He didn't sound troubled when I became the last person to interview him but he took his own life just a couple of days later, and he's sadly missed. Lord Sutch will always be remembered as leader of his party, not least because he always stood for election in the same constituency as the likely Prime Minister and featured in their official victory photographs and news reports, always being the first to offer a hand of congratulations. I chuckle at the thought of Margaret Thatcher always having to look at a photograph of Lord Sutch on her mantelpiece.

Robert Palmer recorded some fabulous radio friendly songs in the 80s. He had a reputation for working hard and enjoying malt whisky, I had an interview 'down the line' with him and I was really looking forward to the chat. Sadly, he appeared to have been sampling the whisky quite early in the day and our interview, fortunately pre-recorded, was little more than a rambling session of unanswered questions. Sad, because although there was no question that he enjoyed a drink, he had a reputation for 'suffering the press' politely. Not that he wasn't polite when we spoke, but I quickly decided that the interview would never be broadcast as he was hardly coherent. However, on my journey home later that day I was listening to the new on air news and chat station BBC Radio 5 Live as the accomplished afternoon presenter Sybil Ruscoe announced, "Next I'm joined by rock musician Robert Palmer, live on the show." This'll be interesting I thought, as I turned the volume up on my car radio. Unfortunately, he was just as incoherent as he had been earlier and I felt quite smug, having dropped my recorded interview. In Sybil Ruscoe's case, there was nothing she could do other than battle on, live on air.

Sometimes technical issues get in the way of a potentially great interview, despite the best preparations. I always like to get into a studio with time to spare, either ahead of a show or before an interview. Fortunately, I have no problem with nerves once an event is underway, but I do like to be prepared and when it comes to remote interviews, happy that the equipment is working properly. Sadly, with my first of several interviews with former Rolling Stone Bill Wyman this wasn't the case. Hearing an intense echo to everything I said resulted in an abandoned interview. Bill didn't sound too happy about the waste of his time, although I still think the technical hitch was at his end. Fortunately, the interviews that followed were far more successful and enjoyable, not least when I asked him about his love of history and in particular archaeology.

"Bill Wyman - I'd like to talk to you about old bones and relics."

"That's no way to talk about my former band mates," he replied. Great. just as I'd hoped he'd respond!

Chapter Fourteen

"Back On a Boat and The Eye in the Sky"

I was now enjoying the security offered by a staff contract on a local commercial radio station, but they say you never forget your first love, and when it came to radio, Caroline was mine and as the 30th anniversary of the radio station's first broadcast approached I had an idea. The radio pioneer's days at sea were over after the near shipwreck of Ross Revenge on the Goodwin sands a few years earlier. She was now moored in the protective waters of the River Blackwater, which was part of the broadcast patch for Breeze.

I persuaded both the Caroline and Essex Radio managements that it would be a great idea to broadcast a special programme from the radio ship on the Breeze frequencies. The broadcast evolved into an eight-hour live documentary from the same studio that I'd started my radio career in seven years earlier. I spent many weeks contacting former Caroline presenters, including those who were household names during the sixties, many now living overseas, eventually tracking down numerous former Caroline people and those who had played their part in this amazing story. Then, off to the House of Commons, speaking to Roger Gale, former Caroline DJ, now MP for Thanet, Tony Blackburn, then at Capital Radio, Tony Prince living alongside the Thames at Windsor and Australian and Canadian disc jockeys who'd been huge in the UK, Graham Webb, Ian MacRae, and Keith Hampshire.

The programme also included those who had worked behind the scenes. I met elderly ships engineer Ernie Stevenson in his home town of Hull. Although I'd not met him before, he and his wife made my wife and I so welcome and amazed us both with stories of his life at sea on deep sea trawlers, including the Caroline ship Ross Revenge.

By the time I had finished I had recorded more than 40 interviews, all of them needed to be edited for the programme. Many hours were spent, after my daily show and several long weekends in the Essex Radio production studio, editing the recordings. This involved marking the recording tape with a chinagraph pencil and then making a splice with a sharp razor blade in exactly the right place. It was easy to discard the wrong section of the quarter-inch-wide magnetic tape by mistake. I would then need to trawl through the huge heap of previously discarded tape in search of the one piece that I needed, being careful to reinsert it the right way round, to avoid the interviewee speaking backwards.

Back to Sea,
The Breeze Broadcast from the Radio Caroline studio

Physically editing tape is now an almost forgotten skill, replaced by digital recording. I enjoyed editing tape and I was very good at it, concentrating so intently that I would often place the razor blade between my teeth if I was working on a complex piece. I'd occasionally use my razor blade trick to good effect when prospective advertising clients were being shown around the radio station. They were usually impressed enough to sign a deal once they'd witnessed my daredevil performance.

Return to Ross Revenge for Breeze Broadcast

Peter Philips, former Caroline programme controller and colleague, co-presented the show, with the signal relayed from the ship back to the Breeze studios in Southend via a relay mast in Great Braxted. The whole event was promoted heavily with the opportunity for visitors to board boat trips available around Ross Revenge; more than a thousand listeners and fans were in Bradwell that day.

The broadcast certainly helped to raise awareness that Radio Caroline was still in business, both with our broadcast and the features on Anglia Television and Sky TV. A few former Caroline presenters came out to the ship before the most unexpected of visitors arrived - Caroline's founder Ronan O'Rahilly. He was welcomed by those that recognised him, but throughout the 30 years of Caroline's existence he'd shunned publicity and seldom made public appearances, so many of the visitors hadn't realised who he was!

Once onboard he made his way to the on-air studio and offered himself for a live interview, something he'd never done before on the radio station that he'd started. To be honest he had little choice, he was there, we were there, and I had a live microphone. There was no escape - but his response to my questions was witty and factual. Twenty-six years later when his death was reported it was a clip of that interview that was broadcast across BBC national radio.

The programme had been a huge success, it'd taken hours of patient negotiations, planning and preparation, but it had worked. The trade newspaper of the time *Radio News*: reported: *'What could have been a disaster on air was actually very good and a great broadcast.'* I have always been extra critical of everything I do: If it's worth doing then it has to be done properly and I felt justifiably proud of what I'd achieved.

*****

More *New York Festival* awards for *Best Presenter* followed over the next few years. On one occasion I found myself competing with Kenny Everett in the same category. I wrote a note to Kenny, congratulating him and wishing him well. It had recently been announced that he was suffering from the awful AIDS virus. He wrote a lovely note back to me and even recorded some personalised jingles. Now that was an amazing thing to have, jingles, made for me by Kenny Everett, the ultimate radio genius.

CAPITAL GOLD 1548 AM

Dwahhling...
thanks for your nice
letter. congrats on your
'gong'. herewith a couple of
'things'.
x Mo.

Congrats from radio wizard Kenny Everett – Mo to his friends!

*****

Essex Radio leased an aircraft for morning and evening travel reports. All the larger radio stations had a 'Flying Eye' back in the day. Based at Southend airport it would fly above the busy main road routes around Essex - the A12, A13, A127, A130 - with the reporter and pilot Paul Hartley. He would fly around the county giving up to date travel information every 20 minutes during peak travel times on both Essex FM and Breeze.

Paul was very good and was considered part of the broadcast team, but his salary and the aircraft costs were paid for from a lucrative advertising deal, usually sold to the more prestigious companies.

In the past, Ford and Access credit cards had been sponsors of *The Essex Radio Jambuster.* All was well with this arrangement until Paul was suddenly diagnosed with a medical condition that immediately grounded him. From the company's view, the *Jambuster* simply had to fly, because it was sponsored. It would cost too much in lost revenue if it was grounded, it just had to keep flying.

Finding a replacement pilot was relatively easy, all pilots have to maintain their flying hours, keeping a log of every hour that they are airborne, and there were plenty of amateur pilots at Southend airport only too happy to take off in the *Essex Radio Jambuster*. But replacement travel reporters were not so easy to find, especially when asked to volunteer for no extra pay. It was therefore 'suggested' that all presenters had to take their turn as an eye in the sky reporter, alongside the temporary pilots.

Now, I've never been particularly keen on flying, and certainly not in small planes. But the time came when I felt I really ought to take my turn to report on the county's roads and become *'Young, upwardly mobile Ray Clark.'*

I drove to Southend airport and met up with the pilot of the day. It was a typical overcast, blustery November day, and even by 3pm the daylight was starting to fade. I was already feeling very uncomfortable about the whole exercise, and that was before I entered the aircraft.

As our small aircraft taxied along the runway, the wind buffeting us and with the aircraft's single engine screaming away, we slowly gained height. I was holding on tightly and I would rather have been anywhere than in that tiny flying machine. As we cleared the airport perimeter we banked sharply, which caused me to grab at a part of the aircraft that I thought was in a fixed position, but it wasn't. A lever of some sort moved as the pilot shouted, "No! No! Don't touch that!" I was already saying my prayers.

My first on-air report came as we flew over Rayleigh Weir roundabout, trying to hide the fear in my voice as I began my broadcast: "There's lots of traffic going in all directions, avoid the area if you can, go home."

That was really the gist of all my reports throughout the evening. The wind was increasing, and the small plane was really being buffeted as we dipped and rose over the Essex countryside, the rain still lashing the aircraft and the completely ineffective windscreen wiper was faltering in its journey across the small screen.

Daylight had gone as we approached Basildon. All I could see were the red rear lights of hundreds of vehicles queuing in long tailbacks. My geography of Essex is pretty good, but I wasn't really looking down long enough to identify anywhere in particular. We flew ever onward, suddenly doing a low swoop over the Thames as the aircraft banked again. I looked down and we seemed to be at 90 degrees above the towers of the newly built Dartford crossing. I wanted to be at home with my feet up, sitting in the warm with my wife – I was genuinely fearful that I might never see her again.

To my immense relief the pilot turned and said: "It's getting a bit wild up here," - something I'd decided nearly an hour earlier. "Are you happy to go back?" he continued. Was I? You bet!

"Well, if you really think we must," I heard myself saying,

"but what about building your pilot's hours?" Was I so stupid to suggest we stay up longer? Fortunately, the pilot had decided to return to Southend airport by the most direct route. The plane's small engine continued to struggle against the increasingly strong winds as we ploughed on back towards Southend, still rising and dipping at a terrifying rate.

I eventually identified Basildon in the distance, and knowing that the safety of the runway was getting closer I started to relax, just enough to start a conversation with the pilot. While still tensing my body with every small jolt and bump I yelled, so that I could be heard above the wind and engine noise: "I suppose if the engine was to stop, we could always glide safely to land, could we?" "Oh yes, of course," he yelled back. Correct answer, I thought.

"How ..how..how far could we glide, assuming we needed to?" was my next question. The pilot's answer was immediate: "About a mile for every thousand feet of altitude." I hesitated before my response - this was to be my killer question: "...And er, what is our present attitude and position?" I asked, by now sounding as calm as I could.

"Our current altitude is 500 feet and we're eight miles from the runway".

Oh, how I wanted to be sitting at home.

*****

From the outside world, radio seems a wonderful industry to be a part of, and yes, it is, especially when your audience figures are good and your face fits, but nothing ever stays the same. With pressure from shareholders for bigger audiences and, consequently, better sales, or new management wanting to make an impression, there are always changes. The Essex Radio Managing Director, Phil, was first to go. I remember writing a note wishing him well, saying that any boss who rolled his own cigarettes couldn't be all bad. Then, within days, the management board had hired a new MD and his first task was to fire the Breeze programme controller, the guy who'd given me a job and had subsequently become a good friend, Keith Rogers.

As word of Keith's demise spread around the building I was called into the boardroom. I was wondering if I would also be heading for the back door of Radio House. However, the outcome of my chat behind the closed door was to be completely different. I was asked to take on the responsibility of running Breeze AM with immediate effect. I'd have been bonkers to refuse, but my loyalties were split between the job and concern for my chum Keith.

I drove home, via the Bull pub where Keith had gone to consider his future, and whilst expressing my concern asked if he minded me, in effect, taking his job … and ultimately, his company car. So, the next morning there I was, in charge of a radio station. Well sort of, you soon learn that in middle management you're only as much of a boss as the boss directly above you allows you to be, but I was determined to give this my best shot.

Within days both higher management and certainly sales had changed their opinion about calm, quiet, placid Ray from Breeze. Ever since the station had come on air, it had been the underdog compared to Essex FM.

Breeze was never going to be the predominant station, but I had decided to fight every step of the way for my new radio station and our small on-air team. On day one I was again called into the boardroom and "Just carry on as usual", was the message.

"No, we need to refresh a few things," was my reply.

We'd been covering the Drivetime show with a succession of freelance presenters, it needed some stability and David Baker, the late-night presenter had been with Breeze since the start and was, understandably, tiring of being on the 'graveyard shift'. Convinced that David had the right voice and ability to take on a show during the daytime, I was happy to tell him his late-night days were at an end and he sounded great on the Breeze Drivetime show.

*Me and what became my home studio – both
still working – CR3 at Essex Radio*

My second request was to tweak the format. The 'light n' easy' style had been very successful under Keith's direction and was certainly the right course to follow six years earlier, but it had changed very little since then and the decline in our audience figures prompted change. Within days we had lost many of the pre-1960s songs, though not all, and had added a few more 70s and 80s - not as many as we needed, but I wanted to change our sound gradually, taking our audience with us.

I was now presenting breakfast and by playing more 'gold hits' and upping the pace the Breeze breakfast show was helping to increase the audience by a percentage point or two in successive audience surveys, which translated to a few thousand extra listeners.

The overall audiences of the AM radio stations everywhere were starting to decline, the switch to FM was noticeable. To any smart observer we were at the beginning of the end for medium wave listening, but the audience was still substantial, and I saw it as my job to ensure Breeze battled for every listener.

Since I had been given the job of running Breeze by the Managing Director there was now to be another tier of management as radio consultant Paul Chantler was taken on as Group Programme Director for all the Essex Radio stations. I liked Paul and we got on reasonably well, but there were to be some stormy meetings ahead. Understandably, his obvious love was Essex FM. It was the biggest station in the group, with a better signal, a fun format, a younger audience, and a team of 'hot jocks'. As such, it was the major money earner for the radio group, but I was determined that its success wouldn't be completely at the expense of Breeze, the poor relation AM station.

There is no doubt that during this period I surprised many people at Essex Radio, including myself, with my determination for our radio station to thrive. While I have always strived to be a smiley little man, polite and friendly, I would fight for our radio station every step of the way, particularly in sales and promotions meetings: Monday lunchtime meetings would always be the hot spot of the week in Radio House.

Promotions: *"We have a new sponsored feature this week for Essex FM and a great prize to give away."*

Me: *"Anything for Breeze?"*

Promotions: *"No, they didn't want Breeze."*

Me: *"You mean they weren't offered Breeze."*

It was a constant battle that I often lost, but by perfecting my newfound talent of being a pain in the arse I was eventually able to secure a number of excellent promotions that continued to make Breeze sound like a big radio station.

The battle for the survival of Breeze was made easier when John Terry, one of the top salesmen in the building, became a fan of the station and managed to persuade several customers to take an 'add on' deal with Breeze. He'd often call the studio while he was with a prospective client asking us to give the potential customer a mention and play them a song: '*This next song is especially for the team at the hardware store enjoying the music from Breeze this afternoon'* and it would frequently lead to the customer signing up for a month's-worth of advertising, just to give it a try. They often signed up for more at the end of the first month.

For a medium wave station, we had a great format, a brilliant on-air team … and advertisers, and on the strength of that we even managed to secure a competition budget. I loved working on the mechanics for new competitions: *Cash Casino* with a budget of a few thousand pounds was devised during a family car trip to London. *Maharaja Magic* offered a trip to India as the prize, *The Skoda Decoder* gave away a new car. My favourite competition, and it worked so well, was *The Crunch*. We offered listeners a chance to win a trip for two to New York, The Big Apple. The competition eventually gave us four finalists, who with their partner, had to travel to Stansted airport complete with their cases packed and their passports ready for a long weekend in New York, but only one couple would win and get to fly directly across the Atlantic. You couldn't do that nowadays because of security clearance and the need for airlines to check passenger details in advance, but back then we were able to build the tension as the winners would, literally, be 'cleared for immediate take off.'

Each contestant had to reach into a bag and select a key to unlock a mini safe containing two tickets for their flight. There were 16 keys, with each finalist selecting a key in each of four rounds, but only one key would unlock the safe, and it went to the penultimate key. The suspense was great and the winner whooped and screamed wonderfully. What made it better still was calling back the three losing couples as they were about to make their way home, obviously disappointed at losing, and giving them runners-up tickets for a weekend in Edinburgh. And all of this was played out live on the radio.

One director of Essex Radio, a former politician, was very good at blagging free holidays for himself from various national tourism boards, but he would usually manage to acquire a further free holiday to be given away on air. Through his efforts we were able to offer a great prize, consisting of a two centre stay in China with internal flights between the cities. I usually had a free hand at choosing the name for our competitions, but try as I may, I failed to get away with calling this one '*Special Fly Twice*' no matter how hard I tried.

There was one potential promotion for Breeze that the sales team offered that came close to causing me great embarrassment, although it has been a family joke ever since. The Breeze breakfast presenter at the time was former Essex FM guy Peter Holmes and, as in previous years, he had a part in the Christmas pantomime at Southend's Cliffs Pavilion Theatre. It was the biggest panto in the county, but coming a close second was the more traditional style production at the nearby Palace Theatre, and I was asked to have a chat with the director, with a view to me making an appearance in *Peter Pan*. Now, whilst I can be very brave when sitting out of sight behind a microphone, I get extremely nervous and self-conscious when I'm on a stage. The idea of dressing up in a theatrical costume and performing nightly in front of an audience certainly didn't excite me, in fact it scared me silly. Fortunately, the director came to my rescue. As I entered his office he looked me up and down and announced, in a very theatrical style, "Ooo, you're a bit hefty for flying aren't you?" My panto career ended there, before it had even started...*Oh Yes it did!*

*****

The Breeze team continued to produce great radio programmes, the original gold format was continually adjusted, and at one time it was suggested that we play just love songs.

Music categories are a bit like survey data, they can be whatever you want them to be, and with a bit of imaginative interpretation the lyrics of most songs can make them love songs. But I was concerned that we'd lose the pace that our music and presentation had if we introduced too many slower, 'lovey' songs, and argued against the idea. Eventually a bit of a bonkers compromise was reached where we played two love songs every twenty minutes: '*All-time favourites and love songs on Breeze*'. Later, another name change was suggested, so we then became *The Breeze.*

Back on the Buses with The Breeze Breakfast Show

It became a constant challenge to avoid some of the ideas that regularly bombarded our small team from those in the marketing and sales departments, but strangely I was soon to find an unexpected ally.

The company now had another new Managing Director - Rob van Poos. With a background in national TV and radio advertising, he was well known within the world of media sales. Rob was a caricature of every sales executive you'd ever seen, his big round glasses had brightly coloured frames and he always wore red braces over his bold coloured striped shirts. Flashy gold cufflinks and expensive leather shoes were essential, and of course, he enjoyed copious amounts of red wine. He was often heard shouting at anyone who disagreed with him, while demanding impossible targets from the sales team and many of my colleagues were fearful of him.

It's fair to say that I would normally steer well clear of a character like Rob, but surprisingly we got on very well. Whenever he tried to ridicule or bully the Breeze team, which he occasionally did, I would challenge him. Always the best tactic - to take on a bully - and it worked. I had very little grief from the big boss. He acknowledged that, while others thought Ray would be a pushover running Breeze, I'd become anything but, and he frequently acknowledged my efforts, both privately and publicly, to make the radio station a success.

I continued to tweak the musical format at every opportunity until I eventually got it the way I wanted. *The Breeze* sounded great, and our audience figures were holding up. The broadcast team were very good: I introduced a few former Caroline names to the station to cover spare shifts: Nigel Harris, Steve Masters and Barry Lewis all did sterling work. I also managed to 'save' one of my all-time radio heroes.

Emperor Rosko had been a huge radio star in the sixties and seventies, starting his European career with Caroline, becoming the top radio presenter in France, before joining Radio 1.

Rosko was still a brilliant radio act, he'd moved back to Hollywood when his father, famous film producer Joe Pasternak, had become ill a few years earlier, and had started offering dedicated recorded programmes from the self-styled "*Trans-Atlantic super jock*". He had been heard regularly on Essex FM, but with a change in the line-up he was now surplus to requirements – it happens, no matter how good you are.

"Hey, Rosko, come and work on Breeze," it was nice to be able to ask, and we had a radio legend working with us, although I was surprised when I met him for the first time. The handsome dark haired former heartthrob Radio 1 DJ was now a middle-aged man with a bald head. Time can be cruel to all of us, but on air he could still do the business.

Flying High with Emperor Rosko

By chance, during an outside broadcast from the Essex County Show I met up with a school chum from my Primary school days. Roland had dedicated his entire working life to saving lives with the Essex Ambulance service and was part of a small team attempting to start an air ambulance service in the county. It occurred to both of us that a relationship with a radio station might help with the launch of the project, and so it proved.

The Essex Air Ambulance service and the lottery that continues to fund it to this day was launched on Breeze, with the weekly winning numbers broadcast on the station. Emperor Rosko was visiting the UK at the time and, as a Breeze presenter, helped to secure more publicity for the venture. Prior to the launch I travelled to Cornwall and recorded a feature with the air ambulance service in that county, which was the pioneer service in the UK. The finished feature was broadcast on the Essex launch day and explained the benefits of having an air ambulance in a large, and surprisingly remote county, such as Essex. I like to think that I played a tiny part in helping my county to get an air ambulance which was so desperately needed and continues to provide emergency cover to Essex.

While working at Breeze I eventually got to meet a man called Dave Gillbee which, looking back, made me think about life's strange coincidences.

Growing up for the first ten years of my life in a tiny hamlet called Ostend, just outside Burnham On Crouch, in the wilds of Essex, I knew most of the families and certainly the family names amongst our neighbours. You can imagine how intrigued I was when I heard a story that someone locally worked on 'one of those pirate radio stations'. I had no idea who it was at the time. Dave Gillbee was known on air in the 60s as Dave MacKay and did work for several of the offshore stations. Many years later I matched the two names when he started working for Essex Radio and later BBC Essex, Melody, and Primetime Radio.

We finally met when both working in the same building, but it still makes me smile to think that, from a tiny hamlet, with a population of less than 100 people, two of the inhabitants became successful voices on the radio.

Chapter Fifteen

"Transatlantic Underpants"

In 1997 the new big thing was the World Wide Web, The Information superhighway, the internet. I remember a very basic demonstration from a young, keen engineer, who had already grasped the potential of this new invention, although I didn't understand it fully then. I still don't, but I could also see that it was to be a major aid in the future for our industry. I suggested we put a message on the system, I suppose now it would be called a message board or forum. My idea was to investigate a potentially useful link with America.

'Radio station in the UK with access to The Sun seeks contact with radio station in the US with access to the National Enquirer'.

Within hours we'd had three responses, a couple from university radio stations and one very interesting reply from a guy called Fred Honsberger: *"Hey, we'd like to make contact, I'm the afternoon Drive guy at KDKA in Pittsburgh."* KDKA was a callsign that I recognised, it was the world's first commercial radio station.

The next day an email asked if we had someone who could talk on-air to the KDKA audience about Mad Cow Disease and Princess Diana's cellulite - both were big news at the time. I could do that, I thought, and I was on the air in Pittsburgh that same evening. It was the start of a great relationship with KDKA that continues to this day.

If the team at KDKA wants someone to comment on a story in the UK, they call me. It was also the start of a great friendship with Fred, a larger-than-life, right wing, hard hitting American talk radio jock.

His politics were certainly different to mine, but we got on so well.

The Voice of Pittsburgh, KDKA's Fred Honsberger

His listeners loved the stories from 'across the pond' and within days I was a regular on KDKA's Friday Drivetime show talking about the news from the UK.

The spot became so popular that it was soon sponsored and earning money for the radio station, and me. At this time British Airways operated a twice weekly service flying into Pittsburgh from Gatwick and they sponsored my regular Friday piece to advertise it. *'News from across the pond, brought to you by British Airways, the world's favourite airline.'*

Our original five-minute chat was soon extended to twenty minutes and became a very popular feature on Fred's show. Better still, Shelley and I were invited to fly out to Pittsburgh, Business class, by BA and we spent a fabulous holiday with Fred and his family. I also had the chance to broadcast from the KDKA studios; it seemed that I had quite a following in the city. Of course, the on-air relationship worked both ways; we introduced *The Double Decade Diner,* broadcast every Sunday lunchtime on Breeze. The pre-recorded oldies show was hosted by Fred and his American radio colleague, Judy, and was very popular with the Breeze listeners.

With reduced budgets, especially for our lowly AM service, I continued to fight even harder for a share of the on-air promotions from the marketing team, not least because it got people talking about our radio station and warranted our survival. Giving away holidays usually went with a newspaper contra-deal of some sort which served to advertise Breeze and always helped to maintain our audience. One such promotion was the annual Disney deal, a major advertising sponsorship for the whole radio group which provided a huge income to the company's bank balance. Essex was a prime target for Disney World in Florida, and thousands from the county regularly holidayed at the resort. Every year a live broadcast from Florida was used to promote holidays to 'the home of Mickey Mouse' and an inclusive family holiday was offered as a wonderful on-air prize, which was set to run mid-way during the all-important audience survey period.

It was certainly a victory for Breeze when the radio station was included in the deal for January 2000. A small team of us flew out to Orlando for a series of live broadcasts back to the UK. At that time flying was still quite a new experience for me. I have certainly added to my airmiles by travelling around the world since that flight, but as we boarded our new Airbus, 'Pure Shores' by All Saints was playing throughout the aircraft, the music encouraged passengers to relax. It worked for me. So, an all-expenses paid week at Disney World. What a wonderful experience - but as enjoyable as it might be, it was very hard work with 18-hour days.

We visited every single attraction that the Mouse had to offer, enjoying huge meals and then broadcasting back to the UK, promoting the wonder of the place on air.

No, honestly, it really was hard work! Understandably, Disney certainly wanted their moneys-worth.

During our live broadcasts back to Essex we were visited by Fred and Judy from KDKA who'd travelled down from

Pittsburgh to join us. Another of our on-air guests was Jonathan Ross, who was working as a Disney Ambassador. I remember asking him if he'd made his first million yet and I'm pretty sure that since then he's added a few more.

The story of my final day and journey home from Orlando continues to be one of great joy within my family and the legend has now been picked up by my young grandchildren.

"Grandad, did you *really* fly across the Atlantic in your underpants?"

Well, the short answer is yes. Not only that, but I also walked around Disney World in them while we waited for the bus to take us back to the airport.

The story goes like this: With my case packed and sent on before me I had no change of clothes for the last day. I had dressed ready for the UK winter weather, but with several hours to kill in the Florida heat, I decided to buy a cheap pair of shorts to wear until we landed back in the UK. I folded my long trousers into my hand luggage bag and wore my newly purchased shorts that looked great. They even had an embroidered Mickey Mouse on the left leg and a buttoned fly and I also bought a matching t-shirt. My attire in the hot Florida sun was very comfortable as we enjoyed our final hours within Disney World. And nobody on our team commented on my dress at any time. Expecting a loving greeting from my wife as I returned home after my week-long absence I was met at the front door with an exclamation of horror…

"You haven't been out dressed like that have you?" she asked.

"Yes," I replied, proudly twirling around in my new shorts, "and for nearly 24 hours now!". Americans are strange people… fancy calling men's undercrackers, shorts. Who knew?

*****

Times were changing in UK commercial radio, and so it seemed for those entertaining thousands across Essex every day. Expansion was on the cards at Essex Radio, and that included the Breeze brand. First was an application for a new FM licence to serve the Havering area of London. Although the bid was unsuccessful it showed that after all the struggles we had produced a successful brand and there was a belief that it could work in other markets. Next was the acquisition of the former Mercury Radio in Crawley, Surrey, the AM service, which had been run into the ground and was now just one computer playing non-stop music. Sadly, the long-standing existing FM service breakfast presenter was also destined for the same AM service – understandably, he wasn't happy. I had the job of trying to persuade him that this new service was a better alternative than what the new management had in mind. He didn't stay for long.

I immediately asked former Caroline stalwart Johnny Lewis to join us. He did and slowly, ever so slowly, with the Breeze music format of unpredictable, yet well-known classic hits, together with occasional 'future gold' spice tracks, we started to build an audience.

I even managed to negotiate a few on-air promotions to steer towards Johnny and his breakfast show, including an outside broadcast from northern Norway. Johnny enthused about his radio station and became part of a small on-air team spread over two completely different counties: Essex and Surrey. The output of both transmitters joined after the stand-alone breakfast shows.

At this time new, major technical advances were coming on stream and we were now in a position to give each service an individual identity, at the same time: recording separate links relating to either Essex or Surrey whilst on air and playing them out at the same time to the two separate transmitters. Our team got so good at it and loved the challenge that colleagues were amazed to see Breeze in action.

All was good, unlike most AM services around the country, Breeze was maintaining both audience and sales – what could possibly go wrong?

Our small, dedicated team was running a cracking little radio station that was bucking the trend for medium wave radio and many people were talking about Breeze in a positive way.

We were running regular listener competitions, managing to give away a brand-new car, something only occasionally offered by bigger FM stations.

We'd also been running a promotion offering listener holidays around the world - our more mature and financially secure older audience were good customers - resulting in an invitation for me to join the inaugural Virgin flight to Las Vegas from the UK.

It occurred to me that I could use the opportunity to present my show from the Gambling City of the World, and searched out a local radio station that could be used as a base to broadcast back to the UK. My first port of call was to my friend Emperor Rosko, who lived in Hollywood, a mere 229 miles away: 'Do you know anyone with a radio station in Vegas?' I asked. 'What are you doing in Vegas?' was his reply. He wasn't able to help me find a radio station, but he did invite me to his wedding. I took champagne with the happy couple on the top floor of the Bellagio Hotel.

'Live from Las Vegas' was just such an enjoyable adventure, even if I had to go without sleep because of the time difference. At random, I called a radio station in the city and explained my situation, maybe not such a strange request in the world of radio, and within a couple of minutes my quest was over. I was left alone in a small country music radio station on the outskirts of the city at 4am. It was almost a case of 'the key is under the doormat', though not quite. I was engineer, producer and presenter of the Sunday morning show, broadcasting back to the UK using interviews and audio that I'd recorded in the city, the casinos, at the Grand Canyon and on the Colorado River. That's where I first heard a phrase that has stayed with me since. Our guide on a white water raft tour offered his advice when we went ashore for a picnic: *'Never put your hands, legs or behind where your eyes haven't been first.'* I'd even got an interview with the pilot of the 747 flying us over, although I

failed to get a word with Virgin boss Richard Branson who was also on the flight. To cap it all, I was able to meet up again with Emperor Rosko.

The show was announced as coming *'Live from the Stratosphere tower on the Strip in Las Vegas.'* It sounded wonderful, even though I have never seen the inside of that tower, but that was the wonder of radio in those days, you could paint pictures in the minds of every single listener, even if it included an occasional fib. Breeze was flying high, and so was I.

Chapter Sixteen

"Great Work Ray"

The morning I returned to the Essex Radio building in Southend following my flight home from Vegas, I was aware within seconds that something was up. Hushed conversations were taking place behind closed office doors and news soon spread around the building that we were being taken over by a rapidly growing radio group, GWR. Consolidation was rampant within the commercial radio industry and this group, financed by the *Daily Mail* Trust, as was Essex Radio, was moving into nearly every established radio operation in the country. Within minutes Rob, our Managing Director had left the building and it was obvious that others would follow, including most of the team that had been involved in the success of Breeze. *Classic Gold* was to be the future, it was the way GWR worked, networking all the AM radio services and using former Radio 1 DJs, such as DLT, Tony Blackburn and Paul Burnett to cover the non-local shows. I knew right then that I would probably be the first to go from Breeze, but I decided that I would try, as much as I could, to go on my terms and not theirs. The weeks that followed would provide a very bumpy ride indeed.

GWR had already taken over other radio groups and in every case networking the medium wave output was the only option. To pre-empt the end of Breeze I wrote, on behalf of the Breeze presenters, to the new group's' MD suggesting a team buyout of our station. We received a half-hearted acknowledgement in reply, but nothing more. It was just as well really – where would we have got the money from to buy a radio station?

Within days we were summoned to a full staff meeting with the new organisation's Australian Programme Director who, with a constant use of unnecessary four-letter words, told us that everything was going to be wonderful, and we'd have more listeners than ever before, or rather Essex FM might have more listeners than ever before. There was no mention of Breeze during his presentation, but he'd invited me to have a chat immediately afterwards. It was obvious to me that there wouldn't be much to chat about.

"Don't suppose you've heard those ideas before… what d'ya think of them?" he asked, in a condescending manner. Politely, I told him I'd heard nothing from him that I hadn't heard before, and much of what he'd said made perfect sense. He gave a surprised smile, which soon dropped when I told him, in a very succinct way, that I disagreed with other parts of his presentation. Our meeting lasted just a few minutes and then I was invited into another office to be told that I would be made redundant at some time in the future, but that I would be required to continue running the radio station until that time.

As I made my way out of the building after the two meetings I saw John Leech, an Essex FM presenter of a very popular daily soul show, taking the awards that he'd won for his show down from the reception wall where they'd been proudly displayed for all to see. As a presenter of a specialist show he'd been told that he wouldn't be part of the new plans. I followed his lead and removed my five International awards as well. The once proud radio station display now looked very bare, leaving just a couple of awards remaining and the faint outline of where ours had once hung. As I removed my last award from the wall, Mick the accountant walked past, and just minutes after he'd had the job of telling me that I would be made redundant he asked, "what are you doing that for?" I just shrugged, it seemed pretty obvious to me. I had always given 100% to my job, and that wasn't just about to change, but the passion and commitment that I'd had for Breeze for eleven years had just evaporated completely. It was now time to look after myself.

The local newspapers were soon onto the story and were regularly asking me for comments, but understandably my mind was on my future redundancy payment, and I feared that spilling the beans about events behind the doors of Radio House might put that in jeopardy. I had no intention of fighting any battles in public. On reflection I might have been overcautious but never having been in such a position before, I wasn't going to risk losing the stash of cash that was due to me.

However, the immediate future for GWR wouldn't be as straightforward as they'd hoped. They were about to become embroiled in a huge public battle with hundreds of Breeze listeners campaigning to keep their favourite radio station exactly as it was. Letters complaining about the proposed changes appeared regularly in the local newspapers, the story splashed over the front pages of Southend's *Evening Echo*. Local MPs became involved, the Palace Theatre in Westcliff was booked and filled with campaigners, with every speech greeted by a full house of cheering fans of the radio station. Due to the public outcry, the Radio Authority was forced to watch every development closely, while the new owners were hoping they didn't, and although GWR were issuing regular press statements saying how much better the new radio service would be, every statement was counteracted by supporters fighting back. The situation surrounding the takeover of Breeze was even debated in parliament, with heated discussion about the consolidation of local radio services. I was mentioned in the proceedings, being described in *Hansard* (the official record of parliamentary debate) as some sort of radio hero, just for doing my job: '*Indeed Ray Clark has, on occasion, presented two different programmes at the same time. Ray, who joined the station in 1989 has won five world-class awards, yet he is to be made redundant…*'

Although facing imminent redundancy was a very unpleasant position to be in, it was fun to watch the new company trying to fight off every new challenge. I was still on the payroll, at least for the time being, but I knew I needed a new radio station and being nearly 50 years old and considered a 'gold jock' it wasn't going to be easy to find a new job. There were very few commercial radio stations that hadn't been taken over by GWR and there were many other radio presenters, some who'd served even more years than me, looking for work. There were very few options, and I'd already decided that the BBC was calling – except that it wasn't, well not at that precise moment. I contacted most of the local BBC radio stations in the region, Suffolk, Norfolk and Cambridgeshire, that might be considered within driving distance. All of them answered my plea with friendly letters, but none had any vacancies.

However, the Managing Editor of BBC Essex invited me in for a chat. Several of my former colleagues from the Essex Radio newsroom had moved to the BBC and were kind enough to mention my name and suggest that I might fit into BBC Essex.

Having come from the recently revamped digital studios of Essex Radio. I was now sitting in the reception of my local BBC radio station, and it came as quite a shock - it looked so twee and old fashioned. I doubted if I would fit in there as I sat opposite a green chaise lounge with curly legs and glanced up at the crystal chandelier hanging from the ceiling. Margaret, the BBC editor, was very kind and welcoming whilst explaining that, unfortunately; she had no vacancies, her explanation being that nobody ever left BBC Essex once they went in through that front door. I was disappointed that there was no job for me, but at the same time I was also a little relieved.

I feared that my radio career was coming to an end. My concerns were made worse by a telephone call from an industry colleague that I was quite friendly with. He asked what I was going to do, and when I explained that the future looked bleak, he replied in a very odd way: *"Oh well, never mind, you'll just have to try something else"*.

It was completely the wrong thing to say and at the worst possible time. I put the phone down and started to sob bitterly. My dream career that I had battled so hard to gain had come crashing down around me because of the men in suits taking over. I was only allowed a few minutes of despondency before my lovely wife, Shelley, shook me out of it, but it was another example of the unpleasantness of redundancy, it's something I would never hope to go through again. I don't think I've spoken to the guy who called me that day since; he probably wonders what he did wrong.

The output of Essex FM was already changing to fit the new format introduced by the new owners and while Breeze continued as usual, it would ultimately become part of the growing *Classic Gold* network.

But the change was to be some months in the future. A new man was seconded from GWR management to oversee all proceedings at Southend. Compared with my experience with some of his colleagues, he turned out to be an OK guy and I got on well with him, but as the AM services within the group were run separately to those on FM, he was genuinely unable to give me dates and details of the future changes. The two guys responsible for the medium wave stations did make one visit to Southend, but they were also unable to answer my questions about the future plans for Breeze, or at least chose not to. They reminded me of Laurel and Hardy, though not as funny. One of them seemed reasonable, at least to my face, the other, a New Zealander, was gobby and rude. *"We're here to run this radio station properly,"* he said. They never did and Breeze, sadly, soon started to haemorrhage listeners. What a surprise!

As for my future, there was still little sign of any suitable vacancies, anywhere. All I could do was jog along with Breeze until I was eventually shown the door. I had no alternative, but after an unpleasant time since GWR had swept in, things were about to play into my hands.

"Quick, phone this number!"

I'd hardly got through the door as my wife explained that a radio station had called and didn't just want me – they needed me. The Beach, a very successful radio station based in Lowestoft, Suffolk was part of the Tindle group. Set up by a lifelong newspaper man, Sir Ray Tindle, the group owned dozens of small, local newspapers; many had been thrown a lifeline by Sir Ray when closure had threatened them, and now he was moving into local radio.

I returned their call and spoke to a guy called David Blake. He explained that the Radio Authority were soon to advertise for prospective licensees for the North Norfolk area, one of the last parts of the UK without a local radio station. Tindle intended to apply for the licence; in fact, getting the licence was a major part of their future plans and they needed someone to set up a trial radio station, a restricted service licence (RSL) as part of their application.

At this time, it was the year 2000, the procedure when applying for a new licence was to show your company's ability and financial resources by operating a low powered, month-long radio station that demonstrated just how your radio station might sound should your group be successful in eventually winning the licence. It was a very expensive way of doing things and a further example of how over-regulated the industry was at the time. The Beach bid for the licence had ground to a halt, almost before it had started, as David had recently employed a radio guy as project manager who had been in the same position as me, made redundant due to consolidation at a radio station in the north. He'd visited the Lowestoft HQ, got the job, driven to North Walsham and signed up for three months rent on a two-floor office above the launderette, gone home and sadly died.

This was so sad, but this was a business, and the temporary licence was due to start in a couple of weeks. Tindle desperately needed someone to take the whole project on *"Can you start on Monday?"* David asked.

I explained that it was exactly the job I needed and wanted, but, much as I had issues with GWR, they owed me a lot of money, and, somewhat foolishly, I felt I couldn't walk out without giving them at least some notice, so I really couldn't help him at such short notice. Fortunately, by the time I arrived home the next day, the date of the licence had been changed with special agreement from the Radio Authority, and Tindle were now offering me the job 'as soon as I could join them'. Done deal – I would be on my way to Norfolk to set up a brand new radio station.

First, I had to deal with GWR, so I told my acting boss that I would be leaving and expected to receive my redundancy pay at the end of the following week.

"But you can't go, we'll have nobody to run Breeze, there are no plans to change things until the New Year…" was his response. "What am I going to do?"

I was on the ball with my reply. "Well, from next week I shall be working for myself as a freelancer, so if you want to hire me I'll ensure Breeze runs smoothly by covering the shifts and scheduling the music, but I will only be on site on Saturday mornings… Oh, and I'm certainly not doing it for nothing, it'll cost you."

What could he say, other than: "I'll get a contract sorted."

Great Work Ray!

Chapter Seventeen

"Life's a Beach"

Tindle were good guys, David Blake was a nice man to work for and I had a free hand to set up and run the temporary radio station as I wanted. I hired studio equipment, a transmitter and a broadcast aerial system from Nigel Hunt, former engineer at Radio Orwell in Suffolk, and we used a *Barrcode* playout system, a digital system that Breeze had been involved with during its development, and cleverly named by its inventor, Brian Barr. The temporary radio station was installed in North Walsham and I invited a couple of former Breeze guys to join me. Steve George had started with Breeze in Southend, but had been running another Essex Radio group station in St. Albans before he too, was made redundant. A presenter from The Beach, Jonathan Woodward, also joined us and a surviving Breeze guy, Barry Lewis sent pre-recorded shows from Essex. Between us we broadcast 24 hours a day. Through the night, we used the recent innovation of the automation playout system.

We were due to broadcast throughout the month of November 2000, starting at midnight on 1st November and with everything set up, we resisted the temptation to go on air before the licence officially started. We figured that the Radio Authority wouldn't be camped out on a windy north Norfolk clifftop in November waiting for us to go on air at 11pm on October 31st rather than at midnight, but we weren't taking that risk.

We fired off the automation system and then drove out into the wet and windy autumnal weather around the deserted villages of North Norfolk to listen in. It worked and sounded great as 'Overload' by Sugababes played out.

We gave up any form of home comforts to run the radio

station. Steve and I were living in the office on camp beds, cooking prepackaged microwave meals and driving three miles every morning to a health club who were advertising with us for a daily shower.

The arrangement worked reasonably well, except on Thursdays when the market traders started to set up outside our window at 4am, and of course we had to fold up the beds and turn the place back into a radio station every morning by 7am. But it was an adventure.

The Beach for North Norfolk sounded just like Breeze at its best, but on FM, albeit low powered. We had a dedicated sales guy and local businesses were queuing up to advertise. We even had a major promotion with a regional electrical retailer for a superb home stereo system as a major prize. From the start we contacted the local paper, *The North Norfolk News*, who were very supportive. The editor enjoyed making a guest appearance every week to chat about events in the district. I respected his attitude towards our radio station, which could have been a major competitor for his newspaper, but we worked very well together.

We approached numerous local groups and gave them the chance to promote their activities on the radio. The area had been served solely by BBC Radio Norfolk until now, but we were offering something different, and it was a success from the start.

I contacted the news editor at Anglia Television. I'd met him once and knew him vaguely, but I also knew that he was a bit of a radio anorak, so we even managed a piece on Anglia news. David, back at Lowestoft thought I was some sort of radio wizard, but after my treatment by GWR I had something to prove, if only to myself.

Even though I had left full time employment at Essex Radio the past was still haunting me. My temporary contract to run Breeze, albeit from a distance, worked smoothly, but I started getting heavy phone calls from the GWR accounts office in Nottingham asking about unpaid newspaper bills dating back six months or so. I had never used the Breeze budget for newspapers, they were sorted by the newsroom, but apparently the bill was over £250 and someone in Nottingham had decided that I should be paying for them. After repeated calls, I told the caller that their paper bill had nothing to do with me and, as I was now self-employed, I would be invoicing them for answering any future calls from them. It was another attempt to intimidate me which failed miserably but I hope the poor newsagent eventually got paid.

Having the two jobs was hard. I would spend Sunday to Friday in Norfolk, then drive home on Friday evening, go into Southend on Saturday morning to plan the week ahead for Breeze, before spending the afternoon at home and then I was up at 2am on Sunday morning to drive back to North Walsham ready for the start of the 6am breakfast show. November felt like a long month, and I obviously missed being at home with my family, but *The Beach, for North Norfolk* was a huge success. We'd shown how good a professional local commercial music radio should sound.

Although the number of listeners was impossible to quantify without proper audience research, the radio station was heard wherever we went in the area; in shops, on car radios and playing out from market stalls.

We'd made many friends in the area and after all the bills had been paid there was even a profit, and I was paid a generous fee. As I travelled home after closing down the radio station on the last day of November, I was satisfied that we'd done a good job.

Throughout the weekend, I put together copies of letters we'd received from the area's great and good, together with a picture album and full day by day diary of events ready to present to the Tindle board in Lowestoft just a few days later. It was good to hear the praise that our station received, but it was even better to hear them ask me to stay on with them for another RSL broadcast six months later and they also offered to pay me a generous retainer.

*****

I returned home, confident that I still had a career in radio. Although I'd been organising the programmes for Breeze, I hadn't presented any shows on the station, but as I was still on the books, I returned to present the *Breeze Breakfast Show*. It was sad to present what was likely to be my last show on the station that I'd worked so hard to build up, and already, after just a couple of months under the new regime, it was showing signs of wear.

I was aware that the *Classic Gold* managers were due to visit Southend and wanted a chat and I was pretty sure what they were planning to tell me, but I had already been made redundant and was still working on my freelance arrangement. Once I'd finished my show, I made my way upstairs to the Breeze office where the dodgy duo were waiting, trying, without success, to gain access to the Selector computer that was used to programme the music. It was password protected and, as soon as I walked into the office, they demanded a copy of the computer files – I assume they feared I might corrupt the output. I couldn't help but chuckle: had I wanted to sabotage the output of the radio station, I could have done that at any time in the preceding three months.

Once again there was talk of how wonderful this radio station would be in the future. I'd heard enough and started packing the few personal possessions I still had in the office before leaving. It was time to exit Radio House in Southend for the last time, the building that I'd gazed at from outside several years earlier, longing to be a part of what went on inside. Well, I did become a part of it for a number of years, but now my time was up. I left the building through the back door to my company car – I still had that for another month, and I'd made a point of parking it in pole position, ready to drive straight out of the car park. Despite having officially left the company in September, I was still sad to go. I was smarting, just a bit, as this was the first time I'd ever been told I was no longer needed in my working career.

Fortunately, that feeling didn't last too long – in fact about an hour. As word got around that Ray had finally gone from Breeze, I received a call from a former colleague, David Baker. He'd left Breeze before the takeover, having been offered a job on a new, smaller radio station serving the Chelmsford area, Chelmer FM. "Would you like to take on our afternoon show, starting at 2pm today?" he asked. It was a sweet feeling, although I suspect very few people realised the significance. But for me it was just the instant ego boost I needed, appearing on a local competing radio station just four hours after leaving Breeze.

Chelmer FM was never going to be a hugely successful radio station, it was run on a shoestring and had a poor signal, but it was to be my new radio home for a few months, and I was very grateful to be heard on it. I moved to presenting the breakfast show and organising the commercial traffic (the ad logs). I wasn't being paid a lot, but at least I was still receiving my generous monthly cheque from Tindle for the Norfolk project. I also came close to accepting an interesting job as a music programmer for a number of music services operated by an international music company based in London, but the deal breaker was that I still wanted time to 'do' radio. I'd fought hard to get on the radio and I wasn't giving up the battle that easily. I was fortunate, I'd managed to keep working after redundancy and I had fingers in a few pies, although nothing that would make me a rich man. I'm still searching for that job to this day.

Now, my ongoing challenge was to arrange the second RSL broadcast for Tindle in Norfolk for later in the new year. The first broadcast had been from North Walsham, a small town towards the east of the area. This time we wanted to show what we could do for those living and working in the west, but it wasn't going to be quite so easy this time. Another group had their eye on the North Norfolk licence, and they'd pretty much got Fakenham, the largest town to the west, tied up, and there were already links between them and an established radio station based in Kings Lynn. I suggested we leave Fakenham to them for the time being, but we would base our next broadcast in the picturesque small town of Holt.

With snow blowing almost horizontally in the biting Norfolk winter wind, I spent a bitterly cold January day walking around closed up Holt, looking for suitable premises for our next trial broadcast, planned to broadcast throughout June. Although this lovely little town would come alive during the summer months, during the winter many shops were closed and much of the population had 'disappeared'. My first stop was the estate agents: *"I'm looking for a short-term rental for the summer months in an office or small shop, have you got anything?"* The response was the same wherever I asked, *"In June, no chance - everythings already taken, certainly not."* Either that or the rent they required was just crazy.

As the sky started to darken on that winter's day, I was feeling concerned. The Tindle management thought I was their Wonder Man, but now, having advised them to go for Holt as a base for our next temporary radio station, there appeared to be no room at the inn.

Not relishing telling them that I might have been wrong, I started the long drive home planning my next move. I wasn't at all confident of finding anywhere suitable or available in Holt and I was starting to think that I'd bitten off more than I could chew. But it took just one telephone call to solve what seemed like an immense problem. If only all difficulties could be solved in such an easy way…

I'd always enjoyed the localness of the commercial television channels. Anglia and Southern had always fascinated me, not with the networked ITV programmes that they broadcast, but the locally produced news and magazine programmes. I especially noticed, and enjoyed, the commercials for local companies, they reminded me of the local ads that were once shown at the cinema: *'Visit your local Chinese restaurant, just across the road from this theatre.'* And one of the regular, local commercials on Anglia Television that had stuck in my mind was for Bettys of Holt, a delightful department store selling furniture, bedding, and household goods. On two separate sites - it had a ladies clothing department across the road from its two-storey treasure trove of a main store. I found it surprising that Holt was home to a department store, it was even more of a surprise to learn there was a second department store operated by another company, just up the road in the same small Norfolk town. The TV ads gave the impression that Bettys store was huge, their advertising budget must have been substantial.

Bettys was the last door in Holt left for me to knock on while looking for a base, and I certainly wasn't confident. Although they appeared to understand advertising, I feared they wouldn't want to entertain a temporary commercial radio station on their premises.

The next morning I sat at home with the telephone number in my hand, held by breath … and dialled, fearing the worst. But how surprising was the immediate response on being put through to the store manager.

"01621? that's Maldon in Essex, isn't it?" said the voice, "My family live in Fambridge."

This was a local village just a few miles from my home and more than a hundred miles away from Holt. What a coincidence, my downhearted mood changed immediately. We chatted briefly about the area of Essex I knew so well, and I quickly concluded that I was dealing with a helpful guy and thought we might be back in business.

"Look, this might sound like a very odd request but I don't suppose you'd have a small office or store room that we could use for a couple of months for a temporary rad…"

I didn't have a chance to finish my sentence. "Radio station? You're the guys trying to win the North Norfolk licence, aren't you? Yes, of course, when can you come and see what we have?" he replied.

If only everything could be that easy. A couple of days later I was back in Norfolk and visiting Bettys of Holt in a torrential downpour, I was made so welcome and offered the pick of the store to position our radio station, even Robin, the manager's office. I chose a small stockroom that contained the company safe, a huge grey monster of a thing, almost ten feet square sitting in the corner. In fact, once we were on the air we placed our audio processor and transmitter on top of it.

*****

Having found a venue to base the forthcoming Beach broadcast I continued to present the breakfast show for Chelmer FM, but also maintained my weekly broadcasts to Pittsburgh via KDKA, now sponsored by The Alleghany, Ohio and Monongahela Hospital Trust - what a mouthful! It was part of the script that I had to read after my 20-minute chat with my on-air friend Fred, however, the sponsorship continued to pay me a considerable number of dollars each week.

The response to the weekly broadcasts grew and the interest in 'The Brit' was such that I was invited over to cover the breakfast show in Pittsburgh for two weeks. Now, for a UK radio guy to cover an American major market breakfast show was extremely unusual, but I was up for the challenge and the KDKA audience seemed very happy with the outcome as I co-presented the *'Daily Morning Drive'* with Fred Honsberger.

The reaction was amazing with full telephone switchboards throughout the programme. I did a couple of television appearances as well, including co-hosting Fred's regular TV show on the Pittsburgh Public Broadcast system. I was even given the freedom of Pittsburgh by the city's Mayor and warmly welcomed into every restaurant that we visited. If you are liked by Americans then expect to be overwhelmed with their generosity. I was quite embarrassed by it all, finding it difficult to feel comfortable in response to what was almost idolisation. I've always felt embarrassed when listeners recognise me in public and although I'm glad that they enjoy what I do, I continue to find it difficult to accept praise from others.

Looking the part on U.S. TV and Ray and Fred on air -
The KDKA Morning Drive wakes up Pittsburgh

The offer of regular work and a possible move to America was hinted at, but I acted quickly to dismiss any ideas of my becoming a Brit in exile, though my wife was initially quite keen on the idea.

Main Street USA looks wonderful, but I'd also had a glimpse of the more deprived parts of Pittsburgh and I became alarmed, as colleagues of my friend, Fred, compared their new pistols, secured in the glove compartment of their cars. They were amazed at my reaction, as I recoiled at the sight of their proud new possessions. I'd never been close to a gun before, and

I didn't like what I saw. The entire gun culture of the States shocks and horrifies me still.

During my appearance on KDKA, the radio station launched a listener trip to London. The plan was to sell 30 places for a ten-day visit to the UK, accompanied by Fred Honsberger and the break would also include a meal and a meeting with 'The Brit' in a top London restaurant. By the end of the week, 75 places had been sold for the visit that would take place during the summer, with more on a waiting list.

What an experience those two weeks had been for me at a time when I'd needed my confidence to be boosted. I'd been flown to the States and back, had a wonderful time and came home with a fabulous Bulova watch as a gift from the management of KDKA and a letter saying I'd be welcomed back at any time. My relationship with KDKA continues to this day, though sadly my friend Fred, a U.S. radio giant, has since passed away.

I returned home from Pittsburgh having had a taste, once again, of broadcasting to a large audience. I was very grateful for the Chelmer FM gig, and although it was a great temporary stopping off place, I knew I was capable of doing far more and needed a much bigger challenge to keep me and my imaginative mind occupied for the foreseeable future.

That challenge came in the form of a telephone call from the BBC.

Chapter Eighteen

"Back To The BBC"

BBC Radio Cambridgeshire were looking for someone to take on the Saturday afternoon show from May until August 2001, between the end of the old and the start of the new football season, and asked if I was interested. The brief was to play a few tunes and chat to a few people. Realistically, I knew that I needed a foot in the door at the BBC, and so I finally returned to their employment, after last working for them in May 1972.

My geography has always been good, but I wanted to know more about the patch that I'd be broadcasting to. So Shelley and I spent the Saturday before I started driving around Cambridgeshire exploring Swaffham Bulbeck, Babraham, Cottenham and Eaton Socon, amongst other places.

The BBC studio was based in the east of Cambridge city centre but was a good 90-minute drive from home, with an all-round journey of more than 100 miles. It might have been a temporary job but I had the luxury of a producer and all I had to do was …do what I do, play songs and chat a bit.

I enjoyed my first BBC programme very much. Not only did I get a lovely letter, full of praise from the boss, or the Managing Editor, as the BBC called the boss, but he also offered me a full-time job on the back of my first broadcast. It was good news, I had regular work, in fact now I had too much of it.

I had a plan: I would continue to cover Saturday afternoons throughout the early months of summer for the BBC. This would allow me to continue daily at Chelmer FM for the time being and also to complete my tasks for Tindle, which included operating a second Norfolk trial broadcast during June. From September, the BBC wanted me to present a daily early breakfast show for six months, by which time the afternoon presenter was planning to retire, then I would take on afternoons. In the meantime, I would need to be in Cambridge by 4.30am every day for the two-hour show, so that would mean getting up to go to work at 2am. I said yes to all of it, not forgetting my regular Friday evening appointment with the Pittsburgh audience.

The second *Beach For North Norfolk* broadcast was on air throughout June. This time the living accommodation was a little more comfortable than before. Rather than sleeping on the studio floor, we rented a holiday cottage to use as a base and I was able to enjoy a pleasant stroll through Holt to get to and from the radio station every day. We even had the luxury of a bath this time. The three daily presenters, myself, Barry Lewis and Jono Woodward, didn't bother cooking meals and were regulars at The Kings Head, in the High Street, living on Jumbo Yorkshire puddings filled with roast beef, our daily diet for most of the month.

Once again, our trial radio station was a huge success and, as the application for a full-time station was being written, I went looking for local 'names' who would be prepared to join the company as directors and endorse our application. Our broadcast had coincided with the general election, and we covered the count. Barry Lewis elected to stay up all night, but it was worth it as we beat both Radio Broadland and BBC *Look East* TV in announcing a change of MP for the district. We also scooped the first interview with the new man – that'll please the Radio Authority we thought. Not only had we got North Norfolk's new MP to say nice things about us, but I was able to persuade his defeated opponent, David Prior, to join the board of the new radio company. The Radio Authority liked applicant groups to have a couple of people representing 'the great and the good' from their area included with every licence application, and a former MP was certainly a big tick in our box.

I excelled with persuading our second director to join the

group. Angela Bond was a radio legend, certainly a formidable woman, but lovely at the same time. Not only had she been Kenny Everett's producer, tasked with controlling him when he first joined the BBC in the early days of Radio 1, but she had been responsible for the British operations of the company that provided the leading computerised music programming system, Selector. The system selects the order of songs played on most radio stations around the world and Angela had taught many radio programmers to use it in her own, unique way. I had spent an afternoon a few years earlier, sitting in her flat in London's Barbican learning just about every shuffle, mood, and tempo control there was. A note here for my radio colleagues: remember to use 'F2' every couple of minutes... Don't ever forget Angela's demand that you regularly save everything!

Angela was one of the radio industry characters, everyone knew her and she lived in a cottage in a nearby village when she wasn't in London... and was willing to join the board for this new radio station application.

So, after two very successful temporary broadcasts, signing up two significant directors and producing two detailed reports relating to the broadcasts, which were included in the official application, the licence to broadcast to North Norfolk was won. My job for Tindle was done, and plans for North Norfolk Radio to start regular broadcasts were made.

It was former Radio Caroline presenters Mike Ahern and Andy Archer who signed up in the radio station's early days. I was asked to take day to day control of the new radio station, but I had already decided that I would never move home for a radio station and declined the offer. However, I was in line for a big cash bonus from the radio group after winning the licence ... which I also declined. By the time the licence was issued I was working for the BBC and I was naive enough to mention it to my new boss, only to be advised that there might be a clash of interests and that, perhaps, I shouldn't accept the payment. I don't think that was the best advice I've ever received, and as good as Tindle had been, they didn't put up much of a fight when I told them that I didn't want their £5,000. An honourable and virtuous act on my behalf, but on reflection, pretty stupid. I was getting older, but certainly not wiser.

*****

Now a BBC man, working early mornings at Radio Cambridgeshire from Monday to Friday, I was happy and settled, especially with the promise of a daytime show in a few months' time.

And then BBC Essex offered me a Saturday morning show. I jumped at the chance. I wanted to return to an audience that knew me and I knew that the Saturday morning audience in Essex was one of the biggest of the week. I'd adapted well to including a lot more speech content into my BBC programmes. It was what they wanted, but I was determined not to talk for the sake of it. I remembered the words of my friend Fred from KDKA: *'Nobody ever turned off because of the hits.'*

I followed the same philosophy - it was simple - If I had nothing to say then I'd play a song.

My first scheduled record on that initial Saturday morning on BBC Essex was The Beatles' 'I Saw Her Standing There'. I played the newly produced jingle announcing my name as the news bulletin came to an end, and opened the microphone, *'You can have the job if you can count to four,"* I said, and the Beatles played straight into my hands as their song started with a countdown: *'One, 'two, three, four'* and we were away. The songs that followed were well known to the audience, I'd picked some good topics to chat about and the phones were constantly busy. Many of the callers, like me, were refugees from Breeze. I was now on the radio six days a week and enjoying the challenge of presenting in a very different style to my previously music based commercial radio shows.

It seemed that the BBC was keen on me being around too, particularly within the Cambridgeshire team. I was one of the first 'escapees' from commercial radio to join them and they seemed to enjoy the way that I 'did radio'.

As the new year started I was counting down the weeks until my promised move to afternoons, and on several occasions I was asked to cover the Cambridgeshire breakfast show. With the programme starting at 7am I was able to enjoy an extra two hours in bed, even allowing an hour for preparation before the programme started.

The Cambridgeshire management were true to their word and with the approach of Spring I moved to my new time slot, three hours every afternoon, starting and finishing at a far more sociable time of day.

I soon came to enjoy the show with a fine mix of music and chat.

I had a producer as well who was lovely. Katy spoke with a very 'proper' BBC accent and had been doing things the BBC way since she started working at the radio station a few years earlier. Our understanding and styles of doing radio were quite different, as were our backgrounds, but we worked very well together, and each appreciated the different ways of doing the same job.

Katy regularly arranged interviews with guests that I would find challenging, such as local academic Germaine Greer. She was great to chat to, but you certainly had to be on your toes when interviewing her, she didn't suffer fools gladly.

Actor Pete Postlethwaite was appearing on stage in Cambridge and came into the studio one afternoon; a fine actor who had appeared in so many films and plays but had only recently become a household name after the success of the wonderful movie *Brassed Off.*

"Steven Spielberg reckons you're the best actor in the world," I said - what a lovely way to start an interview.

Professor Robert Winston was another wonderful interviewee. We enjoyed a compelling chat about the advances in child development and paediatrics.

I now had to work harder and research guests that, in some

cases, I had never heard of and discussions went much further than asking about a new record or film.

Each day I was facing challenging interviewees on air, but every guest told a fascinating story. It was my job to get them to tell it to our audience on what had evolved into a very popular magazine and music style programme, and with each difficult interview I was aware that I was getting better at doing the job that I thought I already knew. I mentally modelled the programme on the ILR style programmes that had been so successful a decade earlier, and it worked. Our audience figures, although not huge, increased with every survey.

How many people have I interviewed over the years? Impossible to say exactly but thankfully the vast majority went well. My favourites? Sir Tommy Steele was brilliant – just an ordinary bloke – who was in at the very start of British Rock & Roll and became a huge screen and Hollywood star and has had a career lasting as long as I've been alive. Dame Barbara Windsor spoke openly about her past and the characters she mixed with, some of them less than savoury. Tom Jones spoke of still meeting his mates 'down the club' when he visited Pontypridd and Lulu was fun, talking of the twists and turns in her long career as she gently flirted throughout the interview. Honor Blackman thought I'd make a very good James Bond, Jerry Hall drawled with her Texan accent, I just drooled, Des O'Connor was charming and humble as he spoke of his amazing career, Michael Aspel, patient and so professional, Michael Palin took listeners around the world without leaving their seats.

Then, there was Midge Ure, responsible with Ultravox for 'Vienna', the amazing song that was kept from Number One in the charts by 'Shaddap Your Face'. During our chat there was a fault in the unmanned studio in Bath that he was speaking from. "I'll see if I can fix it for you," said the man jointly responsible for Live Aid.

I have to admit I wasn't listening to anything that Joanna Lumley was saying - she was just lovely.

There were a number of interviews that didn't quite work out as I'd planned. One of my earliest celebrity chats was with singer and actress Helen Reddy. I'd read up about her career, but every event I mentioned was met with a negative response: *'No, it didn't happen like that'* or *'No that wasn't me'*. When I offered her the chance to tell me her story she declined, she just didn't want to be interviewed. I quickly decided that I wouldn't win with this live interview so there was only one way out.

"You're obviously very busy, I'll let you go," I announced and played another record.

I fear I might also have upset a favourite actor of mine, Timothy Spall, by suggesting he should have been in the *Carry On* movies. I don't think he appreciated that. He even mentioned it in an interview in *The Radio Times* sometime later. I meant it as a compliment, and I might have gone just a bit too far when I asked Christopher Biggins if he'd ever done a hard day's work in his life. It was a fun remark and I managed to win him round, but I couldn't picture him digging holes in the road.

In the days when local radio stations offered prizes to listeners, the BBC had always struggled, whereas the commercial stations were able to find sponsors enabling them to offer prizes such as holidays and cars, just as we'd been offering on Breeze.

The BBC were resigned to giving away stuff that nobody wanted: tea towels and 'goody bags'... radio speak for 'toot'. But I persuaded the Cambridgeshire management to buy a stock of small, quality, digital clocks, so we could offer a fun prize that was worth winning.

Every day we would offer one of these wonderful timepieces to our listeners after answering a question and completing a reasonably simple tongue teaser, *'Tick Tick Tock I'd like a Ray Clark clock.'*

There was always the potential for listeners to stumble, sometimes on purpose, over the words. I still meet listeners who remember trying to win an *'Exclusive, Elusive Ray Clark Clock – sure to become a collector's item in the future'.*

*****

Cambridgeshire is an odd county geographically. The radio station obviously strived to serve the whole county, but in truth the county had never really gelled since three separate areas were lumped together in the 1974 boundary changes. Cambridge, Huntingdon and Peterborough all seemed to be a world apart from each other and had very little in common, but our brief was to serve them all. Every Wednesday my afternoon show came from Peterborough, and I would spend more time driving to and from work than I would on air. I still chuckle now when I drive along the A1 heading north and remember those days of driving from rural Essex almost to the Midlands, just to present a three hour radio show. There was even a period where I was presenting a series of shows from a temporary studio in Wisbech. I was covering nearly as many miles as I did in my coach driving days.

The afternoon show was chugging along quite nicely, but things were about to change and in a very positive way. Someone made the decision to put the noisy, chatty afternoon presenter together with the loud Australian producer who was 20 years younger and at a bit of a loose end. Within days, the new duo, Rory MacDonald and Ray Clark were making some great radio. We were taking chances every day with our choice of guests and topics. We aimed high for guests.

"Who would you really like to interview, mate?" Rory would ask, I'd tell him, he'd get them, and with the experience that I'd gained since joining the BBC I asked all the right questions, even if they weren't always appreciated by the guest.

With the BBC charter up for renewal the Chairman of the Governors, Michael Grade was touring all the BBC establishments, rallying support for the BBC from the local 'great and good.' He had no plans to appear on air as he visited Cambridge, but his visit was on the day that the death of radio personality John Peel was announced and, quite rightly, he agreed to go on air to offer a tribute. As I explained to him that afternoon, I wouldn't be doing my job properly if I didn't challenge him on the future of the BBC. I gave him a hard time with questions about the BBC trying to be all things to all people, but often, appearing to fail as it was such a huge organisation. Another big interview made the national news when I quizzed local farmer Tony Martin. He had recently been released following his imprisonment, initially for murder, but later reduced to manslaughter, after shooting dead a teenage burglar in his home in Fenland.

It was a challenging interview and Mr Martin wasn't the easiest of people to quiz, I had to apologise to our listeners and warn him when he used a four-letter word on air, but it made for a fascinating listen and was reported extensively in the press. Tony Martin is the only person that knows exactly what happened at his remote farmhouse in the Fens on that night, but he did answer most questions that I put to him:

"Have you ever thought that you were guilty?"

"No, never."

"Have you cried?"

[Long pause]

"I'm a very emotional man. I can be slightly lachrymose, but if you're talking about crying about what happened that night, then no. I wouldn't cry about that. If you're asking me to be responsible for the actions of others, then that's the worst form of anarchy I know."

"Do you regret what happened that night?"

"No. You're not listening to me. I can't be responsible for the actions of other people. Roy Hattersley starts babbling about people's lives being worth more than property. But it was nothing to do with property; it was to do with me. He seemed to forget that there was actually a person living in the house."

The interview provided a fascinating insight from the man whose actions became headline news.

On the move – Live from the radio car

Rory and I were given a free hand to go where we wanted and do what we liked, as long as we continued to supply a quality show every day. A situation we certainly enjoyed, not least with outside broadcasts. Rather than the occasional, long planned, day out from base, we took every opportunity to go out to meet the audience. In just one year, we broadcast more than 80 programmes away from the studio, often with the most unusual of topics: I presented a whole show from an onion processing plant, another from a farm north of Peterborough with me driving the combine harvester for much of the show and we decided to challenge ourselves one day by going out to do a three hour speech based show with absolutely nothing planned. We parked up on Parker's Piece in Cambridge city centre and waited for stories to come to us – and they did. Amazing stories like the young couple whose family in China had financed their studies in the city in order for them to learn English and start a business selling Coca-Cola to English speaking tourists at the forthcoming Beijing Olympics. We met a direct descendant of a football pioneer who invented the game – which was first played on the very piece of grass that we were broadcasting from. We just thrived on getting stories and having fun, every show was a challenge and we aimed to make every show a success.

Another fun outside broadcast was from the National Exhibition Centre in Birmingham, reporting from a major food show. It was at the time when food programmes on television had become very popular, due in no small part to Jamie Oliver leading the TV ratings. We were invited to chat with every high-profile chef present, including Rick Stein, Raymond Blanc, Antony Worrall Thompson and Ken Hom, but the one person that we really wanted on the programme was Jamie, the new kid on the block in the world of TV cooks. Despite requests to his promotional people, we were told that he would be unavailable. But, I had a trick up my sleeve and bet producer Rory that we would get to speak to Jamie Oliver before our show was over, and we did.

Jamie would often mention his Gran during his television shows, it was obvious that she was very special to him... and I just happened to be the guy that drove her, and 52 other mature residents of a quiet Essex village to Southend for their weekly shopping trip in the days when I was still a coach driver. As Jamie finished his onstage demonstration, we just happened to position ourselves by the stage exit and as he was whisked swiftly away by his entourage I called out, "Jamie, does your Nan still live in Althorne?" Job done, he stopped and we had our on air guest. Jamie was happy to chat, but his 'people' weren't so keen.

BBC Radio Cambridgeshire, like most radio stations, had a variety of visitors to the reception. Listeners, often lonely, felt that the voices they heard regularly on the radio were their friends, and would pop in for a chat with anyone who might be about. Others would call in to pick up a publicity photo of their favourite presenter, or to pass on details of an event that they wanted to publicise. Some were there, offering a story that they felt would be of interest to listeners or TV viewers in the region, which is how I came to help planetary scientist Colin Pilinger unfold Beagle 2, the British Mars Lander, on the reception floor of the BBC in Hills Road Cambridge. Mr. Pilinger was waiting to be interviewed for *Look East*, the BBC's local evening television news programme. He was sitting with his spacecraft, looking like a small portable barbeque wrapped in gold foil, and transported in a supermarket trolley. I instantly showed an interest and this likeable, very clever man was obviously passionate about the project to send this very craft to the planet Mars. He explained the purpose of this flimsy looking creation with great pride as he explained how it would work.

Months later the world waited for Beagle 2 to send back messages from the red planet on Christmas Day 2003. Sadly, no signal was heard and the project was deemed to have failed, but in 2015, not long after the death of its inventor, it was confirmed that the craft had actually landed on Mars. Only two of the four solar panels had unfolded successfully, blocking the antenna that would allow it to report back to Earth. Perhaps it should have been launched with the protection of the supermarket trolley that was used to trundle it around Cambridge.

My 50th birthday was spent presenting a show from an open-topped double-decker bus that arrived bedecked with flags, ready to drive us around the city while we were broadcasting with the signal relayed via the radio car that followed behind. I'd had no hand in any of the planning and we had guests arranged throughout the afternoon who would simply board the bus at various stops, one of whom was actor Paul Shane, the man with the lived in face, and star of TV sitcom *Hi-De-Hi*. While enjoying the ride and waiting his turn for the interview, we'd acquired a busker onboard. Rory saw him playing en-route and invited him to play and sing a song on the bus. He was awful, probably the most untuneful and non-musical busker you could ever hear. I was frantically trying to shut him up, but he just kept on and on – he was so bad he was funny. But Paul Shane's face was even funnier, as he was obviously thinking, what the f*** Is this all about? He really didn't know if he was meant to laugh or keep an even straighter face than he was known for.

*****

I'm not very good at wind-ups, nor usually a fan of them, at least on air. I've heard some presenters do them very well, but I would never have been able to hold my nerve while speaking to someone who thought I was genuine while giving them a hard time. However, I did manage one wind-up that most certainly wasn't directed at the listeners, but they enjoyed hearing it.

One of my little-known party pieces is a passable Dame Edna Everage impression and boy, did I have fun with it, at my producer's expense.

Every day I would make my way to the on-air studio at least an hour before I was due to go on. I enjoyed just sitting there and mentally working out what would go where within the programme and I'd often spend the quiet time editing or working on production pieces. So, it was nothing unusual for me to be absent from the newsroom, where producer Rory would be working, and consequently unaware that I was about to record a telephone conversation – with him, though he wouldn't know it was me.

"Hello darling, could I speak with Rory MacDonald please?"

The phone was passed over and Rory, acting just as a BBC producer should, attempted, as tactfully as possible, to explain to 'Gladys, the gladiola specialist from Cottenham' that she couldn't come on air just to advertise her flower business. "No, I'm sorry madam, this is the BBC, you can't advertise," said Rory, sticking to his guns. He'd quickly decided that 'Gladys' would be too difficult to control on air.

"But I've heard other people on that Radio Cambridge advertising," 'she' continued, still speaking with 'her' phoney Aussie accent.

"No, they'd have something to talk about that was of interest to our listeners," he patiently replied.

"Young man!" Gladys stormed, "are you suggesting my gladiolas aren't of interest to your listeners, I'm shocked that you could suggest such a thing, I shall see you in your Peterborough studio next Wednesday at noon," and 'she' put the phone down as Rory was left wondering what had just happened to him.

Nothing ever worried Rory…normally, but the potential arrival of Gladys had certainly spooked him. He looked worried as he joined me in the studio, somewhat quieter than usual. "You alright mate?" I asked.

"Yeah, yeah," he replied pensively, and no more was said.

I had planned that when we next broadcast from Peterborough, I would explain the fun I'd had to my listeners and own up to Rory by playing the recording of the phone call of Gladys on air. But it got to be even better than that.

By coincidence, the following Wednesday's Peterborough show would be coming from the BBC's brand-new studio in the city centre and our afternoon show was to be the first to broadcast from the new, state of the art studios, replacing the rundown and dated facilities in another part of the city.

The new BBC complex was very plush with the latest digital equipment and floor to ceiling glass studios so that everything could be seen both inside and outside the studio. So, as Rory and I readied ourselves for the programme, we could see all the comings and goings in the reception area – including a lady delivering a huge bunch of flowers which colleagues back at Cambridge had ordered for the new reception. And, purely by chance, she was delivering the largest spray of gladiolas you'd ever seen. Rory's face looked pale.

"What on earth is the matter mate?" I asked, as the start of the show approached. "Whatever you do, don't let that woman in here," he cried, while cowering at the back of the studio.

The poor flower delivery lady had no idea of the stress she was creating and, like every other visitor to the new offices that day, was being shown around by the receptionist who was rightly proud of her new surroundings.

"Keep her out of here!" screamed the normally mild-mannered Rory, as the poor lady continued her tour totally unaware of the impact she was having on Rory.

As the show started, I attempted to explain the hilarious coincidence on air, that only I knew about, and, in between my laughter and Rory's howls of concern, I pushed the button to play the recording of the phone call I'd made almost a week earlier.

Then came Rory's voice at the shrillest I had ever heard, as he shouted: "One day – one day, I will get revenge, you might well have forgotten everything you ever knew about gladiolas, but one day I will get you ... you ...you..." he spluttered.

I'd never known Rory lost for words before this and I hope the 'listener' enjoyed the joke as much as I did.

The story didn't end there though. We had an excellent working relationship with a member of the Ministry of Defence press team, a retired Major, and he became a good friend of the programme and would help us with interviews when others couldn't or wouldn't arrange them. So, exactly one week later as I drove northwards on the A1 towards Peterborough, I spotted a military helicopter skimming the fields to my left. No, surely not, I thought – even Rory couldn't get the army involved in a revenge. It had me worried though and all these years later, with Rory having returned to Australia many years ago, I am still on my guard for his payback.

Chapter Nineteen

"A BBC 'Pirates' Tribute and Remembering D-Day"

Now an established full time BBC presenter on two BBC stations, I also had the opportunity to return to my pirate ways. Easter 2004 marked the 40th anniversary of Radio Caroline's first broadcast and there were still an awful lot of people, admittedly of a certain age, who romanticised about those far off days when they were much younger.

An email from a listener and fan of the pirates, Vivian, from Chelmsford, prompted me to produce a documentary about the magic of the offshore radio stations that I'd also been smitten with. Vivian had kept a day-by-day diary throughout the 60s and I invited her into the studio to read out extracts from her diary entries, explaining her listening habits and relaying happy memories of taking boat trips out from Clacton and Walton to see the radio ships and the disc jockeys. Her description of those magical days spurred me on to interview more people who held this period so dear. With relevant music added and interviews with the big-name DJs of the day, I produced a documentary to be broadcast over the Easter anniversary as part of the *Pirate BBC Essex* broadcast. This was a huge tribute broadcast, celebrating the offshore stations of the sixties - most of them had broadcast off the Essex coast. The broadcast was made from the *LV18*. Now out of service, it was the last of the serving lightships operated by Trinity House, the seafaring organisation based in Harwich.

The ship was anchored at the mouth of the rivers Orwell and Stour, with access from Harwich via a ten-minute ferry trip. The Editor of BBC Essex gave the go ahead to this major project having admitted to not really knowing much about the pirates at the time. The programmes were to be presented by a mixture of BBC Essex presenters and former pirates, all of whom would be living on the ship, as the original radio pirates had. Former Essex Radio colleague and news guy Tim Gillett suggested that I be signed up as part of the crew. The team included several of the pirate stars from the sixties and many were my radio heroes: Norman St. John, who became a good friend with his lovely wife Maureen: Dave Cash, Mike Ahern, both sadly no longer around, Keith Skues and Roger Day. I presented the breakfast show and was first to go on air. The response was amazing; we were getting emails from every part of the globe: The Falklands, Australia, New Zealand, it was very exciting, and recreated the pirate era extremely well.

Spending a week onboard a former light vessel anchored in Harwich Harbour, midway between Harwich and Felixstowe, was memorable and mostly fun. There were downsides: the ship had been unoccupied for months prior to the broadcast and temperatures in the living accommodation were slow to rise. I was issued with a hot water bottle. As the breakfast presenter, I would leave my cosy bunk an hour before the show and make my way to the galley for a cup of tea and a cuddle with 'Old Fatso', the brand name of an ancient iron stove that was older than the ship itself and provided the only source of heating onboard, it wasn't very efficient either. Colder still were the toilet facilities with a choice of two portaloos securely tied down on the front deck to prevent a potential disaster. You can imagine: *"Hello, Coastguard? Our breakfast DJ has just been washed overboard and is floating away in a blue portaloo,"* thankfully the ropes held tight.

The town of Harwich benefited from the broadcasts with hundreds of pirate fans making their pilgrimage to view the ship from the shore and meet up with their radio heroes. As the closedown approached there were calls for the service to continue as a regular radio station, sadly that didn't happen. However, the *Pirate BBC Essex* broadcasts were repeated with two more recreations of the exciting sounds of the offshore radio stations. Each time another batch of former pirates came on board, travelling to take part from all over the world, all of them had been household names in the sixties: including Johnnie Walker, Graham Webb, Ed Stewart, Keith Hampshire and, of course Emperor Rosko.

Tony Blackburn aboard Pirate BBC Essex and with Johnnie Walker… and the official LV18 Portaloo (tied down securely)

I'd kept in touch with Mike Pasternak, Rosko, over the years, we got on well and he was always very complimentary about my style of broadcasting. "If you'd got yourself an agent, you could have hit the big time," he told me. I'd received similar comments from a few others in the past, but coming from Rosko it was valued, and appreciated.

Our friendship was put to the test though, during one *Pirate BBC Essex* show. He'd requested that I 'drive the board' in effect, do all the technical stuff while he rocked and rolled his way through a three-hour show. We were just minutes away from the start of the programme when we both realised that he'd made no preparations to select the songs for the programme, so it fell to me to select 'Rosko style' songs that were suitable as we went along, not an easy task. Having to do this while playing short songs that would then be interrupted by the Emp doing his *'Hey my man'* stuff', which he was famous for was hard enough, but things were made a whole lot worse by an experienced radio guy from within the BBC who had found his way on board to observe the programmes and was raiding our diminishing pile of CD's while I was struggling to select the next track ready to play.

Radio Caroline Class of 87 Reunion on LV18- Pirate BBC Essex (L-R Peter Philips, Ray, Bill Rollins, Kevin Turner, Michael Barrington)

We got there – the show was as tight as could be and the compliments flooded in, but it was a close-run thing, made far more difficult than it should have been. Rosko and I laughed about it later as we came ashore and enjoyed an evening curry in downtown Dovercourt.

*****

Meanwhile back at Radio Cambridgeshire, producer Rory and I continued our adventures. Our next project was to be particularly memorable and humbling. This time we took the programme to the beaches of Normandy for the 60th anniversary of the D-Day landings. We broadcast live from Arromanches in France, the scene of unimaginable horror sixty years earlier. We'd left it late to book any accommodation and for a while it looked like we'd be sleeping under the stars. Eventually we found what must have been the last bed and breakfast available.

Our team of four, me, news reporter Erica Fisher, Rory and Major Stuart Green, our military expert, travelled all day on Eurostar with a change of train in Paris and, after hiring a car in Bayeux, we arrived. We were billeted in a small cottage that looked much as it probably did at the time of the landings years earlier, but our host was kind and, between us, we communicated with much hand waving, smiles and shrugs. We worked hard on two great days of broadcasting from the town as it prepared for a huge memorial parade, with world leaders due to arrive. We weren't too interested in them, but what we had got were some amazing stories of unbelievable acts of bravery and heroism.

We'd tracked down many of the surviving veterans from Cambridgeshire who had landed on the beaches when they were young men and their stories were mesmerising. Rory and I went to visit some, others came into the studio, and we took our time to listen to their stories and record them. For years, it seemed, they'd tried to forget the horrors and didn't want to speak about what they'd witnessed. But now, being in their later years, they wanted their brave actions, and those of their fallen comrades, to be remembered. I felt very honoured to listen to their tales as they opened up and spoke about what they'd been a part of all those years earlier. In many cases they were speaking about those events for the first time.

D-Day Remembered, on the Beach at Arromanches

The broadcast was excellent and we had scores of complimentary calls and emails about it. Some months later the programme was a winner at the prestigious annual Sony Awards, the top industry awards ceremony, held in the Grosvenor Hotel on Park Lane London and I was very proud to be a part of such a great team.

There was more success in the continuing round of awards just a couple of months later. The Gillards, the acclaimed BBC local radio awards, were presented in Birmingham. BBC Essex had been nominated for several awards associated with the *Pirate BBC Essex* broadcasts including my documentary, *All at Sea.*

A small contingent of those involved, including me, made our way to the Midlands where we mixed with the great and the good from across the BBC and I was dressed in my dinner suit that had served me well on so many occasions at formal radio functions. A real bargain - costing just £5 from the Oxfam shop several years earlier. All of us around the table listened nervously to the nominations, as the different categories were announced.

Gold BBC Gillard award for 'All at Sea'

As it came to my category I quickly called my wife and left my mobile phone on the table in the hope that she would hear the proceedings, including the announcement: *"And the winner for the best documentary goes to... BBC Essex for All at Sea!"*

I was very proud to have won a gold Gillard award for the programme, not least because I felt it went some way towards acknowledging the major part that the offshore radio stations had played in helping to establish modern radio in Britain, and as I walked back to my chair with everyone in the hall cheering and applauding I thought back to my redundancy episode just a few years earlier - never expecting to enjoy another posh event at a top hotel. What a great night.

*****

I've started the countdown to more public firework displays than I care to remember. For several years I would travel as far as Twyford. It was a long way to go just to commentate on a firework display, but the Berkshire organisers seemed to think I couldn't be bettered and were prepared to pay very well for a few "ooh's" and "aah's". Not every event was as lucrative though and I have done my share of favours, writing off, in some cases, a whole day just to attend an event on a freezing cold Saturday evening in November. This would entail organising crowd safety, while all but running the event, as I was the one with a microphone.

"Ray", they would say, "we need to delay the fireworks for half an hour. Can you keep the crowd happy?'

I was often tempted to ask: "How do I do that then?" But they knew I'd sort it, 'cos I did last year and the year before that. I've happily given my time freely to many events over the years. "It's for charity Ray", they'd say encouragingly, and I'd go willingly - but there have been those that have taken advantage.

Sometimes, while standing in the cold and rain waiting to do my bit, I've spent time mentally adding up the money being made by others whose services were necessary for a firework display to go ahead. The public address equipment guy and the lighting guy and the sound guy and the fireworks guy and the roundabout guy and the catering guy… I'd think to myself, who else is working for nothing, 'cos *it's for charity*?' Trouble is, saying NO is very difficult!

One major event that I regularly commentated on, was the Maldon Mud Race. Famous around the world as a hundred or so brave, some would say crazy, souls jumped into the cold waters of the River Blackwater. I think I'll settle for crazy, as I took part once on a freezing Boxing Day many years ago. This fun exercise involves a squelch through the thick, sticky, smelly mud to run across the river at low tide and back again for charity. It is a great spectator event and attracts many thousands who line the picturesque promenade in Maldon to get a view of the competitors, many in fancy dress – though by the time they've crawled to the finish line it is difficult to see if they're dressed in anything at all. This was another of those events where the announcements were always left to me - "Well, you know what you're doing Ray" - and it was certainly an event that I enjoyed.

One race was memorable for the wrong reasons, although I'm very proud of what happened, and I was just doing my job, honestly. Low tide was at 11am, the ideal time for spectators to arrive at the last minute, watch the race and then get home for their Sunday lunch or to go into the pub. But on this occasion the crowds were huge, much larger than normal, and when the planned starting time arrived there were still hundreds trying to get through the gates. The organisers were thrilled at the prospect of making even more money for charity and so a message was passed to me: "'Ray, can you stall the start for 20 minutes?"

Now, I rise to most challenges, but to keep 10,000 cold and hungry spectators waiting for a further 20 minutes, when all they want is to see the participants struggle through the mud and then get into the warm, was certainly a challenge, but as always it was a case of '*Ray will know what to do*'. But this time I was beginning to sense unease within the massive crowd. I desperately needed to keep them entertained, and the answer was my stand by trick. It had worked loads of times before, thank goodness… It was time for a Mexican Wave. Explaining that there was '*a slight delay of about five minutes*', which was met with a huge groan, I started to outline the rules for our attempt on the largest Mexican Wave that Maldon had ever seen. Stalling for as long as I dare, I started the countdown from 10 for the wave to begin on the left. The higher the starting number, the more I could delay the start of the race, anything to buy more time. "7, 6, 5, 4, 3, 2 … wait for it …ONE!

The Mexican wave started, but so too did the race as the runners who'd been lined up alongside the muddy waters of the Blackwater for far too long, decided enough was enough and took off and plunged into the icy waters… And so the race was on! There was no stopping them and no prospect of turning them back, so I carried on commentating like the true professional I am. The late comers were still flooding through the gate long after the first participants had finished the race. I bet my name was mud in the eyes of those who missed the race, but I still laugh at the memory of it every year when the mud race comes around.

I can quickly deal with most eventualities at public events, but I am really quite shy, especially when it comes to appearing before an audience. Part of my job has been to host radio roadshows allowing listeners to meet their favourite broadcasters, participate in silly games and win rubbish prizes at carnivals, fetes and county shows. I have always been happy hosting events and making announcements when I'm out of sight. I enjoy being 'a voice' on a microphone, but it's a completely different matter when you're on stage and people are watching you. Some presenters love this aspect of the job and excel at it. Not me, especially with commercial radio when the roadshow had been sold to an advertiser by a salesperson desperate to offer an unbelievable 'add-on' as a deal maker to get them to sign a contract for a huge on-air advertising campaign.

Often the roadshow was completely unsuitable for the client's business and embarrassing for them and for the poor presenter. They often failed to attract an audience of any size, and those that did attend would have very little interest in the advertiser's product… *"Let's hear it for the radio roadshow coming live from Jones the undertakers."*

Fortunately, it was never quite that bad, but I do shiver with memories of trying to present a roadshow at a golfing professional's day. Those attending the event were really not interested in a signed photograph, in fact I was lucky not to have been told where to stick it. I don't think the radio station ever got paid, but as long as the sales team got their commission, all was fine.

Chapter Twenty

"Billy No-Mates"

My radio life was nicely stable, Monday to Friday, BBC Radio Cambridgeshire and Saturday mornings at BBC Essex. The drive to and from Cambridge every day took nearly two hours each way, but I had three different routes to choose from through pleasant countryside. I was driving home one Spring evening when I received a call, just as I drove into the quaint Essex village of Thaxted, and I was faced with a dilemma.

The assistant Editor at BBC Essex was offering me the daily *Drivetime* programme. I stopped my car, and we chatted about the offer, which would be as a member of staff, rather than a freelance position. That was almost like being offered a job for life, but it would mean giving up my daily show on Radio Cambridgeshire.

I promised to give the offer serious thought and get back to her, though she was surprised that I hadn't accepted the offer straight away. I had much to think about. The positives were obvious: a daily programme, broadcasting to Essex again, staff benefits, less travelling, a good salary. But I had concerns: I enjoyed working with the small weekend team at Essex on my Saturday morning show, but during the week the newsroom, central to all BBC radio stations, seemed to be very insular. They were nice people, I already knew several of them, but there were distinct groups within the radio station who appeared to have an awful lot of say in the way things were done, even though they weren't part of the management team.

The radio station itself, although very popular and one of the largest BBC local radio stations, always sounded very cosy on air and I pictured the chaise lounge and chandelier in the reception as I weighed up my options. I was very happy at Radio Cambridgeshire, and they'd been good to me, but eventually the logistics helped me to decide - I was to join BBC Essex full time, although staying on with Cambridgeshire to present a Sunday morning show, at least for the time being.

So there I was, back on the air in my home county on the BBC, but it felt very different to Radio Cambridgeshire. Although I was the *Drivetime* presenter, I relied on the back up of the news team and a producer, working with different people every day, instead of the one person as I'd done previously, and some of those people were far more interested in what they were doing than others and some had considerably less experience than me.

I would arrive in the newsroom at 11am to find myself kicking my heels, sometimes for hours. Although I was quite capable of arranging interviews and following up stories myself, I was unable to do anything as I had to get guidance from the programme's producer – whoever that might be on the day and I was often unaware of who I'd be working with until an hour before going on air.

Unlike Radio Cambridgeshire, news ruled at BBC Essex. The vision of Lord Reith when the BBC was set up to Inform, Educate and Entertain, was certainly the order of priority given to the output of BBC Essex at this time. The news output was styled to that of Radio Four, always operating in serious mode, rather than the more appropriate, and relevant, lighter touch I was used to at Cambridge. Well that was my feeling, anyway.

So, I wasn't particularly happy when I first moved to my new, local radio station. I started to regret my move there and for a while I'd spend my lunch hour, sitting in the local park on my own, feeling a bit like Billy-No-Mates. I didn't seem to fit in with any of the various teams associated with each programme. I felt I was just going into work, doing the job, and then coming home. I was grateful to be working back in my home county again of course, but everything seemed to be taken far too seriously at the New London Road studios.

Not that it wasn't staffed by good, talented people. They just seemed to operate in a completely different way to those I'd worked with in the neighbouring county.

I wondered if my arrival was seen as some sort of threat, especially by those who had been at the radio station for a while, but I just wanted to be part of a team – any team. I work best either on my own or within a small team, but at that time I had neither, and not knowing who I would be working with until I was due to go on air made me anxious. I began to plan a way out without losing face.

I was presenting the *Drivetime* show in my own county, but after just a few weeks, I was bored. Featuring the same news stories that the breakfast show had already covered in detail and playing repeat recordings of the same interviews wasn't what I wanted to do.

Whilst I was finding the *Drivetime* show uninspiring, I really enjoyed presenting the BBC Essex Saturday morning show, which I'd continued with. Saturdays gave me a chance to be far more creative, play more music and have more fun. A story that I'm often reminded of by listeners many years later, was when a caller told me that she was learning to drive. I told her that I had once been a driving examiner, taking people for their driving test (a job that I did for two years), and we had a lesson on-air. I asked her to get three tins from the cupboard, to use as the pedals and a loo brush for the gear stick. My 'learner' played her part brilliantly as I gave 'instructions' and asked her to describe the other vehicles and obstructions on the road - as she 'drove' along without leaving her kitchen. It was very funny and I would love to know if she passed her real driving test a few weeks later.

I have always thrived on having a project – any sort of project, provided it keeps my mind occupied. During an outside broadcast in Basildon, we came across an elderly lady called Dolly Dear. I chatted with her about life in the town and how much it had changed. Having lived in Basildon all her life, she recalled the days when the area had been surrounded by fields, long before the New Town was thought of. She also told me that she'd never been to London. Already I was thinking about a great programme feature.

Dolly Dear's Big Day Out was a fun project. Together with colleague Tim Gillett, we took Dolly up to town and recorded her reaction as she saw the city's sights for the first time. We visited Covent Garden, watched the Changing of the guard in the Mall and enjoyed afternoon tea at The Ritz.

While we stood on Tower Bridge, an impressive flotilla of boats passed underneath and, on the bridge, armed police were overseeing the safety of those passing below.

Dolly approached one of the officers: "Who's that then – Bin Laden?" she asked. "No, no, no," replied the policeman, "It's President Putin on a state visit"

On reflection, standing directly above Putin's boat on that day, Dolly Dear and I had the ideal opportunity to solve a lot of the world's future concerns.

The 25th anniversary of the Falklands war was approaching, and the islands themselves had always fascinated me. My friend and contact at the MOD offered a return flight to the South Atlantic and we were talking about me going to the islands to record audio and video for the entire Eastern region of the BBC. I was very excited.

My negotiations for this trip were taking place with a new Managing Editor who was in the process of taking over at BBC Essex. Gerald was a career BBC man, having spent time at several local radio stations, including Cambridgeshire where I had worked alongside him. Now he was to be my boss at Essex. At first, he seemed keen on my going to the Falklands, but as the deadline for the final decision loomed I detected hesitancy. Who knows what goes on behind the scenes within BBC management, it's something I've never discovered fully, despite having worked for the Corporation for several years.

Sadly I never got to travel on the flight that was offered by the MOD, as, because of the way the BBC works, even though I'd be flying with the RAF, it had to be paid for and it was decided that the cost wasn't justified in terms of programming opportunities. Some you win, some you lose!

As our new boss was settling in and meeting his new team, my wife and I were looking forward to a holiday to Australia. My former colleague, Rory, had now returned to Australia and was working for the ABC (Australian Broadcasting Corporation) and he invited us out to visit him and his family in Sydney.

"Can't afford it", I said, "maybe one day."

"Mate – don't put it off, you might die!" was his plain-speaking Aussie reply. So we booked – just in case our number was nearly up. But before starting three weeks leave, it was my turn to have my 'chat' with Gerald, our new Editor.

"Where do you see your career within the BBC going?" he asked.

"Well, I'd like to do more documentaries," was my reply. But I think that fell on deaf ears.

"What about presenting the *Breakfast Show*?" he asked - the most prestigious show on any station.

"Been there, done that" was my hasty reply - "All that getting up in the middle of the night? No thanks!"

I was already out the door and off on holiday and it was at least two days later, as we were flying at 35,000 feet somewhere over India, that I sat mulling over what had been said. I realised I had turned down a very good offer of presenting one of the largest local radio breakfast shows on the BBC. So, while we waited to change aircraft in Singapore, ready for our onward flight to Sydney, I emailed a rushed note to the boss: *"OK, breakfast, yes please, let's talk when I get back."*

Although my wife and I were on holiday, I couldn't miss a chance to broadcast from the other side of the world, and with my former producer, Rory, there was an ideal opportunity to create a special show for BBC Essex on Easter Sunday live from Bondi Beach.

We asked BBC Essex listeners to contact us if they had family in Sydney and we soon had more than a dozen young

Brits who we were able to link up with their families back in Essex, speaking to them on air as we enjoyed the sunshine from our vantage point overlooking the surf and sand of Bondi Beach. It was like *Two-way Family Favourites,* the old wireless programme that I'd heard when I was child. It was a great listen and a lovely programme to be involved with, chatting to lots of happy people on both sides of the world.

Naturally, on my return, I was keen to hear what was on offer for my broadcasting future at BBC Essex. The existing *Breakfast Show* was maybe a bit safe and cosy, but it had a good audience and wasn't really in need of too much change. However, a new broom sweeps clean, and with new management changes I was told: "I'd like you on breakfast, I'll pay you a bit more," and that's what I got… a tiny bit more.

"Who would you like as your producer?" I was asked.

Reunited with ace radio Producer
Rory MacDonald and ABC engineer, Bondi Beach

My reply certainly raised a few eyebrows in the newsroom, my immediate choice was Allison, the News Editor. I knew Allie from my days at Essex Radio and we got on well, most of the time.

Our opinions often differed, something that would soon become evident to all.

Allison was passionate about news and known to be quite sparky, she also liked to be right. I am calmer, but I can be very stubborn, and also want things to be right. I think those working in the newsroom could sense some lively confrontations lay ahead.

I had no concerns about presenting the *Breakfast Show*, the challenge was exciting. It was to be a three hour talk programme, packed full of news, and I wanted to be sure that we had the best guests and good content. Essential, then, to have a good, strong news producer capable of finding good strong stories to make it work.

Allison was in her element, we had serious news, heavy news, breaking news, continuous news. The sort of news that excites journalists but is often far too intense for casual listeners, especially at breakfast time. We just had too much of the wrong sort of news for my liking.

I'd been asked to present the *Breakfast Show*, as I excelled at personality radio, but I was also a safe pair of hands, capable of putting my serious head on when needed. However, with the programme overflowing with news, there was very little room left for me to do what I do – and that's to be Ray, which was why I was offered the job in the first place. We appeared to be more news intensive than the *Today* programme on Radio Four, a situation emphasised as this period coincided with a particularly tragic time for British troops stationed in Afghanistan. Every day we would report on yet another dead soldier, essential to report, but in moderation. The content was so heavy, with little room for 'light and shade.'

Allie was excellent at her job, but I'm pretty good at what I do, and it was obvious that our ideas of how the breakfast show should sound were very different. Sparks soon started to fly between us and I started to dread going into work. We both had a different interpretation of what we should be doing. I was sure that our listeners were also getting weary of our constant news agenda – the light-hearted calls that the management wanted just weren't there – nobody wanted to be heard having fun next to yet another dead soldier story. The audience figures were holding up, but our audience was changing with the whole *Breakfast Show* becoming far too serious.

I'm not sure whether it was me, Allison, or our Managing Editor, or perhaps someone even further up the BBC food chain who instigated change, but it couldn't have come soon enough. Allison and I went our separate ways, both, thankfully, remaining friends, but also happy to be working on different projects.

Chapter Twenty-One

"The Hardest Job of the Lot"

My new producer, Claire, had been the regular morning news voice, very aware of finding the right stories for our audience and somebody I knew, immediately, that I could work with. The changes on air were soon evident. Although we disagreed on some of the finer points of what we were doing, we trusted each other enough to make sure the show worked as it should.

Of course, we still covered the serious news stories when we needed to, but I was given enough space to do what I do… and that's something that was always difficult to plan because I never know what I'm going to do or say. I was always savvy enough to know all the details on the news stories that we covered and where I could go with my interviews and how far I could push and challenge. Part of our job description was to 'Hold To Account,' but I also needed space to have fun – and we certainly had fun whilst producing some great creative radio too.

It's fair to say that presenting a single-handed, three hour, all speech breakfast show on BBC Local Radio is the hardest job of the lot. If a guest is held up or a phone connection fails to work, there are very few places for the presenter to hide. You just have to fill with whatever you can find. I always had a pocketful of anecdotes or topics that I could instantly introduce into the show. Claire, my producer in the control room, always knew that something was wrong if I started talking about tractors or cuckoos. It was of great importance to me that the programme would always run seamlessly, and it did, *always*. Even when the studio was falling to bits.

On one occasion a vital lead had come unplugged from a bit of kit during a down the line interview with a member of the government. I was asking him tough questions which he attempted to answer, in the way that politicians do, as I held him to account. What he, nor our thousands of listeners could see, was me crawling under the control desk desperately trying to reconnect an essential keyboard while he answered. I then had to dive for the microphone to put my next question to him.

A good producer in the room next door is essential to make an all-talk show work, and surprisingly much of the communication between the on-air studio and the centre studio control room was non-verbal, with looks, waves and pointing, and sometimes grimaces.

Amazing how you can have a whole conversation without using words, especially on the radio.

Our breakfast team had also evolved and now gelled nicely as we all enjoyed our part in waking up a healthy proportion of the 1.25 million potential listeners in Essex. We had great voices reading the news bulletins: Shani and Sonia, Ben took on sport and Tom - now a vicar, and certainly a brilliant one - was our roving reporter. We were constantly looking for creative ideas that worked for our audience, who came to expect our quirky twist on events around the county and our listening figures were slowly rising.

When the travelling fair was in town, we challenged local driving instructors to compete against each other on the dodgem track. We'd often send roving reporter Tom off on a wild goose chase, or sometimes in search of llamas, which became a standing joke. Anything unusual in our county was on Tom's agenda.

One of the more memorable features was when we arranged an early morning singalong in the beautiful church at Thaxted, one of the county's prettiest villages, with the huge church spire dominating the surrounding countryside. Thaxted had been home to composer Gustav Holst while he was writing *The Planets Suite* – part of which became the music for the hymn 'I Vow To Thee My Country.' Was there any better way to mark St George's Day than with a packed congregation of

Breakfast Show listeners, residents and school children singing the hymn in the same church and listening to the very organ on which the tune was originally composed?

I was back on track, enjoying everything that I was doing - having fun on air, but still with the challenge of tackling serious news stories. The disclosure of the MP's expenses scandal was an issue of particular interest to our listeners. It seemed that very few Members of Parliament were claiming legitimate, minimum expenses, with many pocketing huge amounts of money for unbelievable items and services. The country was in uproar and our listeners were very angry at what they saw as a bottomless pit of money being distributed without control amongst the nation's 650 Members of Parliament, paid for by the public.

It was difficult to get any of the county's MPs to speak on air as a guest about the issue, but one from a safe conservative constituency offered himself for what he probably thought would be gentle questioning from the local BBC guy. How wrong he was. I had the facts and figures in front of me and he had no defence.

"Why should I pay for someone to dig your garden?" I asked.

"I work very hard" was his reply.

"So do the thousands of people listening to this programme," I responded.

I kept pushing, spurred on by the instant response from countless emails and texts we were receiving as well as callers to the studio jamming the switchboard. The message was clear: *"Keep going Ray – don't let him off the hook!"*

I had never received so many messages in such a short time. There was nowhere to run for the hapless politician. I did enjoy the confrontation, but I began to feel rather sorry for the man as he just blustered away with no acceptable answer to the accusations I was legitimately making.

"This is damaging our democracy…" I said. "Yes, I know" he interrupted, "and it's you and your colleagues that are doing it," I continued.

"Well, thank you very much," he retorted sarcastically. It seemed, in his eyes, he was doing nothing wrong.

Another similar debate was with a senior Essex County Councillor who was challenged on receiving free meals, complete with silver service in the exclusive Members Restaurant, at County Hall.

"I work very long and unsociable hours, I'm sure you have perks in your job," he challenged.

When I replied that I was entitled to claim a meal allowance if I was working away from the studio, but I had never claimed it, he took another tack.

"But you receive a very high salary for what you do," he said.

He was certainly mistaken there.

"It's around half as much as you claimed for expenses last year," I was able to tell him, and he went quiet. Thanks to our great team I had all the figures to hand.

As the 2010 general election approached, various politicians were making themselves available to our breakfast team, eager to tell our listeners how good they were and how wonderful the world would be if they won the election. Because we had a couple of high profile and potentially vulnerable constituencies in our county one of those wishing to talk was Prime Minister Gordon Brown.

We were offered an interview just days before the general election and at a peak audience time, 7.45 am. I was quite excited about the opportunity of challenging the most powerful man in the country, and 15 minutes would give me ample time in which to do it. Throughout the early morning I was talking up our interview and as the time came, I was ready to hold him to account - that was my job.

Sadly, 10 Downing Street wasn't ready, although I could hear the Prime Minister and his staff in my ear, it seemed they couldn't hear me. There was a problem at their end of the link, in fact, there was near panic at the other end. *"Can they hear me, shall I start, what's happening?"* I could hear all of this through my headphones while my team in the next studio were desperately trying to establish full contact with Downing Street. If I had opened the fader just then, at that very moment, I could have allowed my, not insignificant audience, to listen in as the Prime Minister floundered and flapped about before I'd even had a chance to question him.

We eventually established contact with about five minutes left to go until our allocated time was up. One question ... and half an answer, that was all we got.

Mr Brown lost the election, and although I don't think my interview was responsible, it certainly didn't help him.

*****

After the success of my pirate radio documentary, I was keen to take on a new project to work on – and there was a village near Basildon that was full of potential stories. Crays Hill was the site of the biggest illegal travellers settlement in Europe and was seldom out of the news. I chatted about my idea with the News Editor, and former producer Allison - Yes, we were still talking to each other!

I wanted to put a documentary together, featuring stories from all those living in the village, the council, and the travellers themselves. I got the go ahead, and once again Allie and I were working together.

We met an outspoken local resident who told us of his run-ins with several of the residents on the site. There were about a thousand people living there, at the bottom of his garden. We talked as we walked to the fence dividing his property from the travellers. Beyond it was a sprawling site packed with chalets and caravans.

Needing the travellers' side of the story, over time, we built up a relationship with their main spokesperson, a lady called Mary and through her we asked for an invitation to visit the site.

Allie and I drove to the site and took tea with Mary in her immaculate chalet, surrounded by railings and ornate iron gates, although the area beyond her property was less well cared for. We were treated in a friendly manner and chatted for some time about the travellers' interpretation of the situation.

Our job was to report on what we saw and let the listener decide which version of events they favoured - the travellers' story or the village residents.

I asked if I could also have a tour of the site and an interview with some of the men, as all contact since the story had started to evolve had been with the female travellers. The menfolk were conspicuous by their absence when anyone wielding a microphone appeared. However, on our next visit to the site, I took a stroll with one of the male travellers who seemed reasonably happy to answer most of my questions, although he was quite guarded when giving his replies. I pushed my luck a bit and started asking questions that I knew our listeners wanted answers to.

"People say there are guns and drugs here," I asked.

"Can you see any?" came the reply.

"What about taxes? Do you pay your taxes? "I went on.

"Of course - We pay VAT on our fuel."

"Yeah, but what about tax on your earnings? I must pay the taxman on my earnings." I said.

"Aah, yes you would pay taxes," he replied, "but when you deal in antique furniture and horses, that's a different matter…!"

We visited the Dale Farm site several times, and, although we were never going to become best friends with the travellers, we always treated each other with respect, and I would always get answers, of some sort, to my questions.

There was no denying that the inhabitants had their own interpretation of the planning laws, and what they could do on land that they owned, but I had a certain amount of sympathy for their predicament. As they often told me: "We need to go somewhere."

Equally, I was accused of being racist when I said I wouldn't want a thousand travellers at the bottom of my garden – I qualified this by saying I wouldn't want a thousand people from *any* background living that close to me.

The relationship that we built up with everyone involved in the Dale Farm story would certainly be beneficial when the eviction of this huge site eventually took place. The council had threatened, and the travellers had challenged until there was nowhere left for either side to go to avoid confrontation.

Reporting with my 'serious news head' on

All I had ever wanted to do was to play records on the radio, and yet on October 18th, 2011, at 5am, I was about to report on the biggest news story in the country as our small team took up position in a field in the village of Crays Hill, as the planned eviction of several hundred travellers commenced. The story had been brewing, with tensions rising for some time, now it was about to erupt.

As the insults and bricks started flying, our team were in the thick of it, broadcasting every move by all those involved, blow by blow. We were working alongside national and international radio and TV crews. They had dozens in their broadcast teams, yet there were just a handful of us reporting for BBC Essex.

A technical team of engineer Chris onsite, ensured our signal got out, while studio manager John, back in Chelmsford, battled to connect 'feeds' from a dozen different sources and send them back to us on site. Producer Claire was juggling with the availability of interviewees and reporters, while shouting in my ear, *'cross to reporter Fliss next, fill for three minutes, phone call coming with traveller next, keep filling,'*

I was hearing everyone at once in my headphones while struggling to listen to the answers to the questions that I was asking of my current guest. It was all a bit fraught, but very exciting. We made a superb job of covering the story that was making world headlines.

On that chilly, bright October morning, our breakfast show was broadcast live from a position just yards from the barricade that had been erected by the travellers and their supporters. BBC Essex listeners woke to the sound of the eviction with shouts, screams and our commentary on events from a piece of controversial land just outside Basildon.

It was serious stuff, not least for those who were being removed by force from their homes.

Although we reported on events in a very professional manner, there were lighter moments too, the best provided by my friend and colleague, reporter Thomas Magill. On the eve of the eviction much had been made of a protestor who was prepared to physically attach herself to part of the barricade in an attempt to slow the eviction, and so during the live broadcast I asked Thomas, via our radio link, if he could give an update on this protestor's current situation from his vantage point next to the huge, barricaded gates.

What happened next still makes me laugh when I recall the near riot taking place around him.

Listeners heard Thomas knocking on the huge gate, constructed of scaffolding poles and corrugated iron, as if it were someone's front door, and then, in his gentle Ulster lilt, he called, *"Hello ... hello ... I wonder, could someone confirm if the lady still has her arm cemented inside the washing machine, please?"*

Nobody replied. I hope the protester survived.

BBC Essex Breakfast Dream Team
(L-R) Ben, me, Claire and Sonia

Our team was trusted by all parties involved in the eviction, so we were able to speak to the councillors, police, and travellers, with access whenever we wanted, while the national newspapers, television and national radio reporters had to wait until we'd got our interviews ahead of them.

At the police press conference, held on site and broadcast live on news channels around the world, I decided to gain a little kudos when I was invited to put my question to the officer in charge ahead of the others: I introduced myself before asking my question, as I'd seen it done at press conferences on the TV… '*Ray Clark, BBC Essex*'. We were playing with the big boys now ...and showing them how it should be done. It was a good feeling.

One year later we were in Gateshead for a huge BBC awards event where *The Ray Clark Breakfast Show* picked up the gold award for the best breakfast show, and this just six months after we'd won a top award at the National Sony event all thanks to taking tea at Dale Farm and the professionalism of our tiny team.

*****

Ocean rowing is now a recognised sporting event, with small teams and individuals attempting to cross the Atlantic via the shortest route, leaving the Canary Islands and arriving in the Caribbean, every January. One of the first crossings resulted in a world record for lone rower and local man Charlie Pitcher. Every day we would make contact with Charlie and chat via satellite phone, taking our audience to a tiny boat in the middle of the Atlantic Ocean.

'*I was standing up last night having a pee in a bucket when I got hit on the back of my head by a flying fish,*' must surely rate as one of the most unusual lines ever heard on a breakfast show. The daily chats and descriptions of events were fascinating, and we certainly played our part in helping Charlie in his efforts. On more than one occasion we were able to offer encouragement when his morale was obviously dangerously low. It would have made great radio had we been able to be there to welcome Charlie and congratulate him on his world record as he rowed ashore in Antigua. We did ask, though sadly our BBC budget wouldn't allow it to happen.

I did manage to take the show to Belfast for the 100th anniversary of the Titanic disaster. We went looking for the Essex links to the ship, and there were surprisingly plenty of them - Marconi wireless, Crittall windows, soft furnishings woven in Braintree, the priest who gave comfort to the doomed passengers came from Ongar. We even had a call from a listener to say his grandfather had packed the jars of Tiptree greengage jam that had been on board – everyone has a story.

The programme was exciting to be a part of, although the subject matter was extremely sad. We'd marked the time it took, from first hitting the iceberg, until the ship sank. It took just less than three hours so our listeners were able to follow the tragic timeline of this horrendous disaster. We finished the show on a very poignant note with the voices of the survivors, mixed with actual recordings of the huge ship's horn as she departed from Southampton one hundred years earlier.

My producer on this occasion, June, had previously lived and worked in Belfast and knew most of those working within the BBC in the province. So, we were able to access many of their guests, including a man who had recently seen the wreck of the ship from one of the few submersibles capable of diving to such depths. As producer June and I left our hotel for a walk to Broadcasting House at 4am in the middle of Belfast, I was aware that this was something we certainly wouldn't have done just a few years earlier during 'The Troubles'.

Things didn't always go as we'd planned them. Of course, taking the breakfast show to the newly rebuilt Broomfield Hospital in Chelmsford for the Christmas Eve programme was a good idea, but despite testing our equipment a few days earlier, when we arrived at 5am we experienced huge technical issues. The walls of the building were very thick and lined with steel, making it practically impossible to move within the building and still get a signal back to our radio car. With minutes to spare before the start of the show we had to move to the main reception and invite, persuade, or cajole our guests, including busy doctors and staff to make their way to us, rather than us going to them.

We got away with it, but only just. I'd also invited the Salvation Army Band to join us to play outside the entrance doors during the show. We thought it would make a lovely festive touch for staff, patients, and visitors to the hospital, but here was our next problem. It had been snowing overnight and the outside temperature was way below freezing, so we invited the musicians inside the building. However, as they struck up 'God Rest Ye Merry Gentlemen' with great gusto, nobody could hear themselves think, let alone speak. The atrium was so cavernous that their instruments echoed throughout the hospital. I had to quickly lead them back out into the cold – but because we were using just one live broadcast microphone, I couldn't tell them why I was throwing them out, especially as I'd only just invited them in! But we needed them to move, and quickly; as they were causing chaos within the corridors of the hospital. I had to beckon the musicians outside with a series of hand gestures, waves, pointing and smiles, resulting in an erratic fast march while they continued to play their hearts out. What troopers they were!

I'd experienced a similar problem with a poor signal before, during my early days at BBC Essex, when I was presenting the *Drivetime* show.

The decision for the City of London to host the 2012 Olympics was to be announced on 6th July, and the day before I suggested that should the winning bid come from London we should present the programme from Stratford station, close to the proposed Olympic site. Having got the go ahead, a colleague did a quick return journey by train to check that our equipment, which was mobile phone based, would work, and it did, quite satisfactorily. So, as the announcement was made I rushed off to present my show from a station platform at Stratford. This time though the station was incredibly busy, unlike the quiet period when the tests had been carried out. The evening rush had started and now, with continuous interference from electric trains passing through the station and the vastly increased number of calls on the mobile network, it was impossible to get a signal back to base.

London Transport came to our rescue, just in time, as they offered an 'ISDN line' (a special, quality telephone line) which enabled a clear signal to be sent from my microphone to the Chelmsford studio once it was plugged in. The problem was the lead on my microphone and portable mixer was little more than a metre in length, and this lead had to be plugged into a wall socket. I had to present the whole programme sitting on the floor at the feet of the ticket office staff while they were selling tickets. I had no view of the outside world and no guests to speak to. It must have been the first time a BBC programme had been broadcast from a London Transport ticket office floor, yet the hundreds of customers buying their tickets were completely unaware of what was going on below the counter. Our listeners had little idea either, they wouldn't have believed me had I tried to tell them.

Both the hospital and the station broadcasts were reminiscent of the day I broadcast live from Ladies Day at Newmarket Races while I was at Radio Cambridgeshire. Our team got all dressed up for a very special day at the races, the ladies in their finery, the guys, including me, suited and booted. We had lots of guests lined up, top jockeys, bookies, punters, and plenty of listeners and our pre-programme technical tests had been fine. I was really looking forward to a stress-free afternoon, speaking to happy people on a delightful mid-summer afternoon. All was good until thirty minutes before we were due on air, when '*VOOM*' our miniscule FM radio signal was obliterated as the huge link transmitter fired up within the giant Channel 4 TV outside broadcast truck next to our radio car and began beaming its signal via a giant satellite dish.

My easy afternoon soon changed. I was now having to

record interviews on a cassette machine and run to our newly repositioned radio car, way down the racecourse, where our signal wasn't affected, in between every song. I ran further, and possibly faster than many of the winners on that beautiful July afternoon.

Now sitting quite comfortably as the breakfast show ringmaster at BBC Essex and with a mixture of light and shade and plenty of humour, *'Planet Ray'* took on life as we saw it and we were on a roll - our hard work had certainly paid off when it came to winning awards. Within one year we were nominated for the top industry accolades, a Sony award, the BBC Local Radio award for best breakfast show and the regional news programme of the year in the EDF awards.

Lots of Men in Suits - another BBC Essex awards night
(L-R) John Mac, Chris Woodward, me, James Melley,
Gerald Main - the Boss, Richard Smith

The popularity of the *Breakfast show* continued with praise from all quarters. I was shown an email from one of the BBC big bosses saying how much he'd enjoyed listening to Ray's breakfast show which was handled in just the right way as the audience returned to work on a cold winter's morning after enjoying their long Christmas break: *"I think it's fair to say that Ray is one of the top 10 breakfast presenters in the country,"* the quotation read. I was happy with that.

The praise continued later in the year when the show was the subject of a very positive review in the *Guardian* newspaper – *'constantly evolving'* they said – I think that's positive.

Throughout my career I've won several top awards. In television or film your value rockets if you are an award winner, but certainly in my experience, with radio you seldom get to see any benefits, either financially or in terms of job security. Radio is a very precarious business to be a part of and, on reflection, perhaps I should now receive one final award for survival within a very competitive landscape. That said, I am proud of the awards that I've won over the years, and they decorate my home studio walls nicely.

Good as we were, occasionally things happened that really shouldn't have. I had several humorous recorded inserts - production pieces, similar to jingles, that I would play out at appropriate times – they were silly recordings and clips that I had acquired. One was a recording from my young grandson's toy police car: *'Let's get going!'* it shouted, and it was ideal to help the morning commute along. Another was the hook from a chart song by The Hoosiers, 'I'm Seriously Worried about Ray'. The clips were on hot keys, buttons on the playout system keyboard that could be pressed to play the clip immediately. Now, a few years back TV chef Delia Smith appeared to have enjoyed an evening in the director's box at Norwich City Football Club – the team were struggling, and Delia decided they, and the Canary's fans, needed some encouragement, so she took over the public address system with a very enthusiastic pep talk. The clip was funny, and I added it to my collection, which was fine, except on the morning when we were playing a heartfelt plea from a grieving mother for the person responsible for the murder of her daughter to give himself up to the police. Unbelievably, and just at the worst possible moment, the pile of daily newspapers placed alongside me slowly started to slide towards the floor, via the keyboard controls, hitting, of all the possible keys, the one for Delia's rant. As the poor mum sobbed, Delia shouted, *'Where are you, let's be having you! Come on we need you, are you with us?'* I was mortified and threw myself at the fader to shut Delia up – I still shudder now when I think about it.

Something else that made me shudder when it came around on a yearly basis was *Children In Need*, the BBC's annual national charity event. Each local radio station was expected to take part in locally organised events based on top television shows and each programme presenter was enlisted. *Strictly come Dancing* was the chosen theme that saw me taking dancing lessons every Sunday evening. I think I was taught Waltz, Cha Cha Cha and Samba … and I still haven't any idea how to do any of them, despite three months worth of weekly lessons.

The night came, I was dressed in my hired tuxedo, at a disadvantage already because of my height, and here I was, competing with my colleagues, all of them taller than me, including the females. The event was held in Chelmsford's County Hall, a grand Victorian building with a wonderful dance floor; it had been the scene of glamorous balls and parties throughout its history. As my dancing partner, who knew what to do, and I were introduced, the crowd cheered with encouragement, the music started and I led my partner to the dancefloor…where I started on the wrong foot and then completely forgot which steps followed. My performance was awful. But the crowd loved it, they cheered, they cat called and they laughed. My boss gave me eleven out of ten for my efforts. I have a DVD of my performance that night, I have never been brave enough to watch it.

Nearly as embarrassing was *'Chelmsford's Got Talent'*, performing on a stage in the city centre in front of more than 5,000 shoppers, there to see the Christmas lights switched on. Various programme teams from BBC Essex performed their version of a well known song, competing against each other. The breakfast 'lads' went for the Queen song, 'We Will Rock You.' We weren't very good. I dressed as Elvis to avoid recognition. Local guy Lee Mead was the judge. We didn't win.

Elvis sings...Queen? (L-R Richard Smith, Elvis, Lee Mead, Ben Fryer

******

I loved producing documentaries, starting with a huge reel of unused recording tape that weeks later would contain a complete programme. Putting together a story lasting one hour would take many more hours of painstaking editing. Of course, nowadays there is no reel of tape, it's all digitally recorded, but the principle is the same.

I would think of a theme that interested me and come up with documentaires such as *Scream If You Want To Go Faster*, featuring the music of the travelling fair, *Where's Weeley?*, the story of a unique pop festival. *Up at Crays Hill*, about the huge travellers site and several others. I enjoyed producing programmes like this much more than the day-to-day news-based programme.

One small idea took off across the entire BBC local radio network. *My Beatles Story* coincided with the 50th anniversary of the release of the Beatles first hit single 'Love Me Do'. It was a brilliant idea – if only it had been mine! But it was my wife, Shelley, who lit the spark that eventually saw it become a *Beatles Day* across the country. As with all the best features it grew from a simple idea.

I was visiting my mum at her home and a neighbour of hers approached me: "You're Ray on the radio aren't you."

It wasn't a question, more a statement. My standard reply when I'm unsure of what's coming next is, *"I might be, why's that then?*

"Well," said the guy, "I've been on a Beatles album."

So, how do you respond to a statement like that?

I looked puzzled as he continued: "You know that double red and blue LP with all their hits on, well I'm one of the kids in the photograph on the sleeve."

He went on to tell me how he and a group of his childhood friends had been playing in a park in north London when The Beatles and a photographer drew up in a car and took pictures of them. He then went on to name the rest of the children.

"What a brilliant story, when can I interview you?" was my immediate response.

A feature to celebrate fifty years of the most famous band in the world was spot on for BBC local radio's target audience; every single listener had grown up with the band. Fortunately, my boss loved the idea of gathering stories from listeners who had met, or had dealings with, the Beatles and together we travelled to Manchester to give a presentation to his fellow station chiefs from across England.

The stories were just waiting there to be discovered, and after my presentation most of the editors signed up to the idea and ran with it, appreciating how simple it was and how their station could benefit from having a fun, music-based feature on air. Amazingly, a few of their number gave the impression of never having heard of The Beatles and looked down their noses at the very idea. But *My Beatles Story* was marked across BBC Local Radio on 12th October 2012, backed up with TV promotion, and for the stations that joined in it was a great success. Simply by asking on air, *"Did you ever meet the Beatles?"* I found a wealth of 'Fab Gear' stories. *"I served John and Yoko tea in bed in the Amsterdam Hilton"* - *"I was their bodyguard when they were filming A Hard Day's Night"* - *"I went to school with Paul McCartney and I've got a portrait drawn by Macca"* - *"I sat on Paul McCartney's knee in Hull"* - *"I travelled to school with John on the bus and was at the Rose Fete in 1957 when Lennon and McCartney met"*. We even found John Lennon's first teenage girlfriend.

Unfortunately, I'd failed to keep the contact details of a listener who'd called me several years earlier, when I was at Radio Cambridgeshire. He was the man who claimed to have called the police when the Beatles performed live on the rooftop of their Apple offices in Savile Row. *"How could anyone work with that row going on?"* he asked. I don't think he was a fan of the Fab Four - That was the one that got away!

*****

In 2018 I was honoured to be invited to become the President of my local RNLI Lifeboat. Living on the coast, I have always been a fan and some years earlier I was asked to help with a campaign to raise money for a special floating lifeboat house. I also enjoy a walk, so I decided to link every lifeboat house in Essex by walking the coast, well at least part of it, and tying it in with the breakfast show.

Starting at Harwich on Monday morning, after presenting the show, I walked on to Walton-on-The-Naze, a much longer walk than it looked on a map. Next day, after the show I took a more gentle five mile stroll to Clacton. The next stage was more difficult.

Had I set out to walk from Clacton to the next station at West

Mersea, then I would probably still be walking now. So a boat trip was needed.

Essex Police offered to help by ferrying me to Mersea Island and then, after an overnight stop and another breakfast show, they took me on the next stage to Southend.

The next morning I left the guest house and headed for the lifeboat station, ready to present the breakfast show from the Lifeboat House. I noticed that the wind had increased considerably and, as 9am approached, I looked for the Essex Police motor launch called Alert that I was waiting for. Moored alongside the jetty was a completely different craft - the Essex Police fast response rib, complete with two huge outboard motors. This was not what I was expecting.

"It's too rough for the boat, how fit are you?" asked the skipper.

"Reasonably, for a guy in his fifties," I replied as I attempted to get into a very tight rubber wetsuit. Our journey to Southend was via the longest possible route due to the low tide.

Helping Essex Police Marine Unit with their enquiries

As we headed out into the shipping lanes of the Thames estuary the sea was getting rougher as the wind increased. The three man crew and me, all holding on tightly as we bounced and crashed over the rises and into the troughs of the choppy sea, were all thinking this was a silly idea. Fortunately, as we made the final approach to Southend pier, the wind was behind us and we zoomed over the water surface at a speed I'd never experienced before on water. It really was breath-taking.

We were all glad to reach our destination, where we enjoyed a warm drink, and in my case, a change of soaking wet socks. The final stage of the journey, from Southend to my home town of Burnham-on-Crouch, was a far more leisurely experience, starting with a gentle seven mile stroll and finishing with a short river crossing to take me home after raising a considerable sum for the RNLI too.

I get bored easily, I need to have a project to keep my mind busy, and I was getting very few new challenges. Trying to understand the latest reasoning of BBC management further up the chain was difficult, you were never told what the present way of thinking was, although most of the time I could sense change, and sometimes throttled back on the fun bits or got more serious with the heavy bits, but it was always a guessing game. I was nominated for another BBC internal award for Best Presenter, but between the nomination and the judging period, I'd detected a distinct change of direction of BBC local radio programming, swerving sharply back towards harder news. So when the presentation evening came my entry felt at odds with the order of the day - I was still very pleased to win a bronze award though.

With every appraisal I was getting a good report and the inevitable question would always be asked, *"Where do you see yourself going within the BBC?"* My response was always the same: *"Where **can** I go?* I recognised that I was presenting one of the biggest local radio station breakfast shows in the country with good audience figures and winning awards. There was no other logical answer to the question. I was unlikely to be offered a position on any of the BBC's national radio services because of my age, or sex. I'd contacted a producer of documentaries at Radio 4 who invited me for a chat at Broadcasting House. He was very nice. We had a great meeting where he asked about my ideas and promised that he'd get back in touch and I'm still waiting. I do accept that I should have done more earlier to further my career and promote myself, I've been almost apologetic about my abilities and ambitions, and seldom pushed for opportunities and I do recognise that I've been very lucky to get to do the things that I have, but maybe I should have refused to take no for an answer more often... that's assuming I was brave enough to ask in the first place.

Ironically, whenever I'm asked for advice by prospective broadcasters I always tell them: *'Whatever you do, follow your dream and never, ever take no for an answer.'* Wise words, if only I'd listened to them. I recently read a tweet from a guy who'd applied for more than 200 jobs within the BBC and was rightly thrilled when he, at last, was offered a position. How brave. My very outdated style was to run and hide if ever I received a rejection letter. That said, I have been very lucky over the years and received very few rejections, but maybe that's because I didn't apply for many jobs!

Chapter Twenty-Two

"You Can Check Out Anytime You Want, But You Can Never Leave"

Until recently, an annual Radio Day event was held in Amsterdam, celebrating the history of the offshore radio stations. It was always a wonderful event to attend and a chance to meet up with former offshore colleagues and friends. Many former pirates would fly in for the event from Britain and Ireland to join their Dutch counterparts. A meal with invited guests was held after a day of reminiscing and serious 'anoraking'. A few days after the event in 2012, the pleasant weekend was still on my mind as I travelled to Lakeside Shopping Centre to meet another former colleague from the Breeze days, Peter Stewart, who, like me, was now working for the BBC and was based in Guildford.

Peter was also an author, having written several books about journalism, and I suppose, as I killed time waiting for him to arrive for our lunch, the thought of books was on my mind. With time on my hands I visited the three shops that guys usually aim for in a shopping centre: Currys electrical goods, The Apple Shop and finally Waterstones, the book shop.

As I browsed through the thousands of volumes, I was searching for books about radio. There were very few: *The Story of The Archers*, a book about Radio 4 and *The Goon Show Scripts...* and that was it. No books about music radio, and certainly none about offshore radio and the part that it had played in the evolution of European Radio. By the time I'd left the store an idea was formulating.

Having spent an enjoyable afternoon catching up on all the radio gossip, something we'd both been quite good at whilst working together at Essex Radio, my mind kept returning to the thought of books, and in particular a topic that I knew something about, the history of Radio Caroline. It also occurred to me that the 50th anniversary of the radio station was just 18 months away.

I have kept copies of many interviews that I've made, though sadly not all of them, but I did still have my interviews with the original Caroline DJ's and by the time I got home I had a new project. I was going to write a book.

I knew very little about writing books, I guessed that I needed a publisher, so I emailed a few top name publishing houses that were responsible for the books on my bookshelf. Maybe I'd set my sights high with the likes of Macmillan and Penguin, but to my surprise, I received replies to the six or so emails that I'd sent.

All of them declined to take me on, but all had a similar message: It's a good topic, but it's not for us. I've often thought that things happen for a reason, and just a couple of days later I was interviewing a local author about a book that he'd written for The History Press. While chatting to him on air and flicking through the pages of his latest book my mind was ticking over. *The History Press, they do history,* I thought - although it usually involved Kings and Queens. But my reasoning was that Caroline had been around for sometime, so I sent them an email about my idea for my book. Within the week, I'd signed up to write the book, and better still, I was to get a generous advance – I felt like a proper author. The book was published in March 2014, just days before the anniversary of Radio Caroline's first broadcast. It has now gone to a second, updated edition and continues to sell in reasonable numbers. I'm very proud of it.

*****

I had been presenting the *Breakfast Show* for seven years, getting up each day at 3.15am. Even though I was presenting one of the biggest BBC Local Radio breakfast shows I still doubted my abilities - though they had long since been proven. I feared that I might be sounding tired on air and would ask myself daily - *'Was I really on the ball and as sharp as I had been?'* Nobody had remarked that I might be past my sell by date, and on reflection I'm sure it was just in my mind and another example of my self doubt, but there'd also been an announcement from the latest Director General of the BBC, that he wanted more female presenters on local radio breakfast shows.

The BBC management have always had a way of unnerving presenters, even if it's not their intention. I started to give my position far more thought than I should have done, but I soon found that this was not the best time to have doubts about my ability.

I had a good relationship with my boss Gerald, I liked him, we worked well together, but I'd remembered his words when I first took on the breakfast show: *"Can we both agree that if ever you want to leave breakfast, or I want to replace you then we'll give each other at least one year's notice?"* I was happy with that, it was fair and I accepted from the start that nothing and nobody is forever, especially when it comes to a gig on the radio.

So, in a corridor conversation just a few days after my summer holiday, I set the ball rolling for my departure from the breakfast show, at some time in the future.

"Good show this morning Ray," said Gerald.

"I try," I replied, with a smile, "but I don't want to be doing this forever."

It was a case of the wrong words, spoken at the wrong time. I assumed that I was setting the clock ticking to my eventual departure from breakfast, twelve months down the line. But success, or otherwise, particularly in radio often depends on being in the right place at the right time, or sometimes the right place at the wrong time. Long surviving national talk show presenter James Whale had recently covered a few BBC Essex shifts. He'd been without a job for sometime, and was very keen to become a more regular contributor. I saw the flash of lightning that went through Gerald's mind as we chatted: *Ray wants out, James needs a job.* I'm sure he could see the headline there and then, '*BBC Local hires top commercial radio shock jock.*' Within days I was asked what show I wanted to present when I gave up breakfast at the end of the year, about three months away. That wasn't quite how I'd planned it.

Inadvertently, I'd set off a whole chain of events over a short period: James took on breakfast and it didn't work out, his style was popular with some, but the audience figures dropped dramatically and continued to slide for some time. He eventually left and returned to a national commercial station. I took on the afternoon show, no longer working with a team, quickly became incredibly bored and surprised everyone, including myself, when I announced that I would retire on my 60th birthday.

And that was it! The end of my radio career. I'd had 30 years of doing my dream job and for most of that time I'd been very happy. The End.

*****

Monday June 23rd 2014 was the first day of my retirement. The sun was shining beautifully as I went to the cash machine and saw more money in my current account than I'd ever had before. Not a huge amount in the great scheme of things, but it was the tax-free part of my small BBC pension.

Those first few days of not having to be anywhere in particular, or having to do anything for anyone else unless I wanted to, were really quite special. But within days I was back on the radio.

I presented a couple of shows for a chum of mine who was running a short-term radio station in a garden centre near Aylesbury – I did it 'cos I could, it was very enjoyable, but also great because it was only for a two-day period – and I didn't have to do it.

But now it was time to take holidays and spend time with my wife as I began to enjoy what would become a whole year off – my gap year.

Then came the call: *"Would you like to do a weekly show on Caroline?"*

I was on a bike ride across the marshes close to where I live, and where Peter Moore, the man responsible for running Radio Caroline has a workshop. Yes, the station name had survived, as had Radio Caroline, against all odds, but it was very different to the Caroline that I'd worked on almost 30 years earlier.

No longer broadcasting from a ship, and no longer operating as a 'pirate,' it was now broadcasting legally via the internet. This wasn't the first time that 'PM' had asked me to join the team, but although I was attracted to the idea, I had retired and was enjoying my free time too much to give commitment to a regular radio programme. It took Peter almost a year to persuade me to sign up to the radio station where I'd started my broadcasting career. *'You can checkout any time you like, but you can never leave,'* That's not just a line from the wonderful 'Hotel California' by The Eagles, it also perfectly summed up the position of most of those who have ever been involved with Radio Caroline,

I have a home studio that is well equipped, though rather dated, it's much of the old CR3 (Control Room) from Essex Radio. A year or so before GWR had taken over at Southend the entire studio complex was refitted and I acquired the Air 2000 mixing desk. It was all official, nobody else had expressed an interest in it. Now, this desk and all the other necessary equipment essential for a radio studio had been professionally fitted into an adapted section of my garage at home.

So I returned to Radio Caroline, presenting a weekly three-hour show, recorded in my back garden. I joked then, as I do now, that I was doing my community service, and this was payback for the career that I'd had since I started on Caroline. I think I have levelled that debt by now.

Around the same time, I was in conversation with the publisher of my Radio Caroline book, which continued to sell well. They were keen on me writing another book, and I offered them a couple of ideas that had originated as documentaries on the radio. They loved the idea of the Weeley Festival, so once again I was writing 70,000-plus words for my next book.

As always, I jump headlong into any idea that excites me, long before I think about the logistics of the challenge, and in this case whether I had any photographs of the Weeley event. You quickly learn as an author that there really isn't much money to be made, unless perhaps you are JK Rowling or Jeffrey Archer, so the art is to hang onto as much of any advance payment as you can. With my first book about Radio Caroline, I'd spent nearly all of my advance payment on photographic rights as I wanted to do it properly, but for the next book I quickly learnt to haggle with photo agencies.

At the time of my retirement from the BBC, there had been a suggestion that I might be called to cover the occasional shift, but no call came, so I'd mentally written that possibility off, until I received an unexpected call from the soon-to-be new Editor at BBC Essex.

There came a very heartening and interesting proposition: "Hello, I'm Lou, the new boss and I'd like you back regularly on the station."

How could I possibly refuse? I returned to the BBC presenting a weekly, two-hour show on Saturday mornings. Just enough to satisfy my need for talk radio, but with a few tunes included. It was good to meet up with a few of those that I'd worked with a year or so before.

So there I was working for the BBC and Radio Caroline and still occasionally reporting for KDKA. I'm still their 'sort of' UK correspondent, so if a news story breaks in the UK that's of interest to the Americans, then I get a call. Invariably it's about Royalty or the government – so I suppose I can legitimately say that I'm the political and royal correspondent for KDKA.

Although I had re-joined Radio Caroline just to present a weekly show, I found myself getting embroiled in more of the station's output when a link was established with Manx Radio, the national radio station of The Isle of Man.

Back at The BBC – again – BBC Essex

Back in the sixties Caroline's northern ship had broadcast from a position off Ramsey on the island's east coast and a loyal friendship between the station and the island's inhabitants had formed. Now, following negotiations with the Manx team, Caroline was offered a couple of days broadcast time, which consisted of interviews with former Caroline North presenters and a few specialist shows. I was involved with one of them, looking back at the history of Radio Caroline in the sixties and its links with the self-governing British dependency, The Isle of Man.

The audience response from the broadcasts was very good and an invitation was extended to broadcast monthly Caroline shows, via the powerful medium wave transmitter of Manx Radio. With its huge radio mast on the highest point of the island at Foxdale, the broadcasts were easily audible throughout North-West England, Southwest Scotland, North

Wales, Northern Ireland and The Isle of Man. The plan was for the programmes to come directly from the Caroline ship, Ross Revenge, now safely at anchor in the River Blackwater, just a few miles from my home, and then to be relayed to the island. Before the broadcasts started, nobody was sure if an internet signal could successfully be sent from the ship, but surprisingly, the system that was devised worked very well and compared with Caroline's historical method of broadcasting, was remarkably simple.

You can check out any time you want, but you can never leave. Ross Revenge, River Blackwater

Using mobile phone technology, the output from the ship was sent to the Caroline land-based studio in Strood, Kent using a dongle attached to the ship's funnel. From the land based studio the programmes were sent via the internet around the world, including Douglas IOM where it was then sent to the Manx medium wave transmitter. A team of Caroline presenters, including Kevin Turner, Johnny Lewis, Dave Foster and myself boarded the ship and set up a temporary home as we returned to our roots. Once again, the ship came alive to pop music from the 60s, 70s and 80s, played from the studio onboard. These monthly live broadcasts from the ship are ongoing. Hundreds of paying visitors have regularly been welcomed aboard Ross Revenge and given guided tours with a genuine flavour of the pirate days when all Caroline programmes came from the ship. Other former Caroline presenters regularly return to the ship, including TV hypnotist, Paul McKenna, whose career started on the ship in the eighties.

Radio Caroline was eventually awarded an AM licence to broadcast, by Ofcom, it was only fifty years late, but the interest in Radio Caroline was still such that the national media became involved, and an interviewee was needed for a news feature to be recorded onboard by *ITV News*. As I was living nearest to the ship, I got the job.

"Will Caroline change now that she has a licence?" I was asked.

"I don't think it'll change, but hey, even Jack Sparrow adapted." I replied.

August 14th 2017 marked the 50th anniversary of Caroline becoming an outlaw and the wheel had turned full circle, Radio Caroline and its broadcasts were now 100% legal. A live broadcast from Ross Revenge was heard on all the Caroline frequencies, plus Manx Radio and, amazingly, BBC Essex, something that could never have been envisaged 50 years earlier, and to be honest, still quite surprising in 2017.

The programme featured the story of all the offshore stations, including Caroline, that had broadcast since August 1967 to date, condensed into a 60-minute programme. BBC Essex provided a producer to assist with the programme, and perhaps as a safeguard to prevent us saying rude things about the BBC - which we would never have done. My former BBC breakfast show producer Claire volunteered to do the job and spent 24 hours onboard Ross Revenge.

As all those on the ship congregated for lunch in the messroom Claire asked, "Am I the first *female producer* that Caroline has ever had?"

Everyone turned towards her in disbelief: "You're the first *producer* that Caroline has ever had," I informed her and we all laughed heartily.

National television coverage from BBC Breakfast, ITV and Sky News marked the anniversary of the Marine etc Broadcasting (Offences) Act 1967, and the radio station that had refused to close down 50 years earlier was once again making the headlines. Interestingly, had Caroline been given a licence to broadcast 50 years earlier it's perhaps unlikely that anyone would even remember it now. The fact that the radio station continued was due to the government of the day having an insane hatred of commercial radio. If Radio Caroline, Radio London and Radio 390 had been granted a licence then, many believe we would be in no worse a place than we are now, with a handful of national commercial radio stations and the same programmes broadcast on scores of local relays. The only difference is the growing number of small community radio stations around the country.

Now, with a licence to broadcast on 648 khz, Caroline had negotiated the use of a huge 300-foot mast at Orford Ness on the Suffolk coast, a remote stretch of land bordering the North Sea and just three miles from the original anchorage of Radio Caroline's first ship in 1964. This redundant radio installation had been part of a secret radar development site, built by the British Government and latterly the home of powerful transmitters for the World Service broadcasts operated by the BBC, and now it was to be home to Radio Caroline. How things had changed.

The first official broadcast via this installation was relayed from the ship just a few days before Christmas 2017. I was on air at midday and marked the event with a few words about the struggles that Radio Caroline had endured over the years as we officially opened the service at noon, though, as is always the case with Caroline, we quickly returned to playing music.

Chapter Twenty-Three

"In Too Deep"

It was always radio that had excited me and although several BBC local radio friends, mainly journalists, had moved onto television over the years, I'd never given TV much thought. But some years ago a memo advertising a temporary posting to *Look East*, the BBC local news programme caught my attention. Thinking it would be a fun thing to try for, and thinking that it might be a way to get some of my documentary ideas onto television, I made an attempt at an audition tape. Fortunately, it never got any further. It was dreadful. My colleague, Tom, was given the task of operating the camera while I reported on a fictitious story. I was rubbish and my attempt, especially for someone who has found it so easy to ad-lib, was embarrassingly bad. I hope, and trust that the video of my audition no longer exists.

However, TV did come knocking in a very strange twist of events, after my 'retirement.' I received a phone call from a television production company based in Leeds who wanted to ask about the Weeley Festival and knowing that I had written a book about it, they decided I was the man to contact. Over the years I've helped a few TV and newspaper reporters by passing on contacts and helping with research, but this time I became the presenter of the entire feature that they had planned, appearing on *The One Show* on BBC One TV. I don't think having me as the presenter was their original idea, but I was becoming more involved with the project every time they called during the research stage.

I returned to Weeley on a beautiful day in May 2019 and spent the day filming with several local people who remembered the festival together with Ray Dorset, lead singer of Mungo Jerry, one of the bands that were present at the original event and my school friend Alan, who had journeyed with me to the festival in 1971.

Filming for The One Show, Weeley

Nobody actually asked me in advance if I'd present the ten-minute piece, it just happened that I became the one in front of the camera and doing the interviews – well, if you're going to start a belated television career, what better place to kick it off than on primetime BBC One? I certainly knew much about this quirky music festival, but I suspect the reason they really chose me to present it was the cost. I was certainly cheaper than Rod Stewart, who'd appeared on stage at the original festival. Anyway, they were pleased, I was thrilled, it was good fun, but sadly this wasn't to be the start of a new career – they've not been back since!

Any chance of a lasting retirement was blown away when

I started getting requests to give talks about my career and Radio Caroline. I really enjoy chatting - you might have noticed! Groups such as U3A and retirement clubs seem keen to pay me to attend for a couple of hours and talk about myself, a task that I've not found too difficult. When I was working full time, I would refuse any payment, but I did learn a lesson some years back. A local lady that I'd known since I was a child approached me and asked if I'd give a talk to a local group. I agreed and when she asked what I'd charge I told her the cost would be a packet of ginger biscuits. When the day of the talk came, I walked into the hall expecting to see a dozen or so members of the WI, but I was confronted with 300 ladies, all dressed up for the occasion and anticipating an interesting talk. Apparently, this was an area conference, and as I soon learned, the budget for the speaker was far greater than the cost of a packet of biscuits. *"We'd like to thank Ray for his generosity in refusing the usual fee for such an event, it's a very generous gesture and I'd like to give this cheque for £300 toward the fund for a PA system at the church."* I smiled broadly as I caught the eye of my wife looking on, both of us thinking what we could have done with an extra £300.

I leave all my financial affairs to my wife now.

The Caroline North live broadcasts from Ross Revenge, via Manx Radio, had now become a regular monthly event, with a team of former Radio Caroline presenters, most of whom had served aboard the radio ship in the 1980s. The journey out to the River Blackwater mooring now took just 30 minutes, with a far more comfortable passage, although it became a standing joke with crew and listeners that the wind would always get up when Ray was due onboard. Although anchored just half a mile from shore, there are still occasional wind and tide conditions that make the old ship move around a bit, just for old times sake.

The ship itself has a wonderful history and one that I find fascinating. Visitors can book on board guided tours and I love to act as tour guide, mixing stories of radio and fish, fishermen and disc jockeys. Who would have thought of such a combination of tales. Recently a charitable trust has been set up to raise enough money to preserve, not only the world's last remaining, authentic, operational offshore broadcasting vessel, but also the *'Rolls Royce'* of the British fishing fleet. Although Ross Revenge became hopelessly obsolete as a fishing vessel following the decline of the deep water fleet after the 1970s cod wars, she is still very much intact. Much of the original fishing equipment survives. When the trawler, the largest of her kind, was converted to become a radio ship, a policy of, if it's not in the way it stays, was followed. I have become fascinated with the history of this wonderful vessel, with her beautiful lines, taking time to research her fishing history and talking to the men who served on her. She would regularly break records. as she sailed out of Grimsby to some of the most inhospitable seas in the world doing what she was originally designed to do, catch fish. The wonderfully friendly team at the Grimsby Fishing Heritage Centre are rightly proud of their surviving trawler, Ross Tiger, but I think they're just a little jealous that Caroline has the Revenge, still afloat in open waters. Restoration of Ross Revenge will take several million pounds. I hope enough money is raised before the rust can take her.

Listening to Caroline North was reminiscent of the hugely successful 558 service from the eighties. The regular team included Peter Philips, the original programme controller from that period: Kevin Turner, Dave Foster, Johnny Lewis, and me. With a format of pop and rock hit songs from the 60s, 70s, 80s and 90s, the programmes were fast-paced and fun to present, with just enough speech giving an insight into events occurring on the ship. But the music seldom stopped – we all enjoyed the opportunity to relive the style of radio that we'd enjoyed so much 30 years earlier and the conversation in the mess room on Ross Revenge often centred on how good a similar format to the 558 days would be if it was available every day.

Peter Moore runs Radio Caroline, we are chums and often chat and enjoy a laugh, but he is extremely protective of the Caroline brand, the ship and all that is associated with the former offshore radio station. Many see him as the guy who has saved Caroline and, without doubt, he's enabled it to have a presence online, on 648AM and on several DAB+ channels across the country, together with the oldies service, *Caroline Flashback*. It's also likely that without Peter's efforts, Ross Revenge may well have made her last voyage to the scrap yard by now. He will often refer to the days when all Caroline consisted of was a wreck of a ship with a large outstanding salvage bill and little else. He is also seen by a few as the man who has no right to operate Radio Caroline – I don't subscribe to that theory, but he would probably acknowledge that he can be a challenging guy to deal with.

I would often meet up with Peter, stopping for a break, as I cycled past his workshop, in the remote part of Essex where I live. We'd often discuss radio and the topic on several occasions had turned to Saint FM, the local community radio station. There had been regular attempts to get a substantial audience since the station first came on air several years earlier, but realistically it was never going to happen. More than once those behind the station had asked Caroline for advice. It had been offered, but it was never acted upon. Although some of those involved with the community station had good intent, in reality it had become a shambles. Often our conversation would turn to 'us' getting more involved, my answer would always be "No."

It was unlike me to be negative, I'm usually up for any challenge, but I could see no good outcome to operating a service that was likely to fail by having to operate within the pages of rules and regulations demanded by Ofcom. It was a radio station run by volunteers who, although very willing, had no idea what they were doing, and worse, it was broadcasting to fields, the signal barely making it into the surrounding villages. *"Don't touch it,"* I'd advised, on more than one occasion, but it was plain to see that Peter was hooked on the idea and could see the possibility of an FM radio station dangling before his eyes.

When the community radio licence for the existing area, plus an extension to include the largest town in the district, Maldon, was due to be re-advertised, Peter asked again, *"Shall we go for it as 'Three Rivers Radio'?"*

Again, my answer was no, even though this licence would cover the area that Doug King had dreamed of broadcasting to, back in 1971, as *'Painter Doug's Dream - Radio Maldon.'* I had also suggested a similar area to The Radio Authority in 1990 when I wrote a 'letter of intent' at a time when I thought a truly local radio station for the area might be viable. There were two applications for the area with the incumbent group regaining the licence to broadcast, but in their efforts to win they'd made near impossible promises of performance in their application that even the BBC would find difficult to fulfil. Having won the licence, they promptly closed down, their plan was to regroup, but it was obvious that they would never return to the air unless they had some serious help.

Paramount in Peter's interest in the licence was his idea of giving the main Caroline album service a platform on FM. Ofcom had allowed Saint FM to use Caroline as an overnight sustaining service in the past and he could see an opportunity to get more Caroline output broadcast in quality. We'd spoken about the possibility of this happening, but from the outset I told him that, in my opinion, the album service wasn't suitable for a community station in this area. If a small local radio station was to have any chance of getting an audience, it would have to use a format of well-known songs, as the often-obscure album tracks that the main service of Caroline were playing was hardly conducive to building an audience of 'non-Caroline' listeners. I suggested that the *Caroline Flashback* service might be better suited, but it might need some adjustment.

Ofcom rules state that any community radio station had two

years from the granting of a licence to start broadcasting, but the newly renamed Crystal FM was showing no sign of life. The equipment was stored on a local houseboat, and there it was likely to remain. Now, whilst it's not possible to buy a community radio licence, existing directors can invite new blood onto the board of the not for profit, limited company who hold the licence.

Two Caroline friendly local residents, of which I was one, were encouraged to join St Peters Studio and Community Radio Ltd, the licensed company, with a view to getting a community radio station for the Maldon area back on the air. A further Caroline friendly director was already on the board... all perfectly proper and legal.

I'd been persuaded to sign up, even though I was convinced that the radio station would never return to the air, and for months that looked likely. An expedition with three cars was mounted to remove the delicate electrical equipment from the houseboat and put it into further storage - under a tarpaulin, covering another boat stored in a barn. Apart from that, nothing happened.

Although a truly local radio station for the area where I'd grown up was something I had dreamed about since I was a child, I was now in my sixties and enjoying retirement and doing just a little radio to keep my interest, but already the warning bells were ringing. I was going to get involved with much of the organisation in getting the thing on the air if I wasn't careful, and so it came to be.

Early in 2020, the licence was just three months away from the deadline to get on air and Ofcom would soon expect to hear the radio station broadcasting. I was a director – it had my name on it - and failure wasn't an option. Against my better judgement, I'd been drawn in and reached the point of no return.

I'd read the original application form over and over, looking for a way to make the ridiculous promises written by the applicants workable, until I believed I'd found the way ahead.

Many community radio stations have failed; indeed, Saint FM was all but one of them, the reason was obvious, they seldom offered a genuine reason to listen. Yes, they were staffed by willing volunteers who had a passion for all things local, and there's certainly nothing wrong with that. But it was the lack of direction and knowledge of the way radio works and why listeners are attracted to the output that was lacking. Why would anyone want to listen to a radio station operated by amateurs with good intent, but little idea of what they were doing? Whilst there are some very good community radio presenters, others have no idea, although it's not their fault, they just have no-one to guide them.

It was obvious that if this radio station had any hope of survival, it needed a strict structure, and although 84 hours of locally produced programming was expected to be broadcast every week, the Ofcom commitments didn't specify at what time of day this local content should be heard. During the evening was the obvious place for the truly local, community output to be broadcast.

Safe, or so I thought, in the knowledge that the former Saint FM transmitter would never be fired up again, I went along with Peter's 'what if' questions. Who was I to discourage a man's dreams? The daytime period from 6am to 6pm had to be filled, and as I was local, experienced, and already involved, it looked like I would be presenting the breakfast show, at least initially.

The possibility of Caroline providing the daytime output had been the topic of conversation between myself, Peter Philips, and Johnny Lewis. All three of us expressed a wish to work on a radio station with a format like the 80s version of Radio Caroline. The suggestion was put to Peter Moore that a third Caroline service, with a format along these lines, could give listeners another choice of programmes from a Caroline station. Peter Moore was certainly not in favour, suggesting a tie up with the existing *Caroline Flashback*, but with presenter presence as the way forward, thus becoming the sustaining service that was needed. But this idea was unacceptable to Peter Philips who had offered to programme the music for the new service. While conversations about the sound of the, as yet, non-existent radio station continued, the need to get something on the air became more urgent, and we also needed a budget. I came up with an idea.

"What if I can find a few people to 'lend' the project £1,500 each on the understanding that they'll never see their cash again, then we can finance it?" – and then, one more of the most bonkers things I've ever heard myself say, *"And I'll put in £1,500 to start things off."*

And so it was, I had a new project, with five friends each donating cash. We had the money to start a radio station. The challenge was on to find and equip a studio, although we had much of the original Saint FM studio gear available. Physically building a radio station was the easy bit: Finding premises, arranging internet providers, organising national and local news service, recruiting local presenters. All of those tasks were an enjoyable challenge, and easily fixed.

What I hadn't bargained for was the continuous grief over the format. I became embroiled in a daily battle between two friends, Peter's Moore, and Philips, both with their own idea as to what music the radio station should be playing. This also differed from my own idea of how the station should sound. I quickly learned a huge lesson, trying to keep everyone happy is just not possible, but by now I had become so entangled within the operation of this thing that if I were to walk away I would have upset everyone. However, it came to pass that on Monday October 17th 2020, in the middle of a worldwide coronavirus pandemic, Caroline Community Radio went on the air, and it sounded excellent. But on day one I was already planning my gradual escape.

Emails and calls bombarded me from everyone with an interest in the setup of the radio station, all wanting this tiny radio station to work in a way that suited them, and everyone expected me to have all the answers.

Enough was enough, I realised that I had taken on far more than I was able or prepared to cope with single-handedly. I had not considered the time and commitment I would need to give to this project, not just to get it up and running, but to ensure that it operated in a professional way. Although others were doing their bit, there was nobody else prepared to take care of the day to day running of the 'not for profit' business, especially for no pay.

As Christmas approached, and just two months after the station first came on air, I resigned as a director. The novelty of running a radio station and being involved in its every day development had run its course – and besides, I'd done it all before, I had nothing to prove and I wanted to continue enjoying my retirement.

I eventually extracted myself from the responsibility of running Caroline Community Radio, well almost. I am still sitting in the background and willing to help when I can. The latest plan is to install a relay transmitter to extend and give better coverage to the area. Despite disagreements between friends during the heat of getting the station on air we all still get on, and that's hugely important to me and my links with Radio Caroline continue. Setting up the radio station has given the chance for several volunteers to get involved in radio, in some cases fulfilling lifelong ambitions. One of the youngest volunteers, Josh, is being courted by two national broadcasters, waiting for him to leave school, and is now Radio Caroline's youngest ever presenter.

Chapter Twenty-Four

"Past, Present, Future?"

The disruption caused by covid had affected everyone in some form or another and had caused huge upheaval for many. The BBC introduced extended hours for their regular local radio presenters during the lockdown periods, and that had a knock-on effect on my Saturday show. I was now presenting a two hour programme, broadcast on Sunday evenings that was recorded in my home studio. I was still smarting from the pressures of the community station, my mental wellbeing had also been rattled by a prescribed medicine that I was taking for a medical condition, which I learned later was causing me to doubt my every move and attacking my self confidence even more than usual. Fortunately, after speaking to my doctor I've since dumped this awful drug. It seems the consequences for some were far worse than the effects it had on me.

"That's it, I'll retire properly at the start of the new year," I said to my wife.

"Are you really sure about this?" asked Shelley, who was already worried about my distress and frustration with the community radio station, and my general self-esteem and wellbeing.

But I'd made up my mind. I'd see out my current BBC contract and bow out gracefully …and then, on the very day that I'd convinced myself that I was giving it all up I received a call from Lou, the Editor at BBC Essex.

"We're going to extend your Sunday show to cover BBC Radio Kent, Radio Norfolk, and Radio Suffolk."

The timing was spot on, I decided that perhaps I wouldn't throw in the towel just yet, although it was a close run thing. It took a while but eventually I fell back in love with being on the radio. I am now a regular on *Caroline Flashback*, presenting a Sunday morning show with a very good audience, certainly for a predominately online show, although it is also broadcast on DAB in Cambridgeshire and Norfolk, and on FM via the community station - yes, that one, the one that I helped to set up.

I am still involved with the Caroline North broadcasts from the ship, but only occasionally now. I still enjoy going out to Ross Revenge, but only when the sun shines and certainly not every month.

I soon came to enjoy my weekly BBC music show, I like it more than any show I'd done before for the Corporation. I have a free hand to play and say what I want and I am working from home. I just play the songs that I love and chat a bit, though not too much, it was all I'd ever wanted to do. The audience figures are good as well, especially for Sunday evening, when radio listening is traditionally light, and the listener response is great, so, it was just ripe for scrapping - and that's exactly where we are now.

At the start of November 2022, BBC senior management announced plans to pull the plug on countless hours of local radio output – and that included Sunday evenings, and my show – hey ho, here we go again. I've been through management changes and disruption before, it goes with the job. But if this is to be the end of my BBC career, then I've ended on a high following a surprise request to produce a documentary about local rock band legends Lee Brilleaux, Wilko Johnson and Dr Feelgood. Making the programme reawakened my love of producing radio documentaries, helped when I was told by several people, including those involved with the band, and my boss, that it was one of the best documentaries they'd ever heard.

So, as I write these words the future is as unclear as ever it was – it'll be fascinating to see where the latest events take me.

When I left the BBC Essex breakfast show an influential

online review appeared a couple of days later, I appreciated it very much: '*Ray will be a tough act to follow. His local cheeky-chappy persona is bang on brand for BBC Local Radio, his personality and Essex credentials comes through in the link work and interactions with his team.*'

I like to think that description of my broadcasting style still applies, although I've always been able to adapt: Presenting all music or all speech formats. From 'light n easy,' with a little classical for good measure, to pop, rock and oldies. News and documentaries and in depth interviews.

I've been so very lucky, eventually getting to do my dream job, via the longest possible route, but there are still questions that I ask myself, just occasionally:

Could I have done more? Yes, probably.
Should I have chased higher profile jobs? Certainly.
Was the big time waiting for me? Who knows.
Will I ever retire fully? Probably not.
Should I have believed in myself more?
Yes, yes, yes… well, maybe…

Ray on top of the world

For more information about
Ray Clark's two previous books visit his website:
www.rayradio.co.uk

Also from Poppublishing:

Printed in Great Britain
by Amazon

30431082R00191